ARCHITECTURE

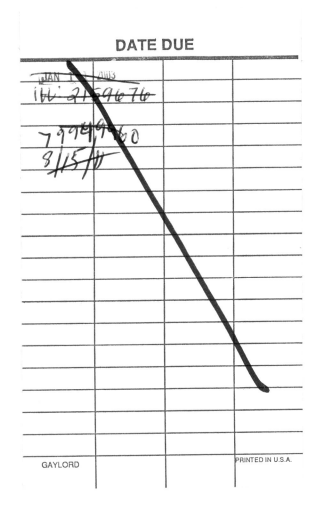

DATE DUE

JAN 2003			
ILL 21594676			
79949690			
8/15/11			

GAYLORD   PRINTED IN U.S.A.

TQM and
ISO 9000
for Architects
and Designers

TQM and ISO 9000 for Architects and Designers

Charles Nelson AIA, FRAIA

Illustrations by Michael Lindell, FRAIA

McGraw-Hill

New York   San Francisco   Washington, D.C.   Auckland   Bogotá
Caracas   Lisbon   London   Madrid   Mexico City   Milan
Montreal   New Delhi   San Juan   Singapore
Sydney   Tokyo   Toronto

4-23-96

Library of Congress Cataloging-in-Publication Data

Nelson, Charles (Charles E.)
    TQM and ISO 9000 for architects and designers / Charles Nelson;
illustrations by Michael Lindell.
        p.   cm.
    Includes index.
    ISBN 0-07-046277-1 (hardcover)
    1. Architectural services marketing—United States—Quality
control. 2. Total quality management. 3. ISO 9000 Series
Standards. I. Title.
NA1996.N45 1995
720′.68′5—dc20   95-45348
                                                                CIP

McGraw-Hill

A Division of The McGraw-Hill Companies

1 2 3 4 5 6 7 8 9 0   AGM/AGM   9 0 0 9 8 7 6 5

ISBN 0-07-046277-1

*The sponsoring editor for this book was Wendy Lochner, the editing supervisor
was Penny Linskey, and the production supervisor was Donald F. Schmidt.*

Printed and bound by Quebecor/Martinsburg.

McGraw-Hill books are available at special quantity discounts to use as premiums and sales promotions, or for use in corporate training programs. For more
information, please write to the Director of Special Sales, McGraw-Hill, 11 West
19th Street, New York, NY 10011. Or contact your local bookstore.

 This book is printed on recycled, acid-free paper containing
a minimum of 50 percent recycled de-inked fiber.

This book is dedicated to my mother,

Laura Nelson,

who could truthfully answer 'always' to
the majority of questions in Peter Mears'
total quality person test, but who - out of
modesty - probably wouldn't.

TQM and ISO 9000
for Architects and Designers

READ ME FIRST
(Some User Notes)

Herman the Odd

Hermione the Even

Every author of a technical work has certain cultural obligations, usually dispatched up front. One of these duties is to grasp firmly the gender nettle. Another is to tackle its companion, the Personal Pronoun Problem. Despite huge strides forward in gender-neutral writing in the last few decades, the forms '(s)he' and 'his (her)' are futile, awkward attempts to de-bias leftovers from our Romance language heritage. With my illustrator's help, I will try to resolve these issues.

There are four characters in this book; you, me, Herman and Hermione (and, occasionally, a contractor, a client, and a helper).

This book is personal. It is written to YOU, the reader, addressed in the second person singular. (This also includes the second person plural form common in Texas, 'you-all', or 'yawl' as it is pronounced.) It is written by me, so identified.

The other two characters, introduced to you here, are our colleagues Herman and Hermione.

Herman is an intrepid architect, the alter ego of his creator, with a penchant for choosing clothes which make him look shorter and fatter than he really is. His hero is Marcel Marceau; he will mime every new idea possible.

Across the street from Herman is the office of Hermione, a cool and unflappable consulting engineer of many disciplines.

Sometimes the two collaborate on projects, but mostly they are on their own. Recognizing that the sexes are becoming equally represented in the design professions (by aggregate sensitivity if not by aggregate body mass), this book equally features Herman and Hermione. He gets the odd numbered chapters and she gets the even numbered chapters. Like most of us, these two are small practitioners. They have occasional staff, but mostly do everything themselves.

One more pronoun: When I use the collective 'we', it usually means you, me, Herman and Hermione: all of us design professionals together. Occasionally 'we' refers to my firm; hopefully the distinction will be obvious in the text.

Taking aim . . .

Another duty of the author is to aim the work; as the publisher says, 'define your target market'. The publishers will tell you that the U.S. is the big market for books like this; that international markets are important but secondary.

A decade of living mostly outside the U.S. has given me a different perspective, which is that the practice of architecture, engineering, and other design professions is remarkably similar wherever you go.

Even though they had been cut off from the rest of the world for two generations, the architects' offices I visited in Leningrad in 1990 seemed completely familiar to me. The language and the hunger for information about their colleagues elsewhere were the only differences worth noting.

There are differences between practice in the U.S., the U.K. and Australia, to be sure. But those differences are inconsequential when compared to the overwhelming similarities. Even the legal systems, with common roots in English common law, are remarkably similar, although the precedents cited will vary. This book, in deference to the publisher's marketing nous, is mostly written in the U.S. version of English, but is completely international in spirit, and written for any design professional who can read English.

The matter of style can be a 'can of worms' for any writer who hasn't settled on one. When McGraw-Hill sent the outline for this book out for review, one reviewer responded, *"Major modifications should be to use a more professional, serious approach to describing quality systems rather than the humorous approach. ... the viewpoint is not serious in nature giving the impression that quality and quality improvement are not serious issues. ... the approach is technically limited and somewhat demeaning of the topic of quality and quality management. ... The author's writing style is a drawback for the proposed audience of highly educated, professional people."* Hmmm.

Thinking about this reminds me of Christian Norberg-Schulz' book *Intentions in Architecture*, which I believe to be the most thoughtful, serious book ever written on the topic. Beautifully written, but *very* heavy going for a Bear of Very Little Brain to digest.

There is a collateral issue to the one of being serious, which is information packaging: the ability to produce easily accessible units of data.

An artist's impression of Frank's machine. There is another on page 136, fittingly at the start of the chapter on tools.

My good friend Frank Stasiowski has made that into an art form; there is no point in trying to compete with him.

There is a rumor that in the back room of his Newton, MA, offices there is a secret machine which will turn great globs of turgid prose into crunchy, bite-size breakfast bits. It's all there at the flick of a switch, like changing organ stops: checklists, helpful hints, step-by-step instructions, fact-packed tips, you name it. (If you doubt this, try his *215 Project Management Tips*, 242 *New Money Making Ideas* or the one that nearly broke the machine, *934 Ways to Better Project Management*.)

How can one position oneself meaningfully between the diametrically opposed styles of these two giants of design thinking? I can't bear people who take themselves and their work so seriously that they can't see the inherent comedy in any intellectual pursuit, but neither do I discount the reviewer's point.

With apologies to René Descartes, *I am, therefore I think.* To get the core understanding out of this book, you too will have to do some thinking, some serious thinking. But you *are*, so you will.

All of my research into and experience consulting on quality management for design professionals convinces me that there is no possibility of a crunchy, bite-sized set of answers that will work. We will need a different approach.

Whether you choose to think of the process as re-inventing yourself, or re-engineering your firm, that sort of action is the only path to the goal. 'Tweaking' the systems you already have will improve your practice, but never create the breakthrough of TQM or ISO 9000 qualification.

So, contrary to the reviewer's assumption, I am very serious about quality management, but I am equally convinced that getting there has GOT to be fun, and that having a little fun at our own expense is well worth doing.

Buffet or baloney?

Designing a book is much like designing a building. Most of the ingredients for the new design came from somewhere else; our own previous experience plus all that we have absorbed from the work of others. To the remains of those previous feasts, hopefully, we bring something special and unique, so we can say we designed it rather than copied it.

In a book, there are two ways to lay the table: a buffet of identifiable choice morsels gleaned from the refrigerator of the mind and the pantry of the library, or grind it all up and serve baloney. Same ingredients, either way.

I've chosen the buffet approach.

What kind of tools do we need?

Finally, to an issue which has helped to shape this book. It is another point raised by the same reviewer: *"The quality tools that are mentioned are ones that have a low level of sophistication and don't get to the core issues of developing a quality system that is based on ISO 9000. ... It is obvious that Mr. Nelson ... has only superficial knowledge of quality systems and quality methods/tools."*

The experts in quality management are obsessed with measuring things, and the measurements get more complex with more sophisticated tools. We design professionals are not, generally, measurers. However, it would be to our benefit to begin to measure some things we've never measured, such as the cost of rework - redrawing, redesign - that we do because of bad design planning.

Without a holistic view of our craft we have little to offer our clients or the public. It may be that there are 'sophisticated' tools which are appropriate for quality in design, but my guess is that they will be developed *by designers* in response to the needs of an evolving and maturing quality construct appropriate to the profession, just as the manufacturing industry has developed the sophisticated tools which it uses.

But crawl before walking, walk before flying. Right now we are at the 'sitting up' stage, and crawling looks tricky.

Peter Mears has written (1995) a thorough and marvelous compendium of quality tools and techniques. It outlines four dozen quality methods which have evolved in response to specific needs. Most of these are specific to the manufacturing environment which created them, and will not be of much value or interest to design professionals. Some we have been using for years, without knowing the names TQM gives them.

It is the purpose of this book to acquaint readers with the range of basic (read unsophisticated) quality tools which are used in other industries, as well as to describe the best of the industry-specific tools and techniques which I have found in researching this topic, in offices, books and in conversation with my professional clients.

I have had fun writing it, and I hope reading it gives you a few chuckles along with some useful information.

Join the journey

Herman and Hermione invite you to to join them in their quest for quality. Some of this journey will be easy:

Some of it will not be easy:

But all of it leads to a happy ending:

WITHOUT WHICH...
(it could never have happened)

For the experiences and thoughts which form the backbone of this book, I owe a debt of gratitude to far too many people to mention individually.

There are a number of people, however, who have been active in the immediacy of its preparation and who deserve special mention. They are:

Michael Lindell, Australian architect and custodian of the magical pen full of the wonderful characters that people this book, who was the first to urge me to write it.

Margaret Lothian and Ray Andrews, for their thoughtful reviews.

Joel Stein, Wendy Lochner, and Penny Linskey of McGraw-Hill, for their encouragement and support.

James Franklin, for sharing his ideas and outline of his own manuscript on the same subject with me, and for his review of the completed text.

Adrian Renouf, for articulating the evolution in client expectations which forms the basis for Chapter 4.4.

The authors of the related works frequently quoted herein; especially James Franklin, Norman Kaderlan, Peter Mears, Stu Rose and Frank Stasiowski. Their previous work has done much to clear the 'boulders from the path', and make this journey easier.

My wife, Jennifer Fall, for her encouragement, for taking on a greater load of the chores so I could have more time, and for careful, thoughtful reviews of the text.

Hermione also deserves a special note; she is Michael's 'photo-fit' of suggestions about her looks and style contributed by nine Melbourne women in architecture. Thank you, Ann, Christina, Clare, Helen, Helen, Jenifer, Maggie, Virginia, and Yvonne.

Part 1

BASICS: Understanding the Concepts

1.1 Design Excellence and Quality Principles

The next time you are with a group of, say, ten businessmen and the conversation lags, try slipping in the word "consultant" and watch the conversation pick up as passions heat. No doubt, the words "crooks" and "incompetents" and "conmen" will be the more printable ones used. - Charles H. Ford [1]

Purpose

This introductory chapter has three purposes:

◆ To outline broadly the relationship of quality management principles to architecture, particularly with respect to design practice.

◆ To identify areas where TQM and ISO 9000 principles can improve design practice.

◆ To outline how quality management concepts offer design professions an opportunity to strengthen public perceptions of their profession.

Do we have any sacred cows, and if so, how should they be guarded?

As Charles Ford points out, consultants can have something of an image problem. Do design consultants have an image problem, and if so, why? You might not agree, but I think that architects in particular have an image problem, in the sense that the way their services are perceived by the public does not always coincide with their own view.

Architecture is one of the few professions, if not the only profession, where lay persons believe their ideas are as valid as those of the professional. This is another way of saying that the profession of architecture does not have any 'secret knowledge', inaccessible to users of their services.

Architects struggle to maintain a community perception that they do have some special knowledge, by virtue of their special training, which (among other things) sets them aside from paraprofessionals or 'pseudo professionals' e.g. drafting services. [2] Architects have sought, with varying degrees of success, to have this 'difference' enshrined in law, by legal restrictions on the use of the title 'architect' by state systems of registration, and by regulations requiring the use of registered professionals.

The rationale for this 'protection' is protection of the public
- health and safety at the minimum - but extending to more
esoteric ideas of environmental harmony and broader
community well-being through good design.

Protecting the Public

These protections of the profession are under threat in most
countries and under attack by advocates of consumer
protection and fair trade practices.

Throughout these debates runs a continuous thread of
'quality' and value for money: How can the public be assured
that it is getting the necessary protection at the lowest cost?
Answering this fundamental question to the satisfaction of
all involved is far from easy, but what is clear is that the
quality management movement has something central to do
with it.

How much this movement has to do with answering this
question concerns the degree to which the design professions
learn how to:

◆ use the tools of quality management to both improve,
  and demonstrate improvement of, delivery of their
  services, and

◆ re-employ the tools they already use and understand to
  relate them to public perceptions of quality.

In the way of these goals are some misconceptions that need
examination.

Misconceptions about quality management

There are two common misconceptions that architects hold about quality management concepts, whether their orientation is to TQM or ISO 9000 quality management. The first of these is that the ability to document good practice should be sufficient evidence of quality management. The second is that - stripped of all rhetoric - quality management in architecture equals good design.

While there is some truth in both conclusions, both miss the mark, with respect to either the TQM or ISO 9000 QM approaches to quality, and the differences that those approaches add to the understanding of quality management.

These differences are subtle but powerful; collectively they may be termed the 'quality culture'. Every industry has its own version of a quality culture; Part 1 outlines the parameters of a quality culture for architecture.

The 'design quality' mental barriers

I have seen three barriers, or biases, operating with respect to quality management in the design professions. The first is that every design professional coming into contact with formal quality management systems for the first time has an instinctive and overwhelmingly characteristic response, which goes something like this:

> *"I already understand design quality. It is my life, my training, my bread and butter. If I didn't understand how to do quality design I wouldn't have any clients."*

This conviction, seen as self-evident truth, makes the design professional feel rather strongly that the wisdom gained in manufacturing better products has little, if anything, to do with his or her profession.

A few (especially those who are disorganized and wish they weren't) have the hope that any formalized system will help them sort themselves out, reduce their risk of mistakes, and possibly even increase profitability. The basic attitude towards formal quality management, however, is at the outset usually one of rejection. This mental barrier stands in the way of understanding what benefits can be derived from the implementation of quality systems.

A second bias universally held in design professions is that formal quality systems will require excessive, unnecessary paperwork, which will create another overhead the firm doesn't need.

A third powerful barrier goes up for most design professionals when they start to dig into the details of a quality system for the first time - say a read of ISO 9000 or a browse through any of the thousands of books available on TQM.

Again the reaction will most likely be *"this stuff has nothing to do with me or my practice or my profession"*.

How much and which parts of quality systems have something to offer the design professional, and why, are the subject of this book.

Its first task is to help you, the reader, past the powerful mental barriers described above, so you can make an unbiased assessment of what quality management has to offer.

What are the benefits?

As one researches quality management issues and begins to get beyond the questions of interpretation of the Standards, understanding the gurus, weighing the costs, and filtering out the 'background noise', it becomes apparent that quality management principles offer real potential for specific benefit.

These opportunities require careful study, as to applicability to individual practices, but broadly they include:

◆ A marketing edge, as perceived by the marketplace.

◆ The potential for real increases in profitability.

◆ Real, perhaps dramatic, reductions in the risk of practice.

◆ Increased accountability, both professionally and personally.

While increased accountability may not in itself be readily seen as an advantage, the complex relationship between increased accountability and commercial success cannot be overstated.

The by-product of increased professional accountability is personal accountability, meaning the responsibility appreciated by every member of the practice. While this topic is worthy of a book in its own right, and cannot be developed in great detail here, the overall implications are explored in Chapter 6.4.

Each of the above points is discussed more fully below.

The quality consciousness imperative

Despite the intuitive natural biases with which most design professions first view formal quality management systems, there is an undeniable, permanent, irreversible, worldwide shift toward these systems. We know this, and it creates a powerful imperative to find out what they are, and how we can use them.

In the United States and Japan, the emphasis is chiefly on "total quality management" (TQM) concepts; in the U.K., most of the rest of Europe, Australia, and increasingly, the rest of the world, the emphasis is on ISO 9000 quality assurance. Both of these systems are discussed in some detail in later chapters, as well as their similarities, differences, and the theory base they share.

Excellence vs. quality

All design professionals understand the concept of 'excellence'; as in 'design excellence'. Most would probably think 'excellence' and 'quality' synonymous. In the lexicon of quality management (especially in the ISO 9000 variety) 'quality' has a more specific context than 'excellence'.

Simple definitions are not all that useful in separating the concepts, but by the end of Part 1 of this book, the reader will have a clear understanding of the subtleties, which will begin to ease the bias discussed above.

Concepts of excellence

The AIA has taken a leadership role in defining design excellence, and it will be useful to review very briefly what the AIA has learned in its 'Roundtable' discussions about excellence and how it is achieved.

In 1989 the AIA published *In Search of Design Excellence* [3] the results of what then president Benjamin Brewer Jr. FAIA called in the Foreword *"an ambitious, careful, and serious investigation into the important subject of design excellence"*.

This compendium of 10 'excellent' papers on the subject included a 55 pp document by AIA Resident Fellow James R. Franklin FAIA entitled *Keys to Design Excellence*. Franklin cites the "Signature Firms roundtable" events as having produced the best answers to questions about design excellence. He defines design excellence as:

"the perceived quality of the experiences a building provides for three groups:

◆ *The Profession - through design awards, publications, etc.,*

◆ *The Participants - client, architect, consultants, etc., and*

◆ *The Public - user groups, tenants, the community, through approval, support and enthusiastic use."*

Few would disagree with this somewhat complex definition, but its implications should not be ignored. By this definition, design excellence is achieved only when the *perceived* benefits are there for all three groups. *Beauty must be in the eye of the beholder.*

Other research in design quality

There have been a number of studies carried out which have focused on quality of design in one way or another. Reviewing some of these will provide a useful basis for relating to the more formal TQM and ISO 9000 structures throughout this book. (The coverage is by no means complete. References for the research outlined are given at the end of Part 1.)

Stuart Rose, in his book *Achieving Excellence in Your Design Practice*, starts out with the dictionary definition: excellence is *'being eminently good'* [4]. His research is summed up in one brief sentence:

"All excellent firms share one trait: an obsession with quality." [5]

He goes on to note:

"Quality, in fact, is almost synonymous with excellence in the eyes of most design professionals."

In discussing this relationship of quality to excellence, Rose states [6]:

"... quality obsession is that last inch, that extra mile, those few extra steps that make the difference between a good job and a great job.

"A quality obsession also includes consistency. It involves a consistent commitment to go for the greatness, and to do what it takes to go from being good to being excellent."

Rose's observations remind us of Peters and Waterman's summary conclusion in *In Search of Excellence* [7]:

> *"Above all,* the intensity itself, *stemming from strongly held beliefs, marks those companies."*

Rose's research, although generated from the viewpoint of practice, comes up with conclusions which are remarkably aligned with those of the quality industry professionals.

Norman Kaderlan, an astute observer of architectural practice, in his book *Designing Your Practice* [8] makes these observations:

> *"Expectations shape the relationship between designer and client.*
>
> *"The client's expectations, however, are likely to be different from yours. ... The quality of service may be more important than the quality of work. Issues that are significant to you, such as design excellence, aesthetic impact, and making a design statement, may be less critical to the client."*

Here we see an important, perhaps fundamental distinction, that of quality of *service* vs. quality of the *design* which results from that service.

Frank Stasiowski, among others, has defined quality assurance as *"meeting and exceeding the client's expectations"* [9].

Kaderlan notes:

> *"Expectations are like land mines. If you aren't clear about them, they can explode at the worst possible moment and destroy the trust you have worked so hard to develop."* [10]

I will return to these points later. Expectations of the client, and of other project "users", are core to quality management principles.

Refer *Total Quality Project Management for the Design Firm,* by Frank Stasiowski and David Burstein. Copyright © 1994 by John Wiley & Sons Inc. Reprinted by permission of John Wiley & Sons Inc. Quotations also appear on pages 27, 46, 52, 57, 138, 172, 273-274, and 288.

Frank Stasiowski and David Burstein have published their research in design quality with the development of a construction industry-specific TQM they call TQPM (total quality project management). In the Preface, the authors assert that *"... an average design project can easily require 30 to 50% of its budget to locate and correct errors!"* [10]

James Franklin has continued his research on design quality, and has developed what he calls (after Juran) the "Big Q, Little Q" concepts of design quality [12].

By 'big Q', Franklin means 'delighting the customers'. This he contrasts with 'plain old' quality, which he says "... *gets measured in terms of how well the specified requirements were met with no quantifiable deficiencies or errors. It means being on time and in the budget with no discernible negligence - doing things the right way in sequential order.*"

Q q

In approaching design quality from a practice point of view, Franklin comes very close to describing key differences between TQM (roughly, big Q) and ISO 9000 (roughly, little Q). See Chapter 1.4 for more on this relationship.

Throughout this book I will discuss relevant aspects of research by others.

Quality vs. excellence

I said above that excellence and quality (in the formal sense) were not synonymous. As we examine the TQM and ISO 9000 approaches more closely, the differences will become more sharply focused. Broadly, however, the relationship can be characterized as follows:

Design excellence tends to be process-focused; intent on creating "good design". For most design professionals, this implies a pure design-oriented ethic which sometimes transcends the client's stated needs.

At an extreme, this ethic translates into not much more than "using" the client as a means to creating award-winning projects. However infrequent, it happens often enough to create a small but enduring negative attitude in the general public about the motivation of designers.

For the vast majority of design professionals, however, the motivations are purer and driven by a real desire to improve the visual environment rather than to exploit clients.

Not infrequently, this involves a delicate balancing act, especially where the sensibilities of the design professional to the environmental context exceed those of the client.

Another key criterion of 'design excellence' concepts is that they are evolutionary -

that they are borne out of the maturation of artistic vision; and that this maturation, in its best expression, liberates the designer to create "great architecture".

Contrast this with TQM - a revolutionary rather than evolutionary concept. Underlying virtually all of the in-vogue TQM theories is the idea that nothing is so good that it can't be improved: radically, powerfully, revisionistically. As a metaphor, one could say TQM creates greenfield sites for design excellence with dynamite, not water flowing over rock. This metaphor would not sit well with TQM experts, who would argue that the "continuous improvement" process so central to both TQM and ISO 9000 theory is, in fact, appropriate evolution.

This is one of the subtle but important quality management implementation problems noted earlier, and will be discussed more fully in Part 3.

What about ISO 9000? Here is another metaphor: ISO 9000 is like laying a street grid over a town plan based on cow paths. It works, it seems clean and efficient, but it also seems arbitrary. ISO 9000 is a "one-size-fits-all" mental framework for organizing approaches to quality issues. Its strength is its universality; the concomitant weakness is its apparent inflexibility to specific professional differences.

Zealots in both the TQM and ISO 9000 camps will argue passionately that the religion must be embraced wholly to be effective. Detractors will cheerfully recite celebrated cases where firms that won the Malcolm Baldridge award one year went out of business the next.

The truth is somewhere in between. The 'marketing imperative' issue aside, implementing an appropriate level of quality management into a design practice in an appropriate way will give the practice powerful operating advantages.

One example: In 1993 I was talking with a group of about two dozen architects in Brisbane, Australia, about quality assurance. There was a lot of participant response about "paperwork"; basically on the idea that QA would dramatically increase overheads, which couldn't be recouped in a competitive environment.

In the middle of this discussion, the quality manager for Conrad & Gargett, the very first Australian architectural firm to get ISO 9000 third party certification, rose to his feet and waited until he had the floor. Paraphrasing his remarks, his message was:

"Before we implemented a QA system, we couldn't afford to do residential projects. Every time we tried, we lost money. So we stayed away from them. Since we have got our QA system up and running, we have become so much more efficient, that we can take on even residential alterations and make money on them. We are taking jobs away from you smaller firms. Think about it."

The hall was quiet for many minutes while they did, indeed, think on that.

The key here is APPROPRIATE technology. In the Australian vernacular, the idea is to 'pick the eyes out of' all the systems going, to get the best parts for our profession.

The zealots may gag, but that is the essence of this book.

A caution, however: the zealots are partly right. There can be no equivocation about embracing quality principles if we want to reap their riches. More on this in later chapters. Management cannot be lukewarm about quality and expect staff will do it - the failure rate will be 100%. Lip service to quality is probably more debilitating to the firm than no quality policy at all.

Where can we lift our game?

Under 'Purpose' at the start of this chapter, I identified as a goal 'to identify areas where TQM and ISO 9000 principles can improve design practice'. Opposite the heading 'What are the benefits?' on page 5, I listed four items.

The first benefit: a marketing edge

The first of those four points was that quality management offered design professionals a marketing edge. There is both a simplistic marketing edge factor and complex marketing edge factor, the latter being quite flexible in the benefits it provides.

The simple factor first: Remember back in the late 70's when CAD was a new idea? The story went around (and there was some truth in it) that if you had a computer in your office, it gave you a marketing edge. You actually didn't have to know how to use it - you just had to have it sitting there, so you could say *"Of course, we are computerized now"*.

QA is a bit like that - if it is the 'cutting edge' stuff, clients expect you to have it if you project yourself as a 'cutting-edge' professional. In some countries, such as the U.K. and Australia, and increasingly throughout Europe, even local governments are demanding evidence of quality system implementation as an 'entry' gate for consideration of appointment. The private sector tends to follow suit.

This 'edge' is *simplistic* because it relies on form rather than substance. It is, nevertheless, real.

At the more complex level, we have to look at client perception patterns to understand how the marketing edge works, and be able to profit from it.

Frank Stasiowski, one design services marketing guru who enjoys an international reputation, states flatly *"clients don't really care about design"* [13]. What does he mean? In fact, clients do care about design - but it is way down on the list of what clients care about. Why? The reason is that clients know that designers care about design. Some clients think designers care too much about design, and will build monuments to themselves at the clients' expense if given half a chance.

Stasiowski is not the only critical commentator on this point. Robert Gutman, Distinguished Professor of Sociology at Rutgers University, and for nearly a quarter century Visiting Professor of Architecture at Princeton University, is acknowledged as one of the most authoritative voices in practice research. In his 1988 book *Architectural Practice: A Critical View* he writes [14]:

> *"I believe architects ought to worry about the heavy emphasis the AIA and many firms now place on marketing programs. It is all too consistent with the view of the profession in many sectors of the community, especially among building users and the general public. Users of buildings and urban environments are very suspicious of architects' motives. The profession is looked upon as venal and selfish. Architects are perceived as people who are mainly interested in advancing, often on the basis of spurious arguments, the economic interests of building owners and developers; and therefore, indirectly, the wealth of professionals themselves."*

Clients care about money and time, and (above all) about being listened to - something that some designers are not very good at.

This characterization probably represents the vast majority of all clients, be they public, corporate or private. They worry about time, money, being heard, and they have suspicions that designers don't worry enough about time, money, listening to their clients, and that they may even try to create award-winning projects at the clients' expense.

These clients, to a greater or lesser extent (depending on their knowledge of quality management systems), will understand that formal quality system implementation *requires* that the "service provider" (e.g. the design professional) puts in place, and works within, a framework of responsiveness to the clients' needs and interests.

The client's knowledge that QM will increase the designer's responsiveness is the KEY to the marketing edge.

The client, with varying degrees of self-awareness, believes that by the design professional's willingness to embrace a formalized quality system, that he has undertaken or is in process of undergoing, a fundamental paradigm shift toward greater responsiveness to the client's point of view.

This presumption of a paradigm shift opens a window of opportunity for the design practice - to be nurtured and developed, or to be missed and lost. It is precisely this opportunity which creates a highly flexible marketing edge for the designer. The best firms sense this, sometimes without framing the thought, and move to set themselves apart from the 'rest of the pack' in the way they both develop and communicate their quality management credentials.

The second benefit: potential for increased profitability

Above I described the Conrad & Gargett experience, where they found that development and implementation of QA increased their ability to undertake small projects profitably.

Profitability is often thought of, rather narrowly, as the difference between the cost of producing the service and the income from the service.

However, in design, where overheads are usually as much as, and sometimes twice, the cost of directly productive labor, efficiencies in overhead can be more powerful generators of profitability than increased efficiencies of production.

Implementation of quality management systems costs money (some authorities say up to 3 to 5% of operations) but if the implementation is successful, operating efficiencies will increase to more than make up this cost. Examples are savings from reduced turnover of personnel, greater sense of job value and increased motivation to work, reduction of time lost due to general office disorganization, reduced re-work through better planning, etc. Part 6 of this book will focus on these opportunities.

The third benefit: reduced practice risk

The third benefit noted above was about the reduction of practice risk. I said those reductions could be dramatic. The whole field of practice risk is currently undergoing very extensive research and is rapidly evolving. The American Institute of Architects, Victor O. Schinnerer and Company, and Design Professionals Insurance Company (DPIC) have been active in pioneering programs of risk management education which have virtually halved the risk of practice for U.S. design practices.

The partnering movement has also proven itself to be a dramatic risk control technique.

There is a very high degree of correlation between quality management concepts and risk management concepts - implementing one powerfully enhances the other, even though they are separate disciplines and systems.

The reason is that both disciplines involve a certain organizational control and rigor: a keener awareness of cause and effect; an ongoing analysis of the long-term effect on the practice of the way various situations are dealt with.

This relationship is explored in more detail in Chapter 6.3.

The fourth benefit: increased accountability

The design professions have been buffeted by the dramatic increase in litigation over the past several decades. This explosion of litigation, well documented by many writers, has created a knee-jerk, self-protective response which has hurt the design professions more than it has helped them.

Herman on the offensive

It is only in the last few years that professional design societies, such as AIA and the RIBA, together with their commercial risk insurers, have discovered that "offense is the best defense" and have started to reverse the defensive posture by advocating the idea that *taking increased responsibility will actually lower the risk of that responsibility.*

I personally believe that this change - still in its infancy - is the single most important development in the design professions in our time. Why? What we, as a profession, began to understand in the late 80's was that we were going to be blamed for all manner of building failures whether or not we were responsible for them.

As the building environment became more complex and more fragmented, we gave away the role of 'master builder', and along with it, virtually all meaningful control over the building process. Yet the public still holds us accountable for the results.

There are two keys to redressing this imbalance. One of those keys is education in risk management, which *is* taking place and has been enormously successful.

The other key, I believe, lies in quality management systems. The reason why: a core feature of quality management (particularly ISO 9000 systems) is the specific assignment of responsibility, and therefore, accountability.

However, both TQM and ISO 9000 quality systems come with some specific problems in this regard, because they are founded in manufacturing and presume a seamless path of responsibility from design through installation. In countries where ISO 9000 systems are increasingly mandatory (such as the U.K. and Australia) design professionals and their clients are working out the fine points of these responsibility relationships and transfers. The outcomes will provide guidance for the U.S. and the rest of the world in the coming years.

The responsibility (and therefore the accountability) of the design professional within a formalized quality environment has significant implications with respect to the standard contracts for construction in use in the U.S., the U.K., Australia, and elsewhere.

Under ISO 9000, the basic relationship is that the design professional starts out as the 'supplier', but in the middle of the project transfers 'supplier' responsibility to the builder, and becomes the agent of the client, acting in a performance audit role.

The mechanics of this transfer are not contemplated by the International Standard, except that it is clear that the 'product' offered by the design professional changes from one of design (primary) to execution monitoring (secondary).

The evolution of the designer's accountability within the world-wide movement toward quality management systems will continue, probably for at least another decade. This evolution, together with the resounding benefits of the joint campaign by the AIA and key insurers of its members, offers the greatest opportunity in decades for the design professions to re-establish their authority and position with respect to decisions about the built environment.

The best firms will sense this and reposition themselves within a quality management framework to simultaneously increase their authority and accountability, while reducing their actual exposure to risk.

If this idea appeals to you, keep reading.

**Chapter 1.1
Summary Checklist**

- ✓ Architects seek to improve the public's perception of the value of their service.

- ✓ The status that architects have traditionally enjoyed has been, is being, and is likely to continue to be, eroded; through competition from within and outside of the profession, as well as by trade practices legislation.

- ✓ The issues of perception of value and status can be resolved only through objective evidence of an increased capability to provide value-for-money to the public.

- ✓ Quality management offers architects and other design professionals both increased capability and evidence of it.

- ✓ Misconceptions about quality management stand in the way of its adoption.

- ✓ In addition to a marketing edge, quality management offers the benefits of reduced risk, increased profitability and increased accountability.

- ✓ Design excellence and management of practice quality, often confused, are not the same thing.

- ✓ Designers equate design and service. Clients do not, and they value service over design. This conflict is a core source of miscommunication between designers and clients.

1.2   TQM and the TQM Gurus

This is, so to speak, an exercise in the art of painting by numbers. You are the painter. The numbers are the data of process quality capability analysis. Your ultimate canvas is the balance sheet of profit and loss. - Frank Price [15]

Purpose

To provide an overview of TQM principles and their interpretation by leading proponents, and to propose preliminary conclusions as to how these principles and interpretations relate to the practice of architecture.

Coming to grips with a new terminology

U.K. quality authority Frank Price, as noted above, has distilled TQM to the relationship between two elements of business.

Profit and loss, we understand. But what on earth is 'process quality capability analysis'? Does it mean putting our draftspeople on some kind of perpetual-motion charrette treadmill to see how fast they can draw without an upturn in the mistakes curve? Does it mean benchmarking the amount of time we can stare out the window while waiting for a great design idea to happen?

Actually, it means something very simple in Price's highly readable approach; the first of four key questions (see p 30) of quality control: *"CAN we make it OK?"*

Waiting for an idea...

Part of the issue here is the unfamiliarity of a new terminology. More importantly (as we will see by the end of this chapter), some of the central tenets of TQM will at least at first sight seem anathema to the average design professional's traditional way of working.

We will find that there is value in translating these concepts, honed to perfection in Japanese factories and now being imitated world-wide, into equivalent concepts in the design professions. We also will see that the application of them will demand great care, if we are to be successful.

Is 'partnering' TQM?

In the U.S., TQM has 'flavor of the month' aura, helped in large part by the success of the partnering movement championed by the U.S. Army Corps of Engineers.

This influence is so strong that, for many, TQM virtually equates to partnering.

Partnering is, in fact, only one quality management strategy, which is equally applicable to TQM or ISO 9000 structures. The relationship between partnering and quality management is discussed in Chapter 4.9.

Who are the experts?

What does 'TQM' mean? It would be fair to say that concepts of TQM are a bit like concepts of 'God': it all depends on which sect you belong to; which disciple you follow.

Most design professionals would probably have heard the names of Deming, Juran and Crosby; few would know of Shewhart, Ishikawa or Feigenbaum; and fewer yet would have any idea what these various 'gurus' of TQM advocate, how different or similar their ideas were, or how one's practice might be affected if one embraced one set of ideas or another.

Besides the tracts written by the masters themselves, there are hundreds of books about them and about applying their theories in various combinations. While there is not room to go over this material in detail, there is value in comparing the basic tenets of each 'master's' philosophies and in beginning to question how these might relate to design practice, especially in the small firm.

This exercise puts TQM into a sharper focus for readers, and begins to suggest a strategy to pick the most appropriate concepts and start thinking about how to apply them.

Dr. W. Edwards Deming

The late Dr. Deming is hailed as the 'founder of the worldwide quality management system' [16]. Dr. Deming, at 50, taught the Japanese to think about quality in a way that has helped them to achieve economic mastery of the world, in just the space of a few decades.

Besides Dr. Deming's own prodigious output, there are dozens of books about the implementation of his methods. Perhaps the most readable is Mary Walton's warm and factual biography, *The Deming Management Method* [17].

Because of space limitations, I will only present here Mary Walton's version of his celebrated 14 points, the basis of his TQM approach. [18] There are variations on these themes; for example; in Peter Mears' 1995 text *Quality Improvement Tools & Techniques*, point 5 is given as *'Find problems'*, and point 7 as *'Institute modern methods of supervision'*. [19]

Deming's 14 points

1   *Create constancy of purpose for improvement of product and service.*

Dr. Deming suggests a radical new definition of a company's role. Rather than making money, it is to stay in business and provide jobs through innovation, research, constant improvement, and maintenance.

2   *Adopt the new philosophy.*

We are too tolerant of poor workmanship and sullen service. We need a new religion in which mistakes and negativism are unacceptable.

3   *Cease dependence on mass inspection.*

Firms typically inspect a product as it comes off the line or at major stages. Defective products are either thrown out or reworked; both are unnecessarily expensive. In effect, a company is paying workers to make defects and then to correct them. Quality comes not from inspection but from improvement of the process. With instruction, workers can be enlisted in this improvement.

4   *End the practice of awarding business on price tag alone.*

Purchasing departments customarily operate on orders to seek the lowest-priced supplier. Frequently, this leads to supplies of low quality. Instead, they should seek the best quality and work to achieve it with a single supplier for any one item in a long-term relationship.

5   *Improve constantly and forever the system of production and service.*

Improvement is not a one-time effort. Management is obligated to continually look for ways to reduce waste and improve quality.

6   *Institute training and retraining.*

Too often, workers have learned their job from another worker who was never trained properly. They are forced to follow unintelligible instructions. They can't do their jobs because no one tells them how.

7   *Institute leadership.*

The job of a supervisor is not to tell people what to do or punish them but to lead. Leading consists of helping people do a better job and of learning by objective methods who is in need of individual help.

8 *Drive out fear.*

Many employees are afraid to ask questions or take a position, even when they do not understand what the job is or what is right or wrong. People will continue to do things the wrong way, or to not do them at all. The economic loss from fear is appalling. It is necessary for better quality and productivity that people feel secure.

9 *Break down barriers between staff areas.*

Often staff areas - departments, units, whatever - are competing with each other or have goals that conflict. They do not work as a team so they can solve or foresee problems. Worse, one department's goals may cause trouble for another.

10 *Eliminate slogans, exhortations, and targets for the workforce.*

These never helped anybody do a good job. Let people put up their own slogans.

11 *Eliminate numerical quotas.*

Quotas take account only of numbers, not quality or methods. They are usually a guarantee of inefficiency and high cost. A person, to hold a job, meets a quota at any cost, without regard to damage to the company.

12 *Remove barriers to pride of workmanship.*

People are eager to do a good job and distressed when they can't. Too often, misguided supervisors, faulty equipment, and defective materials stand in the way. These barriers must be removed.

13 *Institute a vigorous programme of education and retraining.*

Both management and the workforce will have to be educated in the new methods, including teamwork and statistical techniques.

14 *Take action to accomplish the transformation.*

It will take a special top management team with a plan of action to carry out the quality mission. Workers can't do it on their own, nor can managers. A critical mass of people in the company must understand the Fourteen Points, the Seven Deadly Diseases, and the Obstacles.

How do these 14 points relate to the design professions?

Some of the above points will seem obvious and self-evident to most design professionals, who would wholeheartedly endorse ideas such as point 4.

The conditions under which most design firms function would never give rise to issues such as 'drive out fear' or 'break down barriers between staff areas'. Even point 1 may leave more than a few designers scratching their heads - as they see themselves as quite naturally putting service ahead of making money. How else can they explain their lifestyle?

Two people that I know of, Richard M. Miller and James Franklin, have had a try at translating Deming's 14 points into the world of design.

Richard Miller, with Charles Markert and Richard Simon, adapted for his former Florida consulting firm the 14 points to equivalent concepts in architecture/engineering. Their substantial paper is too long to be included in this book, but will, I understand, be included as an appendix to a book James Franklin is writing. The bottom line is that not only does Miller find the 14 points highly relevant, he states[20]:

> *"None of Deming's points can be taken out of context, cut, or applied without thorough study and consideration. Rest assured that there are 14 points and that they are all interrelated. Adopting a new philosophy, creating trusting relationships, proper training, elimination of fear, leadership, removal of barriers, enhancement of pride and joy, continuous education and the participation of all can all be elements of the above constancy of purpose. Each and every one of the points depends on the others, in balance, which with profound knowledge will attain total quality management."*

James Franklin FAIA, Resident Fellow of the AIA, has done a translation of Mary Walton's commentary on the 14 points (as included above) to the practice of architecture, with special emphasis on the applicability to small firms [21].

Franklin believes that TQM is a requirement of successful partnering [22]:

> *"Basic to TQM is the concept of partnering across corporate and contractual boundaries. For true partnering to exist, architects, clients, and contractors must adopt and commit to Deming's points and begin to creatively apply them in design and construction."*

I will come back to this point in Chapter 4.9.

A new religion?

The above few paragraphs bring us to a core issue about the quality movement; one that does not easily resolve itself. The great majority of quality success stories appear to involve - and therefore require - a zeal toward adoption and implementation which can only be likened to the zeal of a religious convert.

To anyone who has not undergone this 'conversion', this idea that obsession is a requirement seems unnecessary, and very possibly dangerous, in that it could replace the real reason to be a designer, which is to pursue design excellence.

This question of necessity is vexing, and one confronted by every manager at some point of learning about quality principles. For that reason I will return it throughout this book. Why this phenomenon? There seem to be two possible answers:

◆ An obsession with quality really is essential - one simply can't access the 'holy grail' without total faith in the process.

◆ What one finds when one achieves a mature quality system is so compelling that one becomes a true believer.

The approach of this book, signaled in Chapter 1.1, is to study the whole panoply of quality tools and techniques, select those that seem to fit the design professions best, and construct a useful system; a 'buffet lunch' approach. I also noted that this fairly pragmatic idea might make the 'zealots' gag.

Consider Miller's statement, quoted above. Essentially, it is 'all or nothing'. Sanford McDonnell, founder and Chairman Emeritus of McDonnell Douglas, is quoted as saying:

"Quality in the broadest sense of the term must become an obsession in every corporation throughout America from the CEO on down if our nation is to remain competitive." (23)

In Chapter 1.1 I quoted Stu Rose's finding that excellent firms all shared one trait, an *obsession with quality*.

When we consider the stunning impact that Japan's adaptation of quality principles has had on the world economic scene, it is tempting to put a lot of the credit to Japan's high work ethic, cohesive society, and other differences we can easily find.

There are two problems with this, one being that in small towns across America, especially in the south, Japanese factories are teaching the same tricks to diverse groups of Americans. The second is that other Asian countries, such as South Korea, Taiwan, and more recently southern China and Malaysia, are demonstrating they can compete head-to-head on quality.

Increasingly, Japanese quality products are made in places *other* than Japan.

I will return to this issue of an obligatory obsession by the end of Chapter 1.4, with an approach for resolution.

Back to the experts:

J. M. Juran

After Deming, the other figure of towering authority in quality management is Dr. Joseph M. Juran, who like Deming, has a long history of working with Japanese companies on quality.

Juran's theories are not as readily condensable as Deming's, since they don't come packaged as 'the 14 points' (pp 20-21) or 'the 7 deadly diseases' (not included in this book).

However, his work is of interest to design professionals, because he has focused on the *design of planning* for quality in *services*.

Now, does that begin to sound familiar? His 1992 book *Juran on Quality by Design: The New Steps for Planning Quality into Goods and Services* [24] details his philosophy in this area.

We will consider some points of relevance to design professionals, from his book:

◆ All quality (including bad quality) is planned. Bad quality planning is usually due to inexperience - it has been done by amateurs.

Noting that the two options are to provide consultants to help the amateurs, or train the amateurs, Juran says the second option is better, and that companies that train outperform those that bring in consultants.

◆ The quality crisis has given rise to the 'big Q, little Q' terminology, where 'big Q' looks at the whole business and 'little Q' equates quality with conformance to standards or specifications. Juran says [25]:

"Some companies have defined quality in terms such as conformance to specification, or conformance to standards. These are dangerous definitions when applied at managerial levels. At those levels what is essential is that the products respond to customer needs. Conformance to standards is only one of many means to that end."

Juran has developed and copyrighted 'The Juran Trilogy', which he calls three universal sequences - they can be applied effectively to any industry [26]. With apologies to Juran, I have added numbers to his sequences, to help identify them in the comparative table in Chapter 1.4.

1   Quality planning:

   1.1 Establish quality goals

   1.2 Identify customers

   1.3 Determine customers' needs

   1.4 Develop services corresponding to customers' needs

   1.5 Develop processes which can create those services

   1.6 Establish process controls

2   Quality control:

   2.1 Evaluate actual quality performance

   2.2 Compare performance to quality goals

   2.3 Act on the difference

3   Quality improvement:

   3.1 Establish infrastructure needed to secure annual quality improvement

   3.2 Identify improvement projects

   3.3 Establish teams to effect improvement projects

   3.4 Provide resources, motivation and training to teams.

Juran's 500 page book is the detail of these steps.

As we will see in Chapter 1.4, there is a clear relationship between The Juran Trilogy and the theory underlying the ISO 9000 standards.

Philip Crosby

If Deming and Juran are the founders, fathers, and guiding lights of the quality movement, Philip B. Crosby is without doubt its most enthusiastic promoter. After 14 years as corporate vice president and director for quality at the ITT Corporation, he started the quality consultancy PCA, Inc., which is his platform for spreading the word. Crosby's big contribution to quality history was the 'zero defects' idea. His best-seller books include *Quality is Free: The Art of Making Quality Certain* [27].

Some key quotes from Crosby's experience [28]:

◆ *"People perform to the standards of their leaders. If management thinks people don't care, then people won't care."*

◆ *"It takes four or five years to get people to understand the need for, and have confidence in, an improvement program."*

◆ *"The cost of quality is the expense of doing things wrong."*

◆ *"One of the reasons I cheerfully share these programs with other companies is that I know that many will probably not be able to use them. Not because they are not capable, but because they do not have a top management willing to be patient while the program is ground out four yards at a time."*

◆ *"The problem of quality management is not what people don't know about it. The problem is what they think they do know."*

◆ *"...we must define quality as 'conforming to requirements.'"* (Compare this with Juran's comments quoted above).

◆ *"Corrective action: It isn't what you find, it's what you do about what you find."*

Crosby has developed what he calls a 'quality management maturity grid', which tracks various aspects of quality planning through five 'stages': [29]

◆ Uncertainty
◆ Awakening
◆ Enlightenment
◆ Wisdom
◆ Certainty

Crosby's prescription for a quality system involves 14 'steps'. [30] Compare these to Deming's 14 points, and to the 20 system elements of ISO 9000 (refer to the next chapter):

1   Management commitment
2   The quality improvement team
3   Quality measurement
4   The cost of quality
5   Quality awareness

6   Corrective action

7   Zero defects planning

8   Supervisor training

9   ZD Day (ZD = 'zero defects')

10 Goal setting

11 Error-cause removal

12 Recognition

13 Quality councils

14 Do it over again

Burstein and Stasiowski rules of quality

Frank Stasiowski and David Burstein, in their book on TQPM [31] have considered Deming's, Juran's and Crosby's prescriptions for quality, along with some examples of how these have been adapted by companies such as Westinghouse and PPG. From this review they have developed the 'Burstein and Stasiowski rules of quality', which are included here as an Appendix to Part 1 (p 57).

Their final point, Rule 13, is of particular interest:

> "Total Quality Project Management (TQPM) cannot be viewed as another program in addition to the firm's 'normal' business; it becomes the way the firm does its business."

At one level, this sounds a bit like the admonition of Richard Miller et al. (p 22) to take every piece of Deming's 14 points as gospel, except to use the B&S 13 points instead. At another (and more important) level, their Rule 13 can be understood to mean that whatever quality system you adapt or develop, it must sit at the very core of business operation.

Stasiowski and Burstein's study of the three experts includes a concise and excellent 7 page summary comparison of the three quality gurus. They note [32]:

> "In establishing a quality improvement process, a company should fit Crosby, Deming and Juran into its process, rather than try to fit its process into one of their programs. Tailor a quality strategy based on all three ideologies, and avoid the conflict involved with trying to choose the 'champion'."

There is considerable value in Stasiowski and Burstein's analysis of how TQM concepts can apply to design practices, especially for larger organizations. I believe one of the few weaknesses of their otherwise excellent study is that they brush aside completely any real consideration of ISO 9000 with a couple of paragraphs [33]:

> "...QA and QC techniques add cost and time to every project. The more thoroughly they are applied, the more they cost."

Putting it all in perspective

What have we learned from this very brief look at the output of three of the most prominent advocates of quality systems?

◆ What look and sound rather like 'motherhood statements' about quality are apparently simple, but they are deceptively so. In fact, they are complex, and can be time-consuming and difficult to implement.

◆ Without commitment bordering on the fanatical, actualization may not be possible.

◆ In addition to monitoring processes, there is a significant emphasis on planning and on evaluation of results.

My experience with the dozens of architectural and engineering practices that I've worked with as a quality consultant is that these three conclusions become apparent to the practitioner at some point early in the learning process, and that they are cause for great consternation.

The first two are perceived as potentially taking more time away from the practice than the practice can afford, and the third is seen as a potentially dangerous re-focusing of energy away from results (design), toward internal processes.

In many cases, employees reach the conclusion that it will be impossible for them to both maintain their output and do the planning and evaluation required to implement a quality system.

These issues of time and focus must be resolved to the satisfaction of both management and staff if the quality process is to continue.

In many cases, these issues are not resolved, the quality improvement process grinds to a halt, and it will not be budged.

Remember Phil Crosby's words? He shares his experience in the knowledge that most of his readers won't have the where-withall to use it! There is a solution, and the logic of it will unfold throughout this book.

Statistical analysis for designers?

There is a powerful baseline of statistical analysis which runs through all TQM concepts. Is statistical analysis relevant to architectural practice? Is TQM relevant to design without statistical analysis?

The role of statistical analysis in controlling the quality of mass-produced goods is obvious, but does the same logic apply to a profession where virtually every project is 'one-off', a unique creation? If so, how?

One does not get very far into this kind of thinking without realizing that there is a law of diminishing returns with the application of any quality improvement strategy, and that strategies must be selected for their ease of implementation and the returns that can be had from using them.

One more expert, and his definitions

I started this chapter with a quotation from Frank Price's excellent book. Price notes [34] that quality control exists in order to answer four questions:

- ◆ "CAN *we make it OK? (Process capability analysis)*
- ◆ "ARE *we making it OK? (Process control monitoring)*
- ◆ "HAVE *we made it OK? (Quality assurance)*
- ◆ "COULD *we make it better? (Product research and development and process evolution)*"

This is very straightforward, elegant in its simplicity, and is a concept we can translate directly to service industries and the design world.

Note: Price's definition of quality assurance is non-standard. 'HAVE we made it OK?' is usually associated with checking (quality control).

Conclusion

There are virtually hundreds of 'tools and techniques' that have been developed as part of the TQM culture. No one firm could possibly employ all of them, nor would there be any reason to do so. The trick is to find those which are most useful to our particular industry, learn them well enough to start using them, and then perfect them over time and with experience.

The trap in that logic - as good as it is - is that we will ignore crucial aspects of some approach because we do not understand its value at the outset: For example, taking only pieces of Deming's 14 point plan, and (if Richard Miller is right) thereby losing the plot.

This brings out the need to find a universal, highly reliable framework for structuring TQM, which is the perfect place to end this chapter and go to the next.

Chapter 1.2
Summary Checklist

✓ Partnering is one quality management strategy. It is not quality management.

✓ There is no single standard for TQM. There are three main TQM approaches, developed by Deming, Juran and Crosby, and hundreds of variants.

✓ There tends to be a zealous 'all or nothing' aura about the teachings of the TQM 'gurus' - as well as about ISO 9000 QM - which gets in the way of a pragmatic assembly of the best features of all, relevant to a particular service industry.

✓ Although there are important differences between the main varieties of TQM, and between them and ISO 9000 QM, these differences are far outweighed by the similarities.

✓ The culture changes required to implement QM frequently pose a stumbling block to staff and management alike, and will derail the process unless resolved.

✓ Statistical analysis is central to all industrial TQM structures, but of limited relevance in the design services.

1.3   ISO 9000 Quality Management

Only a fool would be rash enough to say that quality came anywhere other than first on the universal shopping list - Maxwell Hutchinson [35]

Purpose

To present an outline of ISO 9000 quality assurance and its role in a quality management system; issues of certification, and the broad application of the system elements to design for construction.

What is ISO 9000?

ISO (International Organization for Standardization) is a worldwide federation of national standards bodies. ISO standards, like ASTM standards, are prepared by technical committees. To become an ISO standard, a draft must be approved by at least 75% of member bodies casting a vote.

ISO 9000 is the series number given to ISO quality standards. This family of standards was first published in 1987; the first revision was published late in 1994. The family of standards includes both 'guide' documents and 'requirements' (mandatory) documents. However, it is important to note key language from ISO 9000.1:

> *"The International Standards in the ISO 9000 family describe what elements quality systems should encompass but not how a specific organization implements these elements. It is not the purpose of these International Standards to enforce uniformity of quality systems. Needs of organizations vary. The design and implementation of a quality system must necessarily be influenced by the particular objectives, products and processes, and specific practices of the organization."*

The specific standard which applies to the design professions is ISO 9001:1994: *Quality systems - Model for quality assurance in design, development, production, installation and servicing.*

Up until now I have referred to the whole family of standards as ISO 9000. Hereafter, I will refer to specific documents by number e.g. ISO 9001, but continue to refer to the family as ISO 9000. A list of relevant documents is included in *Resources* at the end of Part 1 (p 56).

The ISO 9001 structure

ISO 9001 contains the following 20 headings, or 'system elements' as they are called (items 1 - 3 are introductory). Subheadings are also included.

4.1 Management responsibility
    4.1.1 Quality policy
    4.1.2 Organization
    4.1.3 Management review

4.2 Quality system
    4.2.1 General
    4.2.2 Quality system procedures
    4.2.3 Quality planning

4.3 Contract review
    4.3.1 General
    4.3.2 Review
    4.3.3 Amendment to a contract
    4.3.4 Records

4.4 Design control
    4.4.1 General
    4.4.2 Design and development planning
    4.4.3 Organizational and technical interfaces
    4.4.4 Design input
    4.4.5 Design output
    4.4.6 Design review
    4.4.7 Design verification
    4.4.8 Design validation
    4.4.9 Design changes

4.5 Document and data control
    4.5.1 General
    4.5.2 Document and data approval and issue
    4.5.3 Document and data changes

4.6 Purchasing
    4.6.1 General
    4.6.2 Evaluation of subcontractors
    4.6.3 Purchasing data
    4.6.4 Evaluation of purchased product

4.7 Control of customer-supplied product

4.8 Product identification and traceability

4.9 Process control

4.10 Inspection and testing *

4.11 Control of inspection, measuring and test equipment *

4.12   Inspection and test status

4.13   Control of nonconforming product
    4.13.1 General
    4.13.2 Review and disposition of nonconforming product

4.14   Corrective and preventive action
    4.14.1 General
    4.14.2 Corrective action
    4.14.3 Preventive action

4.15   Handling, storage, packaging, preservation and delivery *

4.16   Control of quality records

4.17   Internal quality audits

4.18   Training

4.19   Servicing

4.20   Statistical techniques
    4.20.1 Identification of need
    4.20.2 Procedures

Note: Items marked with an asterisk (*) do not have subheads listed as they are generally not applicable to design practice.

The application of ISO 9000 to design practice

Throughout most of the world, quality means quality management systems based on ISO 9000 or its national derivatives. Most U.S. architects - while perhaps being vaguely aware that the ANSI 90 series are exactly equal to ISO 9000 Standards - are unconcerned about them, and have not seen any relevance in these Standards to their practice.

The AIA's records indicate that about 4% of U.S. architects practice internationally. Most of those who do will be aware of the international standards and have some sense of the effect those standards could have on their practice.

ISO 9000 is not a quality management system, but it is a model structure for one; a skeleton or framework that brings order to and establishes requirements for such a system. This idea is developed further in the next chapter.

Accepting this idea does not mean that your quality management system has to follow the ISO 9000 structure in order to comply with it, only that there needs to be a logical relationship to it, understandable to an outside observer.

System elements applicable to design and construction

In the early days of developing construction industry systems to ISO 9000, there was a lot of confusion over how far one had to go to achieve compliance. At the extreme end of foolishness were firms that wrote procedures for buying paper and pencils as a way of complying with system element 4.6: *Purchasing*. Fortunately, those days are past, and most users now understand that 'one size fits none', and that universal systems need tailoring to be useful.

This point is addressed in the 1994 edition of the guide documents, as noted in the extract from ISO 9000.1 above.

There is general industry agreement that there are two tests of whether a system element is or isn't required:

◆ Does the organization perform the function?

◆ Is the quality of the output dependent on the performance of the function?

Consider the example of system element 4.6: *Purchasing*. If the firm purchases something, but the quality of its output is not dependent on the purchase (e.g. pencils) then procedures are not required for the purchase of pencils. Just go buy them!

On the other hand, the design firm also 'purchases' the services of subconsultants. In this case, the capability of the subconsultants is crucial to the quality of the firm's output; therefore, a procedure for appointment of subconsultants is required.

If there isn't a function corresponding to a system element, then no procedure for it would be required. An example would be that system element 4.11: *Control of inspection, measuring and test equipment* would not be applicable to an architectural practice that had no calibratable equipment, but would be applicable to a land surveyor, whose instruments would require calibration. Specific application of this rule is discussed in Chapter 3.1.

Certification

Certification is unique to ISO 9000 systems, and can be a source of confusion to those who are first learning about quality management.

In its simplest analogy, certification is like a driver's license. One can learn how to drive without getting a driver's license, but to prove you can drive, you need the license. The proof is not in the ability itself, but that an external judge of driving ability found you fit to drive.

Telling a star architect with dozens of award-winning buildings to his credit that he needs an impartial agency to certify his quality credentials is seen as an insult. He *has* already been judged by both his peers and his clients, not to mention armies of nit-picking civil servants, conservation fanatics and fervent historic preservationists.

Of course, being able to design quality buildings is not the same as having a quality operating system in place in the practice, where the standard of measure is either ISO 9000 or any of the mainstream TQM choices.

I will return to the issue of certification in Chapter 3.3.

ISO 9000 myths

There are a few myths about ISO 9000 QM, particularly with respect to how much it costs to implement and how much paperwork is involved. It is possible to create huge, expensive, complicated, unwieldy structures that technically comply with ISO 9000, and some well-publicized cases have been good examples. Exactly the same is true for TQM, of course.

Firms are allowed great flexibility within the ISO 9000 structure, but (unlike TQM) there are limits to minimizing system design within the structure. These are discussed in subsequent chapters.

The cost of quality management is, obviously, a most important consideration, and is explored in Chapter 6.2.

Chapter 1.3
Summary Checklist

✓ ISO 9000 systems are the world standard outside the U.S. and Japan.

✓ ISO 9000 is a structure for organizing a quality system.

✓ Each industry, and firms within those industries, can use the parts of the ISO 9000 structure that are appropriate to their industry.

✓ Certification is not a requirement of ISO 9000, it is an optional demonstration of having reached a standard of compliance with the principles of the standard.

1.4   Common Ground: TQM and ISO 9000 QM

There is also the conflict between the two philosophies of 'total quality control' (TQC) and 'quality management systems'. The former being dependent upon the statistical approach to problem-solving, whereas the latter sets out to develop and implement systems to control each activity..." - Lionel Stebbing [36]

Purpose

To outline the similarities and differences between TQM and ISO 9000 systems, and to propose a synthesis of their common ground.

How similar are the choices?

Stebbing refers to TQC in the quote above, a term I have not used otherwise in this book. I believe the point he makes about TQC is also generally applicable to TQM; however, TQC is that part of TQM which is most focused on statistics.

In all the rhetoric about TQM vs. ISO 9000 QM, few writers have drawn attention to the similarities between the two philosophies. There is, in fact, a very substantial common ground, as we will see.

Not only does understanding this help to clarify some of the misunderstanding about what one or the other approach requires, but as one gets into the details, it becomes apparent that the baseline message is not fundamentally different from one to the other.

All TQM methods share one thing in common, which is that they are the developments of one person or group, formed through experience and awareness of what others had done. This contrasts sharply with ISO 9000, which is a structure developed globally, from the broadest possible inputs, and 'ratified' by over 3/4 of the countries belonging to the International Standards Organization.

As such a common denominator of quality management principles, ISO 9000 has none of the allure that comes from having a personal champion.

In thinking about these different versions of TQM, I am reminded of the old story of the three blind men feeling the elephant. If, by the end of this book, readers feel comfortable with the idea that all the variants of TQM, together with ISO 9000, are only aspects of the same thing, different ways of 'feeling the elephant', I will consider the effort a success.

Elephant X-rays

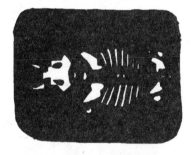

If I can milk that metaphor just a little more, we need to see the whole elephant, at least at a distance, to get an idea what we can do with it. We need to harness it to accomplish a purpose - that is our need. We need to do so without going broke feeding it, growing weary of cleaning up after it, or getting trampled by it - those are our fears.

So, what does the QM elephant look like? Let's start with its framework. If we were to take a giant X-ray of the elephant from the top, and another from the side, we would get two quite different pictures of the same skeleton.

For simplicity, imagine that one of these X-rays is Dr. Deming's 14-point structure, and the other X-ray is the ISO 9000 20-element structure. We get different views of the structure from different perspectives.

Let us try to reconcile those two views, those two skeletons - and at the same time, to relate them to the principles established by Juran and Crosby. Stasiowski and Burstein ran a similar exercise, but without considering ISO 9000, and came up with their '13 Rules of Quality' (refer to the appendix at the end of Part 1 (p 57).

Ten Keys to Quality

So far as I have read, nobody has published a comparison of the ISO 9000 structure to the prevailing TQM structures. My efforts in this regard this should be regarded as a first rough draft for a comprehensive framework. The result of this exercise follows overleaf - the 'TEN KEYS TO QUALITY'.

A Basis for Comparison of ISO 9000

The Ten Keys to Quality	Deming's 14 Point System
1 Management must establish, inspire and lead quality system implementation	1 Create constancy of purpose for improvement of product and service 2 Adopt the new philosophy 7 Institute leadership 14 Take action to accomplish the transformation
2 Drive planning and delivery of services from a thorough understanding of client needs and expectations	
3 Base purchasing (inward services) on value rather than cost	4 End the practice of awarding business on price tag alone
4 Develop process controls which ensure that quality requirements *can* be met	3 Cease dependence on mass inspection 11 Eliminate numerical quotas
5 Monitor processes to ensure that quality requirements *are* being met	
6 Provide processes which improve the service as it is being produced (in-process improvement)	
7 Evaluate the effectiveness of process controls and operate a positive feedback process to ensure increased capability of quality delivery	5 Improve constantly and forever the system of production and service
8 Institute a program of continuous training, to adequately respond to changing markets	6 Institute training and retraining 13 Institute a vigorous programme of education and retraining
9 Provide a work environment which motivates staff to do their best	8 Drive out fear 9 Break down barriers between staff areas 10 Eliminate slogans, exhortations, and targets for the workforce 12 Remove barriers to pride of workmanship
10 Keep good records to demonstrate quality capability and performance	

and Deming, Juran and Crosby TQM Systems

ISO 9001 System	The Juran Trilogy	Crosby's 14 Steps
4.1.1 Quality policy 4.1.2 Organization 4.2 Quality system	1.1 Establish quality goals	1 Management commitment 2 The quality improvement team 5 Quality awareness
4.3 Contract review	1.2 Identify customers 1.3 Determine customers' needs 1.4 Develop services corresponding to customers' needs	
4.6 Purchasing 4.7 Control of customer-supplied product		
4.4 Design control 4.8 Product identification and traceability 4.9 Process control 4.15 Handling, storage, packaging, preservation and delivery 4.20 Statistical techniques	1.5 Develop processes which can create those services 1.6 Establish process controls	7 Zero defects planning
4.10 Inspection and testing 4.11 Control of inspection, measuring and test equipment 4.12 Inspection and test status 4.19 Servicing	2.1 Evaluate actual quality performance	3 Quality measurement
4.13 Control of nonconforming product	2.2 Compare performance to quality goals 2.3 Act on the difference	3 Quality measurement
4.1.3 Management review 4.14 Corrective and preventive action 4.17 Internal quality audits	3.1 Establish infrastructure needed to secure annual quality improvement 3.2 Identify improvement projects 3.3 Establish teams to effect improvement projects	4 The cost of quality 6 Corrective action 11 Error-cause removal 14 Do it over again
4.18 Training	3.4 Provide resources, motivation and training to teams	8 Supervisor training
	3.4 Provide resources, motivation and training to teams	9 Z D Day 10 Goal setting 11 Error-cause removal 12 Recognition 13 Quality councils
4.5 Document and data control 4.16 Control of quality records		

Certainly this is not the only set of 'keys' which could be developed that would accommodate logically the diverse structures considered. I imagine that some would think that elements of some of the QM structures would fit better in categories other than as shown. Nevertheless, this structure *works*, and really does demonstrate that the four systems all have much in common. I will return to it in Chapter 3.1.

Some lessons from this comparison

In looking at the table on the preceding pages, some conclusions leap out, which are worthy of discussion:

♦ In-process monitoring and improvement do not appear in Deming's 14 points. Of course, the Deming method is very deeply involved with process monitoring and improvement, through statistical analysis. These steps are implied within Deming's 5th point.

♦ Deming's and Crosby's systems do not specifically address the relationship of product/service design to customer needs. This is because their systems are more inward looking. In *Quality Is Free*, Crosby gives the customer two pages on the subject of complaints. Deming focuses on improving quality as the path to customer satisfaction.

♦ The Juran and Crosby systems do directly address purchasing, although defects in incoming goods would be identified under their respective process improvement systems.

♦ Deming and Crosby stand out in addressing the importance of people in building quality. In ISO 9000, the human element is addressed in guide documents, but, in the standard, only with respect to training needs.

♦ Only ISO 9000 deals specifically with requirements for document control and records. The other systems assume an appropriate level of record keeping, sufficient for purposes of managing the quality system, but under ISO 9000, document control and records are key to the certification process.

This last point is an important issue for the design professions, who often find that getting their document control 'up to scratch' is one of the hardest parts of implementing quality management. Obviously the difficulty of this will vary greatly with how organized or disorganized the practice is!

Some key differences

A key to understanding the differences between TQM and ISO 9000 QM is that the latter demands accurate process statements, and compares performance to those statements, as a starting point. TQM gets there in the end, but (depending on your choice of systems) it is possible to experiment with 'continuous improvement' for some time before confronting the basic description of what one does.

Note, however, that if one were using The Juran Trilogy as the basis for a TQM system, the preplanning requirements would be the same as they would under ISO 9000.

The problem of statistical analysis

In the introduction to this chapter, I quoted Lionel Stebbing on one key difference between ISO 9000 and TQM. The point he makes is a serious one. Anyone raised on TQM finds it very hard to imagine a viable quality system that isn't founded in process measurement, with incremental improvement based on numbers.

It is not impossible to imagine incremental measurements in the design process, but the very idea is abhorrently alien to most design professionals; managers and staff alike. The concept of choice, rather, is a holistic one.

One of the reasons for this problem is that design is not widgets. Design is almost always 'one-off', and measuring defects between different designs is practically meaningless as a way of improving design.

Another problem is that most design defects are not caused by process deficiencies, but by input deficiencies and by insufficient coordination with others ('technical interfaces', in the jargon of ISO 9000). Rectifying either of these deficiencies is best done by means that do not require statistics.

Some designers do use statistical analysis as a design tool, of course, and therefore would address that use appropriately within their quality procedures under system element 4.20 in an ISO 9001 - based quality system. However, that use is quite different from the use of statistics underscoring TQM theory, as Stebbing notes.

Synthesis and the paradox of pragmatic obsession

In Chapter 1.1 we discovered that the quality movement had many of the earmarks of a religion, and noted that this complicated 'pick and choose' system design strategies. Others have used the analogy.

In 1986, Ted Lowe and Joseph Mazzeo, senior quality managers at General Motors, published a comparison of the Deming, Juran and Crosby methods entitled *"Crosby*Deming*Juran: Three Preachers, One Religion"* [37].

It was Deming, the founder of the movement, who says (in his second point) that we "need a new religion".

In reviewing the research into design excellence, we saw the word 'obsession' more than once, and have noted the requirement by quality experts that commitment to quality be *complete* in order to succeed (hence the 'T' in TQM).

The dictionary defines 'obsession' as 'the dominating action or influence of a persistent feeling, idea, or the like, which *a person cannot escape*' (emphasis added).

Pragmatic obsession

As noted above, Stasiowski and Burstein urge adapting the thoughts of the experts to your firm's processes rather than the other way around. This is good advice, and helps to draw the distinction between being 'obsessed' with the need for and importance of quality, and being 'obsessed' with implementing the teachings of any one guru.

Pragmatism and obsession normally don't go together; they are mutually exclusive ideas. But in this case an accommodation needs to be found, a paradox appreciated.

Have *total commitment*, but be cool and level-headed about it! I believe this approach is reflected in the ISO 9001 structure, which mandates (in system element 4.1) 'commitment' at 'the highest level of management'.

Perhaps we could re-define 'commitment' as 'pragmatic obsession'.

If the 'unpragmatic' obsessions can be shelved, what begins to emerge is an awareness that 'appropriate QM' is some mixture of the concepts and tools of TQM *and* ISO 9000 QM, thus setting the stage for Part 3: PROCESS: Designing Your System.

Chapter 1.4
Summary Checklist

✓ TQM systems reflect the experiences of their developers. ISO 9000 reflects an international distillation of global quality experience.

✓ All QM systems have a common philosophical basis.

✓ The best way to study QM systems is to study their structures, and compare their structures.

✓ It is possible to arrive at a single structural framework which encompasses the mainstream TQM systems and ISO 9000. One such framework is *The Ten Keys of Quality*.

✓ The two most significant differences between TQM and ISO 9000 are TQM's reliance on statistical techniques and ISO 9000's reliance on documentation.

✓ Replace zealous conformity with pragmatic obsession.

1.5 Prevention vs. Cure

*No matter how well planned, every design project
will be plagued with errors and omissions.* -
Stasiowski and Burstein [38]

Purpose

To investigate how quality management principles relate to
problem prevention and problem 'curing' strategies in the
context of design.

**Is Frank being a bit
rough on us?**

Most architects wouldn't agree with Stasiowski, at least
publicly. If they did agree, a little bit, it would be about
OTHER architects' offices, not their own. Stasiowski makes
his living by talking to practitioners - thousands of them
every year - so presumably he has a basis on which to make
this claim. The above quote continues:

> *"The purpose of quality control is to find and correct
> these errors before design goes to the field."*

Note here the use of the words 'quality *control*'. In archi-
tectural/engineering terms, quality control is, essentially,
checking. It is one part of quality management - the *'HAVE
we made it OK?'* question which is the third quadrant of
Frank Price's approach mentioned in Chapter 1.2.

The incidence rate of errors and omissions is not so much the
point as is the reality. Every design practitioner knows that
one single stupid little uncaught mistake can turn into a
nightmare: claims of negligence or even incompetence, a
headache to resolve, and a deep scratch in the patina of
reputation.

Yet, he also knows that it is virtually impossible to check
everything; to find every potential problem. The economics
of practice require that some degree of risk be taken every
day with respect to errors and omissions, and he knows that
this risk must be hedged with insurance coverage.

**Prevention reduces
the need for 'curing'**

It is precisely here that one can find the first payoff in
looking beyond the fragility of relying on a quality control
(checking) procedure to keep out of trouble.

The whole emphasis of quality management is on PREVENTION rather than CURING. Curing is still important, because no prevention program is likely to fix all production faults, especially in the early days of running it.

Obviously, though, if we can prevent problems from occurring, it is better than finding and fixing them afterwards.

It is instructive to look back at Frank Price's 'quadrilogy' - *'CAN we?, ARE we?, HAVE we?, COULD we?'*. The *CAN we?* and *COULD we?* of these are about prevention, rather than cures, and the *ARE we?* is about both prevention and curing. Deming, in his third point, admonishes us to *"Cease dependence on mass inspection"*. In our terminology, Deming is talking about checking drawings before they go out to bid.

Why haven't we design professionals, with all our emphasis on quality and excellence, worked very much on prevention strategies? I would suggest that there are two probable answers:

◆ Our focus has always been on the 'product', not the 'process'.

◆ One can't see the mistakes one hasn't made yet. They are never obvious.

Checking will always be a very important part of quality management, and being consistent about checking would be a major improvement for most design firms. But checking alone will NEVER reduce the rate of making mistakes, and has very little to do with the many other ways design professionals could make their practices more reliable and competitive.

To get beyond quality CONTROL, let us look again at the **Ten Keys to Quality** (refer to pp 40-41):

1   Management must establish, inspire and lead quality system implementation.

2   Drive planning and delivery of services from a thorough understanding of client needs and expectations.

3   Base purchasing (inward services) on value rather than cost.

4   Develop process controls which ensure that quality requirements *can* be met.

Herman checking mistakes
not yet made by client

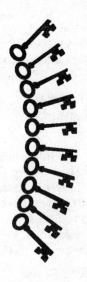

5   Monitor processes to ensure that quality requirements *are* being met.

6   Provide processes which improve the service as it is being produced (in-process improvement).

7   Evaluate the effectiveness of process controls and operate a positive feedback process to ensure increased capability of quality delivery.

8   Institute a program of continuous training, to adequately respond to changing markets.

9   Provide a work environment which motivates staff to do their best.

10 Keep good records to demonstrate quality capability and performance.

Key 1 establishes an *environment* in which quality management is possible.

Keys 2 and 3 ensure establish requirements for *inputs* to the design process.

Key 4 is the *planning* Key, which structures quality control.

Keys 5 and 6 are the *process* Keys.

Key 7 is the *feedback* Key, which makes the system self-learning.

Finally, Keys 8, 9 and 10 are *enabling* Keys, which establish conditions necessary for quality management to work.

Deceptive simplicity

As I noted previously, the logic of some of these 'keys' seems quite obvious, but their apparent simplicity is deceptive. For example:

◆   The founder of a design practice may be a great designer, and even an excellent communicator to his clients (the external ones) but at the same time be a terrible communicator to his staff (the 'internal clients'), and completely unaware of it.

◆   The prinipals of the practice may have gotten so used to never receiving proper briefing from the client that they always assume they have to do it for him, rather than expect it of the client and structure the relationship such that he is guided in the briefing process.

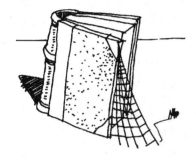

- The practice may have worked so long with mediocre or even barely competent subconsultants that it routinely and unconsciously tolerates inferior performance and the compromising of its own work this performance brings.

- The practice may have an office manual which sets out performance standards, but only one person in the office actually knows where it is, and that person hasn't opened it in years.

- The practice may have an unwritten rule that every job gets checked before it goes out, but checking is rarely programmed in the schedule, and usually happens during the bid period if at all.

- The partners have been meaning for years to do a general overhaul of office procedures and tighten things up a bit, but there never is enough time.

- Training is by demand, occasionally by sheer necessity, and often as a reward for good service. There is no long range training plan related to where the practice wants to be in 5 or 10 years.

- Nobody in the practice, including the partners, could succinctly express where the firm wants to be in 5 or 10 years.

The above list could go on and on, but there is no need. If one or more of these points brings a thin, grim smile of recognition to your face, then your practice would be improved by a quality management program, and the Ten Keys, and the rest of this book, will be of relevance.

Pogo was right

However, the common symptoms of practice malaise noted above are likely to have crept deep into the bones of the practice, and won't be fixed by a quick shot of antibiotics. There are no 'quick fixes' in quality management.

The enemy is nearly always systemic, there because it was created out of the personalities of those who created the firm and those who now make it run. In what is reputed to be the most quoted line in all of English literature, Walt Kelly's Pogo mused *"We have seen the enemy, and it is us"*.

Chapter 1.5
Summary Checklist

✓ Checking may be the profession's most important quality control tool, but it is rarely carried out to the degree intended by practice management.

✓ The reason that checking, and other quality control measures, are often not as effective or consistent as management wants is usually because other conditions necessary for overall quality assurance are absent.

✓ Prevention is better than cure, but good prevention planning will include cures for problems that slip through the prevention net.

✓ Pogo was right.

1.6   Separated by a Common Language

America and England are two countries separated by the same language. - George Bernard Shaw

Purpose

To outline the need for a greater appreciation of the role of communication in professional services delivery, particularly with respect to quality and risk management.

Can I hear you?

Shaw's famous quotation puts into plain words the concept that the appearance of communication, or possession of the tools of communication, does not necessarily mean that communication succeeds.

Communication is, in my view, the single most important aspect of quality management in the service industries, perhaps equal in importance to statistical analysis in manufacturing.

Good communication is not one of the keys. It is the key ring.

Communication is the point where the paths of quality management, risk management and professional services marketing all cross - it is the single most important aspect of all three practice functions, and not one that is understood widely, despite the fact that we all do some version of it most of the time we are awake.

Many authorities on risk management in professional services identify a failure to adequately communicate as the root cause of most claims made against design professionals.

In other words, it is not bad design that usually gets architects into trouble, it is not listening to the client; not hearing the client.

Since quality assurance is defined as 'meeting and exceeding the client's expectations', clearly risk management and quality management are very closely related, with ability to communicate as the common ground.

A low-risk practice is a quality-conscious practice and vice versa.

To some degree the communication problems between architect and client also exist between architect and builder; architect and other members of the consultant team. As the architect is usually entrusted with coordination of the consultant team, the communication issue is an especially important one.

Many writers in our industry stress this importance. For example:

◆ Norman Kaderlan: *"Perhaps the most critical communication skill you can develop is listening."* [39] In Chapter 3.6 we will review Kaderlan's eight 'tips for good listening'.

◆ Fred Stitt: *"Designers sometimes aren't much fun to talk to because they are so deeply involved in the world of ideas they would rather listen to pig grunts than endure normal conversation small talk."* [40]

◆ Stasiowski and Burstein: *"... if you truly don't know how to listen, you will never get to the crux of the client's issue. If you can't get to the heart of the client's needs and wants, you won't get hired again, your firm will not be talked about by the client, and it will not be recommended to others!"* [41]

◆ Lionel Stebbing: *"Communication is, unfortunately, the most abused of the attributes."* [42] Stebbing here is referring to the 'attributes of efficiency', his '12 C's' of the total presentation of quality assurance.

◆ David Maister: *"Having observed quality improvement efforts in numerous professional firms, there is no doubt in my mind that the primary source of quality failure in the professions is miscommunication and misunderstanding between the client and the professional. In turn, the largest single component of this miscommunication is over how 'success' for the matter is to be defined. Professionals think they know what clients want of them, but frequently this differs from what the client truly wants or expects."* [43]

◆ Stuart Rose: *"Probably the one practice that is not widely used by any of the design professions - whether a small or large firm, an architectural, engineering, or interiors firm - is an active program for listening to users."* [44]

Communication is at the core of Dr. Deming's point 8: 'Drive out fear'. He says [45]

"Most people on a job, especially people in management positions, do not understand what the job is, nor what is right or wrong. Moreover, it is not clear to them how to find out. Many of them are afraid to ask questions or to take a position. The economic loss from fear is appalling."

Most texts on quality management, however, do not talk about communication. For one thing, it is too hard to measure. For another, it is seen as a matter more related to human relations, marketing, or some facet of business other than quality. Yet, the bottom line is that unless any quality function can be clearly and effectively communicated to everyone else affected by it, the value of that function is, at best, compromised, and at worst, rendered ineffective or even misunderstood, causing a negative effect.

**Chapter 1.6
Summary Checklist**

✓ Communication is the ring that holds the keys of quality.

✓ Communication is the bridge between management of quality, risk and marketing.

✓ Of all the communication skills, the one most needing improvement is that of listening.

Part 1 Resources

References

(1) Ford, Charles H., *Developing a Successful Client-Consultant Relationship;* Chapter 1 in *Clients & Consultants: Meeting and Exceeding Expectations,* Chip R. Bell and Leonard Nadler, eds., Gulf Publishing Company, 1979 (2nd ed. 1985).

(2) This idea, and struggle, has been with the profession since its earliest beginnings. In Vitruvius' *The Ten Books of Architecture* (written in the 1st century B.C.; translated by Prof. Morris Morgan and published by Harvard University Press in 1914; republished by Dover Publications in 1960) our Roman predecessor discussed the special knowledge needed to practice. He quotes the ancient architect Pytheos, builder of the Temple of Minerva at Priene:

"... an architect ought to be able to accomplish much more in all the arts and sciences than the men who, by their own particular kinds of work and the practice of it, have brought each a single subject to the highest perfection."

Vitruvius comments that *"Pytheos made a mistake by not observing that the arts are each composed of two things, the actual work and the theory of it."*

Vitruvius started a debate about theory vs. practice that has continued for over 2,000 years and doubtless will continue into the future.

(3) Franklin, James R. FAIA, *In Search of Design Excellence,* The American Institute of Architects, 1989, p 5.

(4) Rose, Stuart W., *Achieving Excellence in Your Design Practice,* Whitney Library of Design, 1987, p 7.

(5) Ibid., p 60.

(6) Ibid., p 62.

(7) Peters, Thomas J. and Robert H. Waterman Jr, *In Search of Excellence: Lessons from America's Best-Run Companies,* Harper & Row, 1982, p 16.

(8) Kaderlan, Norman, *Designing Your Practice: A Principal's Guide to Creating and Managing a Design Practice,* McGraw-Hill, 1991, pp 99-100.

(9) In a workshop at the Royal Australian Institute of Architects 1992 National Convention, Melbourne.

(10) Kaderlan, p 100.

(11) Stasiowski, Frank A. and David Burstein, *Total Quality Project Management for the Design Firm,* John Wiley & Sons, Inc., 1994, Preface p v.

(12) Franklin, James R. FAIA, *Big Q Practices: Counter Culture Architecture for the 90s* (work in progress). The 'big Q - little Q' concept is described in some detail by Juran. Refer to footnote 24.

(13) As a headliner in mailings to past clients, promoting the journal *Project Management*. To back up this statement, Stasiowski cites "results from (a) recent Nationwide Survey conducted on clients whereby design ranked behind schedule-budget".

(14) Gutman, Robert, *Architectural Practice: A Critical View*, Princeton Architectural Press, 1988, pp 20-21.

(15) Price, Frank, *Right First Time*, Wildwood House (UK), 1986, p 87.

(16) On the cover of Mary Walton's biography of Deming (see footnote 17).

(17) Walton, Mary, *The Deming Management Method*, Mercury Books Division of W. H. Allen & Company plc (U.K.), 1989.

(18) Ibid., pp 34-36.

(19) Mears, Peter, *Quality Improvement Tools & Techniques*, McGraw-Hill, 1995. pp 232-234.

(20) Markert, Charles D., Richard C. Simon and Richard M. Miller, *Dr. W. Edward Deming's 14 Points - Adapted for the A/E Firm*, a paper prepared for the Design & Construction Quality Institute, August, 1992.

(21) Franklin, James R. FAIA, *Total Quality Management: TQM for Architects* (work in progress, 1992).

(22) Ibid., Appendix A: *Deming with Quaint Phrase: The Fourteen Points*, p 1.

(23) Quoted on the dust jacket of J. M. Juran's *Juran on Quality by Design* (refer to footnote 24).

(24) Juran, J. M., *Juran on Quality by Design: The New Steps for Planning Quality into Goods and Services*, The Free Press, 1992.

(25) Ibid., p 11.

(26) Ibid., pp 14-15.

(27) Crosby, Philip B., *Quality Is Free: The Art of Making Quality Certain*, McGraw-Hill, 1979. Page references below are to the 1980 Mentor paperback edition.

(28) Ibid., pp 8, 9, 11, 12, 13, 15 and 65.

(29) Ibid., p 33.

(30) Ibid., pp 149-222.

(31) Stasiowski and Burstein, pp 33-43.

(32) Ibid., p 39.

(33) Ibid., pp 32-33.

(34) Price, pp 10-11.

(35) Hutchinson, Maxwell, President, Royal Institute of British Architects, in the Foreword to *Quality Management: Guidance for an Office Manual*, RIBA, 1990.

(36) Stebbing, Lionel, *Quality Management in the Service Industry*, Ellis Horwood, 1990, p 29.

(37) Article in *Quality*, Hitchcock Publications, September 1986.

(38) Stasiowski and Burstein, p 59.

(39) Kaderlan, p 98.

(40) Stitt, Fred, *Designing Buildings That Work: The Architect's Problem Prevention Sourcebook*, McGraw-Hill, Inc., 1985, pp 15-16.

(41) Stasiowski, p 10.

(42) Stebbing, p 22.

(43) Maister, David H., *Negotiating Quality*, The American Lawyer, April 1994. Reprinted in TAS/The Architecture Show, Summer 1995.

(44) Rose, p 67.

(45) Walton, p 71.

For more help on...

Design excellence: Obtain and read *In Search of Excellence*, Thomas Vonier AIA, Editor, AIA Press, Washington, 1989. Chapters by James Franklin FAIA, Robert Shibley AIA, Dana Cuff, Weld Coxe Hon. AIA, Marvin Adelson, Robert Gutman Hon. AIA, Ellen Bruce and Sibel Bozdogan. Extensively illustrated with Franklin's marvelous drawings, it is an excellent primer on current thinking about excellence in design.

Excellence in design *practice* (a different topic): Stuart Rose, *Achieving Excellence in Your Design Practice*.

The difference between quality of design and quality of service to the client: David Maister, *Quality Work Doesn't Mean Quality Service*, DCQ Forum, Winter 1992, published by the Design & Construction Quality Institute.

Relevant ISO Standards: Those referenced in this book are:

◆ ISO 9000.1: 1994: *Quality management and quality assurance standards, Part 1: Guidelines for selection and use.*

◆ ISO 9001: 1994: *Quality systems - Model for quality assurance in design, development, production, installation and servicing.*

◆ ISO 9004-2-1991: *Quality management and quality system elements, Part 2: Guidelines for services.*

◆ ISO 8402-1986: *Quality - Vocabulary.*

◆ ISO/DIN 10011-1990: *Guidelines for auditing quality systems, Part 1: Auditing.*

**Appendix to
Chapter 1.2**

Burstein and Stasiowski's 13 rules of quality

1. Quality is defined as 'conformance to *requirements*'-all requirements, including budget and schedule.

2. Requirements must be *mutually* agreed upon with the client and among the entire project team.

3. Requirements must be defined *quantitatively* so that nonconformances can be measured and made visible to everyone involved.

4. The traditional concept of the 'project team' must be expanded to include all 'suppliers' (people who provide input) and 'customers' (people who use the products of our work).

5. Solving quality problems requires the efforts of a broad *cross section* of this extended project team.

6. There must be *a firmwide* system to seek out nonconformances that recur from project to project.

7. Nonconformances should be expected, but not tolerated. In striving for 'zero defects,' everyone must *continually* reduce the number of nonconformances.

8. Nonconformances that affect client satisfaction are the most serious; they should receive the highest priority.

9. Prevention is cheaper than damage control; the *earlier* you catch a problem, the *less costly* it is to fix.

10. There must be a *firmwide* commitment to quality from the CEO all the way down to the most junior clerical assistant.

11. Everyone in the firm must be trained so that they *understand* the new ways of looking at quality.

12. Individuals and groups who achieve the goals of quality improvement must be appropriately *recognized and rewarded*.

13. Total Quality Project Management (TQPM) cannot be viewed as another program in addition to the firm's 'normal' business; it must become *the way the firm does its business*.

(From *Total Quality Project Management for the Design Firm*, p 43.)

Part 2

START NOW: Evaluating Your Needs

2.1 Mirrors, Navel Gazing and Self-Assessment

2.2 Where Have You Been, Where Are You Going?

2.3 The Diagnostic Audit

2.4 Experts and How to Use Them Wisely

2.1 Mirrors, Navel Gazing and Self-Assessment

As the buildings and spaces you create are a reflection of you, so is your practice - Norman Kaderlan [46]

Purpose

To discuss the importance of accurate self-assessment as a precondition to successful implementation of quality systems and typical impediments to self-assessment, and to describe useful assessment techniques.

One of the most important (but little appreciated) aspects of a formal quality management system is its ability to focus management attention on potential problem areas that would not otherwise be seen, and thus alert management to the need for resolution before it is confronted with a manifestation of the problem.

There is general agreement among those who study organizational change that effective change requires objective analysis of the present and a plan for the future.

How can we get an objective analysis?

Can you see your reflection?

The problem with self-reflection as a self-improvement strategy is that most of us are too close to the problem to see it clearly. That's navel gazing. Looking in the mirror is a notoriously unreliable method of self-evaluation, as the image is distorted by all the biases (positive and negative) of the subject.

Problems facing practices are, for the most part, those of which the practice is unaware.

The reason for this is that we all value quality performance very highly, and as soon as a problem is manifested - or at least apparent to management - it tends to be addressed and resolved. Unfortunately this is knee-jerk management, and it can never structurally address the unknown problems. It is problem solution, not problem prevention.

Planning which is not based on present reality is doomed to failure. There is quite a body of literature available on this process, much of which would be relevant in varying degrees to design practice.

I have seen many well-meaning attempts at organizational change never get off the ground because the starting point - the launching pad - was vague and fuzzy. Management either didn't understand its firm very well, or was hanging on to unrealistic ideas about the capabilities of the organization.

One reason for this 'vague and fuzzy' corporate self-awareness probably springs from the idea of the design professional as a 'generalist' - a concept characteristic of architects, but usually not of engineers. The idea is 'We can do anything' and its corollary, 'Get the job first and figure out how to do it later'. As we will see in later chapters, this approach is not compatible with any concept of quality management.

For the present, we will consider some of the simpler methods of introducing objectivity into self-awareness.

The process of getting from where you are to where you want to be is called Strategic Planning.

PREPARING THE PLANNING BASE

ESTABLISHING STRATEGIES

COMMUNICATING & IMPLEMENTING THE PLAN

Figure 2.1: Strategic Planning Model

One particularly useful, accessible and inexpensive source on this topic is Neville Smith's *Down-to-Earth Strategic Planning* [47].

Smith sees strategic planning as an iterative, three stage process, represented by Figure 2.1 at left.

In describing strategic planning, he borrows an idea invented by the science fiction writer Frank Herbert, called 'overstanding'. Smith defines overstanding as 'to over-view the entire context' or 'seeing the big picture' and notes [48] *"Overstanding is possibly the outstanding characteristic of strategic thinking"*.

But how do we come to this point of 'overstanding', especially with respect to our current situation? Management consultants have invented a number of ways of doing this.

All of these techniques necessarily involve some method of introducing more objectivity into (and weeding subjectivity out of) our introspective processes.

SWOT analysis

One of the most common techniques is called the SWOT analysis. SWOT stands for strengths and weaknesses / opportunities and threats. The strength/weakness evaluation is internal, about your firm; whereas the opportunities/threats evaluation is about factors external to your firm. Obviously the goal is to match up strengths with opportunities and to avoid competing where weaknesses correspond with threats.

The SWOT analysis should not be undertaken by management alone, as the biases in management's perception can get in the way of real understanding. Everyone in the practice should be involved. Some firms invite trusted colleagues and/or past clients to participate.

Some sample categories for a SWOT analysis are shown opposite. These headings are very general, just to stir your imagination. The ones you develop should be as specific as possible.

The time frame is also important. The SWOT analysis should take as long a view of the situation as possible; two to five years.

Peer review

Peer reviews are acknowledged as one of the best ways for the owners of small professional firms to gain objectivity in understanding their practices' strengths and weaknesses.

Although there are endless variants on the concept, peer review techniques can broadly be categorized into two types, formal and informal. Taking the second first, an informal peer review system is one where you agree with another professional to be 'on call' and to give frank, honest and direct advice about those matters on which the other person seeks advice. The arrangement is reciprocal and there is no payment for the service either way.

One of the most productive peer review arrangements is to cross-share design reviews. That is, you have a principal from another practice come to all of your design reviews, and you go to all of hers.

Outline for SWOT Analysis

STRENGTHS	WEAKNESSES
Market position: • General reputation • Recognized market niche leader • Design awards **Resources:** • Stable, well qualified staff • Expert knowledge in specific building types / specialist skills • Experienced, self-starting support staff **Financial:** • Comfortable cash position • Predictable cash flow • Good receivables exceed debts • Good backlog of work • No claims of negligence	**Market position:** • Firm not well known • No track record in growth areas • No real differentiation from competitors **Resources:** • High staff turnover • Retirement/loss of principal • Support staff need constant direction **Financial:** • High overdraft /paying interest on operating capital • High receivables; some may be uncollectable • Low backlog of work • Subject to claims of negligence
OPPORTUNITIES	THREATS
Market: • Market growth in areas of firm's experience • Competitor has closed practice • Previous client has announced expansion plans **Economy:** • Improving business climate • Interest rates lowering **Government:** • Government spending on infrastructure to increase	**Market:** • High profile competing firm adding staff in our areas of expertise • Overbuilding to cause slowdown **Economy:** • Interest rates on rise **Government:** • Increased governmental requirements

  The 'fresh pair of eyes' from across town will see things that the design team could never see because they were too close to the problem. Of course, your peer review partner needs to be someone you can trust, and should not be chasing the same group of clients. This technique works for firms of any size, but is particularly useful for the very small practice.

Organizational peer review

Formal review is called "Organizational Peer Review". It was developed by the American Consulting Engineers Council (ACEC). The American Institute of Architects (AIA) saw the positive effects of the ACEC's method, and rather than re-invent the wheel, it joined the ACEC system.

Here's how it works. If you are an AIA member, you request a peer review from the ACEC. The ACEC runs the AIA's Peer Review Program, but an AIA representative sits on the ACEC Steering Committee. When you apply to the ACEC, you get a list of qualified, trained peer reviewers, with information on each reviewer's experience, firm size, and other relevant data. You can choose anyone on the list.

What happens in the peer review? I quote from the AIA's document on the subject: [49]

"At your request, one or more specially trained reviewers, who are practicing architects and engineers, will visit your firm to examine its overall business health. They'll talk with you and your employees and take a look at manuals, business plans, and other materials describing your firm's operation. They will evaluate the extent to which your firm is doing things the way you think they should be done. When they've finished their examination, they'll discuss their findings with you.

"The goal of the peer review is not to criticize, make comparisons, or cast judgment but to provide insights that will help you build a stronger, more productive, and more competitive firm. The primary topics reviewed are general management, human resources, financial management, professional development, business development, and project management."

Confidentiality is, obviously, crucial. Prior to the review, each reviewer signs a nondisclosure agreement. No written records are kept and any materials supplied to the review team are returned at the conclusion of the review.

There are many mirrors

There are other evaluative methods for understanding your practice and the environment it operates in, such as environmental scanning, organizational analysis and portfolio analysis. It is outside the scope of this book to detail all of the 'mirrors' available. The key thing to remember is that you must ensure the objectivity of viewpoint.

Chapter 2.1 Summary Checklist

✓ Gain objectivity in your self-view - see your practice as others see it. Ask them.

✓ Problems facing practices are, for the most part, those of which the practice is unaware.

✓ Business planning is not a requisite for success, but most authorities agree that it helps.

✓ Business planning requires realistic assessment of the practice (strengths and weaknesses), and of the practice environment (opportunities and threats).

✓ Strategic planning is the best method for achieving your long-term goals.

✓ Peer reviews are a good way of increasing your objective knowledge of your practice.

2.2   Where Have You Been, Where Are You Going?

You must know where you are if you wish to go somewhere else!- Neville Smith [50]

Purpose

To emphasize the importance of understanding of the role of business planning in quality service improvement.

Are you doing what you want to do?

Norman Kaderlan introduces his chapter *Vision and Planning* with a quote attributed to Yogi Berra: *"If you don't know where you are going, you'll probably end up somewhere else"*. [51]

Where are we, and where do we want to go? Where is our 'somewhere else'? There are many variants on the old story about a traveler who asked a Maine farmer directions; the response was *'I know where it is, but you can't get there from here'*.

Regardless of one's orientation to quality management, it is impossible to structure an effective quality system without answering these fundamental questions - questions which many practitioners ask themselves frequently, but answer rarely.

Kaderlan has researched the reasons why those questions do not get answered, and his findings are interesting. He says [52] that *fear of failure* is the most common reason why practitioners don't plan, *fear of success* is next, and third that they feel that *the planning process is unsuited to their temperament.*

Advice you can count on

Yet, we encourage our clients to overcome anxiety about new design, believe that our designs will contribute to their success, and sell planning as a service we are better at than anyone else!

Indeed, the process of establishing a quality management system often highlights the importance of a business plan, along with an analysis of the practice's skills base.

In this regard, one of the great benefits of a QM plan can be a systematic focusing on the firm's strong links and weak links (to use the old chain metaphor).

This process identifies the weak links and gives them the highest priority, such that, gradually, all of the things the firm does are as good as what it does best, but in a way which does not unreasonably strain its resources or induce culture shock.

Under an ISO 9000 system, the self-discovery process is called *internal auditing*, but the term is usually used to refer particularly to discovery about how the quality system is working. That topic is covered in the next chapter. Quality management relies on the establishment of business goals and objectives, which are part of the outcome of the process of business planning. Without such goals and objectives, the audit function has no benchmark or standard against which operation can be compared.

Refer *Staying small Successfully: A Guide for Architects, Engineers & Design Professionals,* by Frank Stasiowski. Copyright © 1991 by John Wiley & Sons Inc. Reprinted by permission of John Wiley & Sons Inc.

There isn't room in the scope of this book to describe in detail the business planning process; it is a subject worthy of its own book. There are excellent resources available: Frank Stasiowski's *Staying small Successfully* has a 55-page chapter devoted to business planning for small design practices. Stasiowski defines six elements or steps to the development of a business plan: [53]

◆ Mission and culture statements

◆ Marketing plan and direction

◆ Financial plan

◆ Organizational plan

◆ Human resources plan

◆ Leadership transition

Although the business plan itself is not part of either TQM or ISO 9000 QM, there is a close relationship between the business planning process and both quality management approaches. For example, ISO 9000 requires that the firm have a *quality* mission statement (which might be part of a larger business mission, or identical to it).

It also requires an organizational plan and, at the project level, human resource planning.

Another excellent source is Norman Kaderlan's text, noted earlier. Kaderlan devotes the first part of his book [54] to describing in detail the business planning process.

On the specific subject of external forces acting on the practice (opportunities and threats), there is no more precise analysis than Robert Gutman's, whose book gives it a chapter [55].

Another excellent piece of research in business planning is that of The Coxe Group, published as *Success Strategies for Design Professionals* [56]. This text develops a concept the authors call 'SuperPositioning', which is a business/ marketing 'game plan' based on the idea that all design firms can be organized according to a six-cell matrix as shown below, and that a successful strategy can be developed if you know where you fit into this matrix.

Strong Delivery		A	B
Strong Service		C	D
Strong Idea		E	F

Design Technologies

Practice-Centered Business   Organizational values   Business-Centered Practice

Figure 2.2: SuperPositioning Matrix

The Coxe Group's book describes the characteristics of these six categories, and how firms in each can best 'position' themselves in the marketplace, depending on where they fit in the matrix. Basically, this system is a way of matching the firm profile to the client profile. It is not possible in the space available here to outline the complete approach. It is also not possible to understand how their system works in the absence of substantially more detail.

Whether or not you agree with The Coxe Group's matrix structure, there is much of value to be learned from studying their research and conclusions. They even question whether or not the same rules that apply to businesses generally are applicable to design firms. Their conclusion [57]:

"For a decade, management 'authorities' have been writing article after article for both the professional and business press telling design professionals that they need to be more businesslike to survive in today's economy. Yet when professional service firms that have applied business principles to the fullest are examined, few cases that confirm the conventional premise of what being 'businesslike' implies can be found.

"In fact, for every engineering or architecture organization that is doing well under full application of business management, there are probably ten times as many firms doing as well or better by operating under a rather different set of rules - or no rules at all."

Well! Where does that leave us? That knowledge was the reason that The Coxe Group developed their SuperPositioning theory. It can fairly be said - as far as the quality management issues are concerned, for both TQM and ISO 9000 QM, that the drive for a more businesslike approach comes from the business community that developed the QM methods.

The fact that design firms can succeed without necessarily working to some recognized form of business planning may have something to do with size: over 80% of all practices are less than 10 persons, and nearly 60% are 1-4 persons in size. At this level, 'management' can function as the direct extension of the personality of the leader(s) of the practice. An organized person will, simply, *be* an organized practice.

If you accept the import of The Coxe Group's conclusion (and certainly many design professionals would agree) it follows that development of quality management principles unique to the design disciplines is relevant, if not the only way to go. That is the position this book takes - more on this in Part 3.

Chapter 2.2
Summary Checklist

✓ Most design practitioners think about what they want for their future, but few actively plan for it.

✓ Quality management can help a practice find its weakest links and fix them, thus strengthening the firm.

✓ The first step is to define your goals and objectives.

2.3   The Diagnostic Audit

I would guess that more than 90 percent of our lives are governed by established routines and patterns. Certainly 100 percent of our perceptions are. - Edward de Bono [58]

Purpose

To outline one method of achieving an objective view of your practice, as a helpful precondition to planning a quality management system.

Diagnostic audits vs. quality audits

The *diagnostic audit* is a term I use to describe an initial assessment of a company's readiness for quality system implementation. It is not a definition found in any of the quality standards.

There are some important differences between this concept of a diagnostic audit and quality audits, which are defined and discussed in Chapter 4.4. All quality audits are formal affairs, and must be conducted with objectivity and impartiality. There are three tests in the definition of a quality audit for *'quality activities and related results'*:

◆ compliance with planned arrangements,

◆ implemented effectively, and

◆ suitable to achieve objectives.

Prior to adoption of a quality management system, 'planned arrangements' and 'objectives' are not likely to be formalized, so it is not appropriate to use these measures as yardsticks in a diagnostic audit.

By contrast, a diagnostic audit can be more informal and relaxed. The main purpose is not to test the practice in any way, but to help it to evaluate itself as a first step in embracing the introduction of new systems.

A secondary purpose is to inform the assessing consultant about the practice, if that consultant will go on to help the practice develop its quality system.

Objectivity and finding the 'weak links'

Refer to Chapter 3.2 for a further discussion of this process

An important observation from my work with professional design firms is that because almost all firms value excellence, they focus attention on any perceived problem and fix it as soon as they can. While this tends to be a reactive approach which sometimes results in overlapping systems, in general these efforts are successful, and serve to continuously improve the firm's operations in terms of efficiency, reduction of risk and increased reputation.

This approach does not usually find the firm's 'weak links', however. Determining where the weak links are is an important purpose of the diagnostic audit. Doing this permits priorities to be established which result in the most dramatic improvement at the least cost and tends to build overall staff confidence in the implementation of quality management.

A classic example from my experience was a superbly managed Canberra practice, with well developed systems and a lot of pride in those systems - where the receptionist/secretary had not backed up any computer files since her employ many months earlier. The directors were completely unaware that this dangerous lapse of quality management (and common sense) was happening. If this firm were to conduct its own diagnostic audit, it is entirely possible it would have missed the problem, because - having assumed that the secretary understood and was following procedures - the firm might not have thought to ask.

An outsider will ask the dumb questions that might not occur to the people within the practice. Thus the objectivity of the external auditor can be an important factor in discovering the firm's 'weak links'.

Setting priorities for evolutionary change

We can see from the above discussion that key objectives of the diagnostic audit are to identify the firm's strengths and weaknesses, and to thereby identify those areas which, if improved, will most benefit the firm. This simple 'cost-benefit analysis' has several goals:

◆ Identify and schedule for improvement those areas most likely to cause a firm to fail a formal system audit.

◆ Protect the firm from exposure to risk.

◆ Increase the firm's efficiency.

◆ Help to shape the firm's quality objectives.

◆ Help to create a framework for writing of quality procedures.

What does the diagnostic audit involve?

To complete a diagnostic audit for a typical small to medium sized practice, I find I need to spend two, or sometimes three, half-days in the firm, interviewing many of the employees and collecting information on the firm's systems. This is followed by a half to full day of evaluation and preparation of reports.

The kinds of things we look at in the firm are related to the informal quality management systems the firm has evolved in order to survive in business, such as:

✓ filing systems

✓ file naming of correspondence and other documents

✓ general office organizational systems

✓ standard forms and how they are used

✓ organization of design briefs and client instructions

✓ design reviews

✓ staff role descriptions

✓ staffing assignments

✓ task scheduling

✓ specification data bases and updating

✓ checklist use

✓ Standards and codes

✓ checking of contract documents

✓ tendering and contract administration procedures

✓ post-occupancy evaluation (POE)

From this assessment we normally produce two reports:

◆ One for general distribution to all members of the practice which highlights the positive results of the diagnostic and which responds to questions raised by those interviewed.

This report has several purposes, but the most important one is to assist management in selling the benefits of quality systems to a still-wary staff; in terms that are very practice specific and which expose in a non-threatening way a few of the things everybody would like to see fixed anyway.

◆ A confidential report to senior management which is completely candid about specific problems as well as strengths. This report focuses on finding the best and most efficient way forward and includes specific recommendations for system design and implementation.

**Chapter 2.3
Summary Checklist**

✓ Diagnostic audits are a good way to assess your firm's readiness for introduction of quality management systems.

✓ Key objectives of the diagnostic audit are to identify the firm's strengths and weaknesses, and to thereby identify those areas which, if improved, will most benefit the firm.

✓ The average practice is rarely aware of its weak links - they represent the areas where no problem has yet manifested itself.

2.4 Experts and How to Use Them Wisely

X is an unknown quantity and spurt *is a drip under pressure.* - A temp we once hired.

Purpose

To describe the kind of specialist assistance available in setting up quality management systems, and offer advice on how to most effectively use such help.

Finding experts

With every perceived shift in the relationship between a services industry and the public, another new industry springs up overnight of helpful entrepreneurs. Some professions (notably accountancy) see themselves as men and women for all seasons, and add every new fillip to the range of consulting provided. This situation can create confusion for users of these services.

Picking from the 'Gallery of Experts'

Busy professionals who recognize they need assistance in coping with the relationship shift have to assess widely varying claims about how much and what kind of help are appropriate, and what it should cost. There is almost nothing written about finding the right help.

The key questions

There are a number of questions to be resolved in engaging quality management consultants:

◆ Is it better to do everything ourselves, rather than rely on consultants?

◆ If we use consultants, will there be a problem of 'ownership' of the resultant system?

◆ How important is it that a quality system be unique to our practice?

◆ If we decide to employ a consultant, how should the brief be structured?

◆ What should we watch for in interviewing prospective consultants?

◆ Are there any key points to be included in a contract for consultant services?

There are other related questions which are of concern to some practices, but if you can get satisfactory answers to the above six points, your chances of a good consultant relationship will be greatly improved.

In thinking through the answers to these questions, we will see that the answer usually is 'it all depends'. But depends on *what*? Let's take the questions in order.

Q1: Is it better to do it ourselves?

From my experience, there are two main determiners as to whether or not you should engage consultant help in designing and/or setting up a QM system:

◆ Firm size: Small firms rarely can afford the down time of a senior person to become educated about QM, design a system, and structure its implementation; whereas larger practices can.

◆ Time: The more in a hurry you are to get results, the more important it is get someone on board who knows what she is doing. It usually takes 12 to 24 months to get from start to a fully operational QM system, and can take a lot longer when the people planning it are also starting from point zero.

There are also some other issues related to this question, pro and con:

Advantages:

◆ If the consultant is any good, she will bring to the firm the best ideas of dozens or hundreds of other firms, and your practice will be enriched in the process.

◆ The outsider will always have an objectivity; a perspective; that is extremely difficult for management to gain.

Disadvantages:

◆ There is an 'ownership' issue (see next question).

◆ If you make a mistake in picking the consultant, it will cost you a lot of time and money to get back to the point of re-starting.

Q2: Is 'ownership' of the system an issue?

The answer is, IT DEPENDS. It depends on how fully the consultant appreciates the ownership question, and guides the entire process so that the system really belongs to the practice every step of the way.

I have heard it said that if a consultant really does her job well, the clients will believe all the ideas were their own. I believe this, and think it particularly apt in this situation. Unfortunately, I have seen some quality consultants push (in the name of quality management) their own concepts of how firms ought to practice. The result is that they create systems in their own likeness, not that of their client.

There always comes a time in a client-management consultant relationship where the client should be taking over from the consultant; transferring the responsibility in-house. The actions and meetings leading up to that point are crucial to the successful transfer of ownership, and demand a certain amount of skill on the part of the consultant.

Q3: Do we need a system unique to our practice?

This question is closely linked to the previous one. I have provided quality management systems and support servicesto over eighty design firms; ranging in size from sole practitioners to multi-office practices with over 100 staff. In working with these firms, I've seen a tremendous range in the desire for unique system design. Certainly this interest isn't a function of firm size - some tiny firms believe everything they do must be unique, as do some very large offices.

Nor does this interest appear to be particularly related to the firm's design ethic e.g. the 'uniqueness' with which it approaches design problems. In thinking about this, it would appear that design firms are more similar (at least compared to other professions) than most designers think is the case.

We design professionals have a mobile work force. Designers and draftspersons float from office to office, and in most cases 'slot in' to the new environment very quickly. They *know* what to do when they get there.

Why? Because the way design firms work is so similar, not only across the country, but around the world.

As a quality management consultant, I respond to this differing need by supplying a 'model' system to those with a low index of need for uniqueness, and advising them on how to adapt it to their practice, while helping those with a greater need for uniqueness to develop 'one-off' systems.

What is interesting is that almost always, the system design and development process sees those with a greater 'need' for uniqueness lose some of that 'need' - it rarely stands up to scrutiny; it was just an idea they had.

Similarly, many of those who start out working with a model system (so they could save money) end up modifying it extensively to suit their practice. In other words, they had a fairly unique practice, but never saw it that way until they started to compare their way of working to standardized procedures.

Q4: How should we brief a consultant?

We have a lot of experience working with co-consultants e.g. other design consultants. However, most design consultants have relatively little experience with management consultants - for many practices, their attorney and accountant are the only model, and not one that is all that useful.

Let's say that you have decided to seek some help in improving your quality systems, and you want to write some kind of program or specification of the service, so you can 'compare apples to apples'.

A good way to get at the issues here is to look at them from the perspective of *your* clients. If you are an architect, you know from experience that most clients of architects either don't really understand what architects do, or have significant, erroneous ideas about what to expect from an architect.

You know that you have to educate the client, and that it is wise to do so before entering into a contract. *You are in the same situation as your client.*

So, get yourself some free advice before you prepare that brief. Talk to several consultants and compare notes, and *don't* let yourself be talked into a deal before you are ready.

Here are some issues to consider when talking to the pros, and when writing your 'request for proposal':

✓ Do you want a generalist or a specialist? In this case, a generalist knows a lot about QM but not much about design practice. A specialist knows a lot about design practice and enough about QM. (My bias is showing here.)

✓ How deeply do you want QM to seep into the bones of your practice? This is the most crucial question, and is discussed more fully in Chapter 3.1. The answer will likely determine the generalist/specialist question.

✓ Do you prefer fixed fees with fixed scopes of work, or hourly fees with estimates, or what? As design professionals, you deal with this question every day, from the other side. The issues are the same.

✓ How willing are you to let a consultant inside your practice? Do you have a fear about privity? Do you think you have advantages that you want to keep from competitors?

This cuts both ways. If you want a consultant to bring you the best ideas of all those other firms she has helped, then you have to be willing to share yours. If you want the confidentiality of a lawyer-client relationship, make that clear. But don't expect to have it both ways.

✓ How much of the needed resources can you bring to the equation? You will find that some tasks are best done by a consultant, some best done by your practice, and there are a number where it doesn't matter. But it will cost you one way or the other to get them done. If you elect to do them in-house, you must be prepared to allocate budget and time to see that they get done.

Q5: Interviewing issues

These comments apply both to informal discussions while you are educating yourself on the consultant's marketing nickel as well as to interviews of short-listed contenders.

✓ Is the consultant a *good* listener? Does she ask more questions, or offer more opinions? Do you feel as if she cares more about your practice, or about her credentials?

✓ Is she a generalist or specialist? If a generalist, what is her awareness of your particular specialty? If a specialist, test her awareness of broad QM knowledge.

✓ Raise the 'ownership' issue and pay particular attention to the responses. How does she manage ownership transfer?

✓ Talk through the resources question. What are her strengths, her weaknesses? Does she admit to any of the latter? What does she expect from you in the equation?

✓ Get a list of references, and talk to all of them. Raise the points made above.

Q6: Key points in a contract for QM consultant services

If you put yourself in *your* client's position, you will be more likely to get this right. However, there are some very important differences.

The most important product that the QM consultant produces is not pieces of paper with words on them, or flowcharts and graphs, but rather is a very intangible commodity: a truly workable awareness of the benefits of improving the quality of *your* services. And not just to you, the manager, but right throughout your practice.

The operative word here is *workable*. Do you feel it is workable? Do your staff? You can see that this is not so easy to measure, because you *yourself* are the greatest contributor to, or obstacle in the way of, the consultant's success. Aha! You are in a partnership with the consultant. *You both win, or you both lose.*

Perhaps this is a good place to end this chapter, and this section of the book.

Do not engage a quality management consultant you wouldn't be comfortable with as a business partner.

For, in truth, for the duration of her employ, she will be - to some degree - your business partner.

**Chapter 2.4
Summary Checklist**

✓ Deciding on whether or not you should hire a consultant is largely a matter of timing and available resources.

✓ Picking the right consultant is not easy, but is crucial to the success of your system; perhaps even your practice.

✓ Think carefully about specialists vs. generalists.

✓ Pay close attention to the issue of transfer of 'ownership' of your system.

✓ Your practice may not be as unique as you think.

✓ Your practice may be more unique than you think.

✓ Try before you buy.

✓ Put yourself in your clients' position when thinking about hiring a consultant.

✓ Think about the privity question; be clear on it to prospective consultants.

✓ Be ruthlessly realistic about your own resources and ability to commit them.

✓ Your QM consultant is your partner until she passes you the torch.

Part 2 Resources

References

(46) Kaderlan, p 1.

(47) Smith, Neville I., *Down-to-Earth Strategic Planning*, Prentice-Hall, 1994 (published in Australia).

(48) Smith, p 10.

(49) *Organizational Peer Review;* American Institute of Architects, Practice Management Professional Interest Area, 1993.

(50) Smith, p 24.

(51) Kaderlan, p 9. Other sources, however, have attributed this quote to Casey Stengel.

(52) Kaderlan, p 12.

(53) Stasiowski, Frank: *Staying small Successfully: A Guide for Architects, Engineers & Design Professionals*, John Wiley & Sons, New York, 1991, p 13.

(54) Kaderlan, pp 9-50.

(55) Gutman, pp 97-111.

(56) Coxe, Weld, Nina Hartung, Hugh Hochberg, Brian Lewis, David Maister, Robert Mattox and Peter Piven: *Success Strategies for Design Professionals: SuperPositioning for Architecture & Engineering Firms*, McGraw-Hill, New York, 1987.

(57) Coxe, p 22.

(58) de Bono, Edward, *Sur/Petition*, Fontana (HarperCollins), 1992, p 51.

For more help on...

Strategic planning:

◆ Neville Smith's *Down-to-Earth Strategic Planning* is an excellent resource for mission statements, SWOT analysis, development of a strategic plan. Good worksheets.

◆ James Franklin's *Current Practices in Small Firm Management: An Architect's Notebook* (American Institute of Architects, 1990) includes good advice and forms for doing a SWOT analysis and strategic planning. Refer to Introduction and Chapter 6. I consider Franklin's collection of practice ideas, wonderfully presented in mostly graphic form, to be (after *Architectural Graphic Standards*) the second most useful architectural book published.

◆ Juran (footnote 24) has an excellent chapter (pp 299-333) on strategic quality planning, but it will be of more relevance to large practices than small ones.

Peer reviews: Contact the ACEC Peer Review Program Administrator at 1015 - 15th Street, NW, Washington DC 20005 (telephone 202-347-7474). You can also write to the American Institute of Architects at 1735 New York Avenue, NW, Washington DC 20006 and request its document *Organizational Peer Review*, a publication of the AIA Practice Committee.

Change: Alan Patching's *Partnering and Personal Skills for Project Management Mastery*, Published by Alan Patching & Associates, PO Box 1359, Double Bay NSW Australia 2028, 1994. Chapters VI: *Belief Systems*, VII: *The Process of Change*, and VIII: *Personality Types* offer an excellent description, written for design professionals, of the psychology of change and how that process is affected by personality.

Part 3

PROCESS: Designing Your System

3.1 **Structuring Your System**

3.2 **Implementation Planning: Respotting the Leopard**

3.3 **Certification Pathways for Design Professionals**

3.4 **The Continuous Improvement Pathway**

3.5 **Restructuring Your System**

3.6 **Improving Communication**

3.1   Structuring Your System

Almost invariably there is found to be a lack of consistency between what management believes it is concentrating on, what it has said it will be doing, and what is actually happening - Roy Fox [59]

Purpose

To outline how to create a quality management system which suits the practice and achieves what the principals want to achieve.

The approach

The substance of this approach is to treat every 'ism' of the new religion of QM as having a piece of the truth, but none as embodying all of it.

The core assumption is that a good QM system must be customized first to the industry and second to the practice.

To achieve customization of QM practices to our industry, it is necessary to do two things:

◆   Peel back the onion of our own profession to see clearly and be able to state quite precisely what we do and how we do it, and

◆   Prudently match the core themes of TQM and ISO 9000 QM to what our particular design industry does. The parts that don't match can be left out, provided we can do it with confidence that we haven't compromised any key features of the QM theory.

Firms that want to achieve ISO 9000 certification will, at first, have difficulty reconciling the second point, as it will appear that some of the mandatory requirements under ISO 9000 are NOT essential to good practice. This can only be resolved by accepting that the goal of certification is to provide proof that the firm does what it purports to do, and that such proof requires a formality of reporting that few practices would voluntarily undertake.

Customizing (or 'personalizing') the resultant industry-specific QM system to your own practice follows, and, in many ways, it is the more demanding task.

It is tempting to skip the first stage, the more generic reduction, but in my experience that would be a mistake. I think it is valuable, probably even essential, to undertake the mental exercise of actually defining how your industry relates to the logic of QM, and then working out how close to, or far from, that baseline your own practice is.

This exercise brings objectivity to how you see your practice. It also forces you to think about the impact of quality systems in a more remote way; e.g. in the abstract, rather than personally.

One of the prevalent traits of design professionals is that they have a keen understanding of good practice; they always mean to get around to putting 'systems' in place to ensure that good practice happens. All too often there is a lot more good intention than real action.

A classic example is pre-bid checking of documents. 100% of architects and engineers believe in it, but probably not one firm in ten is sufficiently organized to do it on every project. One big reason for this failure to check is that practices often do not include time for checking when they prepare a schedule for design and documentation. And then they wonder why they didn't have enough time to do it!

Steps to structuring a QM system

There are six steps to creating a quality management system for a design practice:

◆ Outline the actions our industry has developed to ensure consistency and quality of output.

◆ Consider the extent to which your practice uses, or should be using, these actions.

◆ Decide what your goals are in developing a QM system.

◆ Either settle on an established framework, or invent one of your own.

◆ Resolve any discrepancies between your framework and TQM theory and/or ISO 9000.

◆ Using the above five steps together, create process statements (called 'procedures') which describe your quality system.

We will consider these steps in order.

Step 1: Quality actions in our industry

Pre-bid checking, as noted above, would be seen as a quality assurance system by most design professionals. Actually, checking is more properly termed a *quality control* measure, as it consists of proofing finished work before it is sent out. In fact, pre-bid checking is our industry's equivalent of 'mass inspection' that Deming rails against[60].

Roy Fox states unequivocally[61]: *"In my view all inspection activities should be classified as quality failure cost. This means our quality improvement activities should be aimed at eliminating inspection activities as well as the failures they are used to detect. Even more profoundly, we should consider inspection as the technique of last resort when developing new quality assurance processes."* This is an important point, which I will return to in Chapter 4.7.

In Part 1 we saw that all design firms desire quality of output; for the better practices, it becomes an obsession. In reality, every single part of your professional life is connected to the quality of design. Your quality procedures are everything you do. Simple things like updating trade literature catalogs improve the chances that you will specify products which are still available. These are quality procedures every bit as much as is design review.

Because of this complete linking of the routine of practice to quality management, most practitioners find that the easiest way to think about quality systems is to use the familiar order of how we work; e.g. project-based actions. Of course, there are a number of practice-wide actions which are not project-based, which we lump together as 'overheads'.

You can see that describing practice is also a good framework for describing quality systems for our industry. One example of how to do this is shown on the next page. It is the most recent version of the structure of the quality management system which I originally developed in 1992 for a group of 23 practices in Canberra. It is by no means the only way to organize the information, but it works for those who use it.

You can see that all administrative procedures are grouped together, as are project procedures. This is because most staff just need one set or the other. There is little point in providing them with documents they don't need. The Administrative Procedures become, in effect, the firm's 'office manual'.

ABC Architects Administrative (Non-Project) Procedure Structure

A **Management Responsibility**
- A1 Responsibility & authority
- A2 Verification resources & personnel
- A3 Quality manager
- A4 Management review

B **Quality System**
- B1 System structure
- B2 Implementation

C **Internal Quality Audits**
- C1 Audit scheduling & procedure
- C2 Audit forms

D **Training**
- D1 Training
- D2 Personnel records

E **Quality Improvement**
- E1 Review, evaluation & feedback
- E2 Preventing nonconformances
- E3 Client communication
- E4 Responding to change

F **Resources**
- F1 Consultants register
- F2 Technical library
- F3 Master specification
- F4 Pro formas

G **Document Control**
- G1 Information & communication
- G2 System document control
- G3 General document control

H **Quality Records**
- H1 Maintaining records
- H2 Document security
- H3 Archiving records

I **Practice Management**
- I1 Time management
- I2 Personnel management
- I3 Business planning
- I4 Financial management

J **Marketing**
- J1 Marketing policy & research
- J2 Promotional materials
- J3 Project assessment

ABC Architects Project Procedure Structure

K **Project Control**
- K1 Project setup
- K2 Project planning
- K3 Project quality plan instructions
- K4 Project quality checklists
- K5 Project cost plan & program
- K6 Project document control
- K7 Internal cost control
- K8 Partnering

L **Agreement & Brief**
- L1 Expression of interest
- L2 Client/architect agreement
- L3 Preparing the brief
- L4 Updating the brief

M **The Consultant Team**
- M1 Consultant needs assessment
- M2 Agreements & recommendation
- M3 Briefing, input coordination & progress monitoring
- M4 Subconsultants' output verification

N **Design**
- N1 Design input
- N2 Design process
- N3 Design output
- N4 Design review
- N5 Design verification
- N6 Design validation
- N7 Design changes

O **Contract Documentation**
- O1 Documentation setup & controls
- O2 Production
- O3 Coordination & checking
- O4 Completion & acceptance

P **Bidding**
- P1 Bidding process
- P2 Bid evaluation/contract negotiation
- P3 Contract award

Q **Contract Administration**
- Q1 Administration setup
- Q2 Administration
- Q3 Completion & payments

R **Quality in Service Delivery**
- R1 Resolving discrepancies
- R2 Resolving nonconformances

S **Post Completion**
- S1 Post-occupancy services
- S2 Post-occupancy evaluation
- S3 Facilities management

T **Other Services**
- T1 Service planning
- T2 Input coordination
- T3 Output verification

You can also see that Project Procedures are in sequential order, except for *Other Services*, which are short procedures for services other than design, and *Quality in Service Delivery*, which applies to all project procedures. There is no reason why they have to be in sequential order; it simply is more familiar to design professionals.

This system is ISO 9000 - compliant, which accounts for certain headings, such as N5 and N6. However, it goes well beyond ISO 9000, as it makes provision for many practice-related activities that are NOT required by ISO 9000. Examples are the whole of *I: Practice Management* and *J: Marketing*.

Some aspects of quality management apply to both administrative and project activities, and (at least with ISO 9000 systems) there is the tendency to lump them together. Document control is a good example. In the earlier version of this system the client group wanted to equate procedures to ISO 9000 system elements, so it directed that both project and administrative document control procedures be in one place. You can see that in this version, document control is split to reflect the way we work (refer to G1, G2, G3 and K6).

Before reading further, it would be worthwhile to go back to review the TQM and ISO structures and the *Ten Keys* model; and compare the *ABC Architects* model to them:

✓ Deming's 14 points (pp 20-21)
✓ Juran Trilogy (p 25)
✓ Crosby's structure (pp 26-27)
✓ ISO 9001 system elements (pp 33-34)
✓ Ten Keys (p 40)

Responses to the *ABC Architects* model have been generally positive, but one reviewer and a significant number of users have found it too complex and daunting. This brings up a couple of points that every person who tries to document a system will bump up against sooner or later:

◆ It is harder to develop tighter systems and shorter procedures. The fewer the words, the more important each one becomes, and the more situations they have to accurately describe.

◆ Only experience in using a system will tell you what you can leave out in improving it. The process of system design tends to be inclusive; to cater for all situations.

Step 2: How does your practice relate to the industry?

The ABC Architects model is, obviously, only one of an almost infinite number of ways of structuring a QM system. However, you can use it as a starting point for thinking about the way your practice works. Look at the list again. Cross out any headings and subheadings that don't seem to apply to your firm's activities. (If you borrowed this book, make a photocopy and work off that!)

Of course, you might be crossing out something fairly sacred to either TQM or ISO 9000 logic, but that is a later step. The idea is to start to think about your practice as a cohesive set of task groups or activities, all of which relate in some way to the quality of the services your firm provides. This then provides you with a structural starting point for your own system.

Part of this crucial analysis has to do with the way your practice actually works. Is the design/documentation process sequential, or all in together? Is your practice departmentalized? Is your thinking departmentalized, or holistic? Do you have multiple disciplines in your practice? Do you have several partners, each with her own production teams?

In short - WHAT IS YOUR QUALITY CULTURE? (More on this in future chapters...) Roy Fox notes *"Culture change is what TQM is really all about."* [62]

To take Fox's point: If you're NOT interested in changing the culture of your practice, you are reading the wrong book. In that case, give it to a restless colleague; one who is not your competitor.

A very important part of this 'culture' issue is what sort of people you and your partners are, and what you want out of your practice. That is why Chapters 2.1 and 2.2 are there, to urge you to focus on this 'Why am I here?' question.

Step 3: What are your goals?

Mission - Vision - Goals - not exactly the same, but closely related concepts. Experts have written reams about how to find out what your goals are. You could be forgiven for thinking that your goals are self-evident. If they are to you, you are a rare design professional. If you think they are self-evident, try writing them down. If that works, put them aside for a few days, then see if you have changed your mind.

If you haven't changed your mind by the end of a week, try them on your practice partners, your personal partner, your staff. Do they agree? Most of the design professionals I've worked with do a lot more work with the square end of the pencil (chewing, erasing) than they do with the pointy end, before they get to written goals they are satisfied with.

Most authorities stress the importance of keeping your goal statement concise, but you will find that this is NOT easy to do. Many practitioners start out by writing a page or two - a sort of stream of semi-consciousness about the zen of making a living through design.

My view is that a good mission statement can fit on the back of your business card in legible type. In my practice, we've got it down to four words, on the bottom of our letterhead:

Quality management in architecture.

It may not mean so much to anyone else, but it describes all that we do, and it is a constant reminder of the goal.

Like many rural kids, I grew up with the Sears, Roebuck catalog as the ultimate guide to consumer products, and I have often thought that Sears' *'good, better, best'* marketing definition was a benchmark statement of quality marketing. As the customer, whatever your budget, you always knew where you were with Sears. If you bought the 'good' level of quality and thought it could be better, well, you should have bought 'better'. If only we could make our products that clear to our clients!

Actually, I did use the Sears' technique once, with fantastic success. From about 1972 to 1982, I operated a design-build firm in Boston. We had our own painting department, and had an ongoing problem with communicating to our customers about the level of quality they expected in paint finishes. It seemed that no matter how hard we tried to explain what they could expect for a given price, their expectations would be higher, and we would have to come back to make good some minor details.

This was both wearisome and expensive, and after some time we analyzed the problem carefully, and discovered that the problems were never with the *painting*, but with the level of *preparation*. We then prepared a paper which gave each customer three prep options - yes - *good, better* and *best*.

We offered only one level of painting - the best, but we would spend as much, or as little, time making substrates perfect as the client wanted to pay for. The prep levels were fully defined, and the relative cost of *better* was, say, 2x of *good*, and *best* was 3-4x of *good*. What we found was that clients completely understood this system, generally used it to benchmark our competition, and NEVER AGAIN got cranky about the resultant work.

I'm still not quite sure how to translate this experience over to design, but it was a completely effective solution to a very annoying problem. One of the unanticipated by-products of that solution was that customers began to use *our* standards of quality to measure our competitors' proposals, which of course meant that we were suddenly setting the standard rather than competing in the dark against some unknown or vague, undefined standard.

At that time, we were only trying to solve a problem, not invent mission statements. But in real sense, out of that exercise came a mission for the painting department, which (if articulated) would be something like:

We have only one standard of painting - the best.
The standard of preparation shall be as defined by
the customer.

In quality terms, the customer was becoming our partner in this process; we jointly defined the standard of prep quality desired. That's why they quit complaining about the results - the decision was theirs, not ours.

As noted above, there is a lot of help available if you are still chewing your pencil instead of writing your mission statement. A list of good resources is included at the end of Part 3.

Objectives vs. goals

Many people, when starting out on this process, get confused over the difference between *goals* and *objectives*. In workshops I run for my clients, I sometimes use the following analogy:

If your goal is to create great architecture, your
objective is to find a client who wants some.

If your goal is to make money, your objective is to find
a client who has some.

That's a bit tongue-in-cheek, but it conveys the key idea: your objectives are the *means to the end*, the *methods for realizing your goals*.

Objectives are the 'enablers' of your goals. There is general agreement in the quality industry about what makes a good objective; perhaps best summed up by Roy Fox [63]:

> *"It is most important that objectives be definitive, quantifiable and measurable."*

If you write objectives which do not meet that simple test, they will not be of much use to your quality system. It is the function of being able to measure change against your objectives that tells you whether or not your system is working.

Step 4: Decide on a quality system structure

As noted earlier, you need to either adapt an existing structure for your use, or invent one of your own. Which you do will probably reflect your personality and your need to be an individual. After many years of working with a variety of large to tiny practices on quality management, I've developed a bias about that, which is: *if you can find a round wheel, don't re-invent one.*

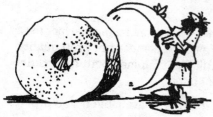

You can spend a lot of time working and re-working system structures. At some point, the incremental gains cease to be of value. You will learn something in doing that, but you have to ask yourself if it is really worth it. Our entire industry (at least in the U.S. and Canada) has become comfortable with the 16-part materials classification system. It is not perfect, but is an acceptably round wheel, so we use it.

Many firms that have an office manual that they really use and like find that the best place to start is to amend that manual to include the quality categories. That is fine, but don't make the mistake of simply adding another section called 'Quality'. As noted above, the quality function will need to thread throughout every other function.

You will need to compare each function against the quality principles that you want to achieve, and rework them to suit. That is quite a good way to go if you want a TQM structure. If you want an ISO 9000 structure, you will find that it may be easier to reorganize your office manual to be more consistent with (or at least translatable to) the ISO system elements.

If you do not have a good, useful office manual, you probably would be better off to take either the Ten Keys model (if your orientation is TQM) or the ABC Architects model (if your orientation is ISO 9000), and adapt your choice to suit your practice. Note that the Ten Keys structure is without any subheadings; you will need to develop your own [64].

Overleaf is a pro forma for a short version of the *ABC Architects* model that you may find appealing, especially if you have a small practice and want to orient your system to ISO 9000.

Step 5: Rationalize your system to QM theory

If you are serious about changing the culture of your company, you will have to spend a fair amount of time to understand how to ensure that your structure responds appropriately to the quality theory you feel comfortable with. In many ways, it is easiest to simply buy into the belief system of one of the gurus, and try to make his* system work for you (* the gurus are all male).

That solution may not give you the result you want or need, however. Remember that in this religion, all of the disciples have some of the truth and none have all of it. And none walk on water.

My opinion is that, among the TQM gurus, Dr. Juran's teachings (rooted, as they are, in planning) come the closest to being applicable to the design professions. However, they still were developed for the manufacturing sector, and require significant interpretation to apply usefully to a design practice.

Some authorities counsel care in adapting ISO 9000 to industries outside manufacturing. Members of the Royal British Institute of Architects and the Royal Australian Institute of Architects have had considerable experience in this adaptation, as increasingly, governmental and large corporate clients in those countries (as well as throughout Europe) are demanding that design professionals have ISO 9000 systems in place.

Applicable ISO 9001 elements

It is generally agreed that the following ISO 9001 system elements apply to the design professions:

4.1   Management responsibility
4.2   Quality system
4.3   Contract review

Pro forma for an ISO 9001 Quality System
for a small design practice

(© 1994 Building Technology Pty. Ltd. Reproduced with permission)

This structure includes only those design practice functions which are subject to ISO 9001.

Administrative Procedure Structure

A   **Management Responsibility**
  A1 Responsibility & authority
  A2 Verification resources & personnel
  A3 Quality manager
  A4 Management review

B   **Quality System**
  B1 System structure
  B2 Implementation

C   **Internal Quality Audits**
  C1 Audit scheduling & procedure
  C2 Audit forms

D   **Training**
  D1 Training

E   **Quality Improvement**
  E1 Review, evaluation & feedback
  E2 Preventing nonconformances

F   **Resources**
  F1 Consultants register
  F2 Technical library
  F3 Master specification
  F4 Pro formas

G   **Document Control**
  G1 Information & communication
  G2 Quality system document control
  G3 General document control

H   **Quality Records**
  H1 Maintaining records
  H2 Document security
  H3 Archiving records

I   (reserved)

J   (reserved)

Project Procedure Structure

K   **Project Control**
  K1 Project setup
  K2 Project planning
  K3 Project quality plan instructions
  K4 Project quality checklists
  K5 Project cost plan & program
  K6 Project document control

L   **Agreement & Brief**
  L1 Client/architect agreement
  L2 Preparing the brief
  L3 Updating the brief

M   **The Consultant Team**
  M1 Consultant needs assessment
  M2 Agreements & recommendation
  M3 Briefing, input coordination & progress monitoring
  M4 Subconsultants' output verification

N   **Design**
  N1 Design input
  N2 Design process
  N3 Design output
  N4 Design review
  N5 Design verification
  N6 Design validation
  N7 Design changes

O   **Contract Documentation**
  O1 Documentation setup & controls
  O2 Production
  O3 Coordination & checking
  O4 Completion & acceptance

P   **Bidding**
  P1 Bidding process
  P2 Bid evaluation/contract negotiation
  P3 Contract award

Q   **Contract Administration**
  Q1 Administration setup
  Q2 Administration
  Q3 Completion & payments

R   **Quality in Service Delivery**
  R1 Resolving discrepancies
  R2 Resolving nonconformances

4.4   Design control
4.5   Document and data control
4.6   Purchasing (but only with respect to subconsultants)
4.13 Control of nonconforming product
4.14 Corrective and preventive action
4.16 Control of quality records
4.17 Internal quality audits
4.18 Training

In the case of a design professional who purchased materials to be used in the project e.g. interior designer or landscape architect, the full provisions of element 4.6 would apply.

Lionel Stebbing, recognized internationally as an authority on ISO 9000, advocates the use of a quality system with 'ten essential elements' [65], which is the same as the above list, except his list does not include design control. He argues that these ten are 'essential', because they will apply to any organization, regardless of product or size.

It is also generally agreed that the following ISO 9001 system elements DO NOT apply to the design professions:

4.10 Inspection and testing
4.11 Control of inspection, measuring and test equipment
4.12 Inspection and test status
4.15 Handling, storage, packaging, preservation and delivery
4.19 Servicing

In the case of 4.10, 4.11 and 4.12, the 'inspections' which architects or engineers might do on site are not related to the design professional's quality output, but rather represent acting as the client's agent in monitoring the contractor's quality performance. These activities come under sub-element 4.6.4: *Evaluation of purchased product.*

Note, however, that if the design professional uses equipment which requires calibration e.g. a transit level, then he would be governed by element 4.11.

Although some would argue that element 4.15 applies to wrapping drawings when they go out of the office, in fact the quality of the output is not dependent on this function, and it is not required.

Element 4.19 applies to 'after sale' care of the product sold; e.g. the contractor's warranty period activities.

The following elements may or may not apply to design practice:

4.7   Control of customer-supplied product
4.8   Product identification and traceability
4.9   Process control
4.20 Statistical techniques

An interior designer who had possession of a client's goods, e.g. having furniture sent out for recovering, would be subject to the provisions of element 4.7.

Authorities do not agree as to whether or not elements 4.8 and 4.9 are required in a design quality system. Proponents insist that 'product identification and traceability' applies to the identification of drawings. However, the Standard itself does not make identification mandatory; stating 'where appropriate', procedures shall be established for identifying product through stages of production, delivery and installation. It is clear that this clause was written to apply to the manufacturing process, rather than the design process. The requirement for traceability is limited to contracts where it is a 'specified requirement'.

If the design procedures include identification of drawings (which is what happens in reality), then any requirement for identification could be deemed to be satisfied by the design procedures.

There is also disagreement about the application of process control. Some authorities have suggested that the whole of design is a 'process' and therefore element 4.9 applies. However, this element requires the supplier to 'identify and plan processes which directly affect quality' with respect to 'production, installation and servicing'. Again, it is obvious that this clause was written for manufactured goods.

Subelement 4.9(c) requires 'compliance with reference standards/codes, quality plans and/or documented procedures', which sounds like it may be talking about design. However, if the design control processes adequately describe safeguards with regard to these items, then any requirement for process controls could be deemed to be satisfied by the design procedures.

There is considerable debate about the applicability of element 4.20. In particular, authorities with a TQM orientation argue that quality management is not possible without statistical analysis of that which must be measured.

It is clear that if your profession involves statistical techniques, e.g. finite element analysis or complex computer applications, then element 4.20 applies.

There are a great many tools in the TQM toolbag which do not require statistical analysis, however. I believe that one can argue reasonably that statistical analysis may not be a required tool for every line of work. But you won't convince a committed measurer.

It is important here to differentiate between the need for measuring quality performance (such as achievement of your objectives, or reduction in rework), and the need for running statistical analysis programs on these measurements.

Step 6: Write your procedures

It is only a matter of time until some latecomer to the quality mine writes a whole book just on how to write a quality procedure, but, quite frankly, following the advice of any good guide to technical writing would suffice, unless you are developing an ISO 9000 system. (In that case, note carefully *Writing ISO 9000 Procedures* below.)

A typical quality procedure is usually composed of the following five parts:

◆ Purpose
◆ Scope
◆ Responsibility
◆ Related documents
◆ Actions

In some cases there may also be a need for a *Definitions* section; this would normally follow *Scope*.

Standard forms and flowcharts are often appended to the procedures. Flowcharts contain the same information as actions, but in an abbreviated, graphical form.

◆ **The *Purpose* statement**

The *Purpose* description should answer, as simply as possible, the question '*Why* is this procedure needed?'

From the auditor's viewpoint, the purpose serves as a requirement which the procedures need to fulfill.

Thus, there is a direct link between the purpose and the actions. If the actions do not fulfill the purpose, the auditor could reasonably conclude that the quality system was not 'effectively' implemented.

◆   The *Scope* of the procedure

The *Scope* description should answer the question 'What are the activities to which the procedure applies?'

The *Scope* statement typically includes *inputs* and *outputs*, beginning and end points for the procedure. The actions in the middle create the outputs from the inputs.

◆   *Responsibility*

The *Responsibility* section establishes the overall responsibility path as well as specific task responsibility.

◆   *Related documents*

This section provides a cross reference to other documents within and outside of the quality system: to clauses in the quality Standards, to the Quality Manual, to other documents the practice uses.

◆   The *Actions* statements

The *Actions* part of the procedure should answer the question: 'How are the tasks to be performed?'

Each action usually contains one or more closely related tasks, but usually begins with a verb and contains tasks which have a single responsibility.

Writing ISO 9000 procedures

If you have decided to develop an ISO 9000 system, you will need some education in procedure writing, particular to the requirements of the Standard. You can either educate yourself, or employ a consultant with experience in ISO 9000 systems. If you decide to educate yourself, get at least one book (and preferably two or more) specifically on ISO 9000 systems. If you get only one, Stebbing's *Quality Management in the Service Industry* is highly recommended.

The reason that I recommend more than one book is that there is value in comparing notes and thinking about what different authors say.

The ISO 9000 standard (at this writing) is only eight years old, and just into its first revision. It has been used for only a few years in the design and construction industry, and its interpretation is still in an evolutionary process.

Another very good reference is AS/NZS 3905.2:1993 - *Guide to quality system Standards AS 3901/NZS 9001, AS 3902/ NZS 9002 and AS 3903/NZS 9003 for construction* [66].

This Australian/New Zealand joint guide standard was developed to assist the construction industries in those countries in understanding how to interpret the standards.

In particular, it gives definitive guidance on which parts of the standards apply to which aspects of the design, management and construction processes.

Not all authorities agree with the interpretations of this document, mind you, but at least it has the authority of the national Standards associations in those countries.

Putting it together

The collected procedures form what is called a Procedures Manual, which is a confidential (non-public) document that governs how the practice operates.

The Quality Manual

The Procedures Manual is typically pared down to outline form which, together with the firm's goals and objectives and a description of the organization, is assembled into a separate document called a Quality Manual.

The Quality Manual is a public document, given to clients and prospective clients.

Frequently, quality systems will include *Work Instructions*, which add detail to the procedures, and act as training guides for less experienced staff.

The quality hierarchy

The relationship of the various parts of the quality system documentation is often depicted as a 4-tier pyramid:

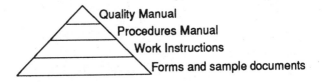

In this model, the higher up the pyramid, the more important the document in the quality system. Each level of documentation supports the level above it, as in the real pyramids.

Another view...

By way of comparison to the steps in this chapter, Roy Fox says that there are the following six phases in the implementation of modern total quality management [67]:

1   Demonstrate top management commitment
2   Establish the current state of quality
3   Determine the quality strategies
4   Educate management in TQM
5   Raise quality awareness everywhere
6   Institute never-ending improvement

**Chapter 3.1
Summary Checklist**

✓ Implementation: Customize QM theory first to the industry and second to the practice.

✓ Step 1: Outline the actions our industry has evolved to ensure consistency and quality of output.

✓ Step 2: Consider the extent to which your practice uses, or should be using these actions.

✓ Step 3: Decide what your goals are in developing a QM system.

✓ Step 4: Either settle on an established framework, or invent one of your own.

✓ Step 5: Resolve any discrepancies between your framework and TQM theory and/or ISO 9000.

✓ Step 6: Using the above five steps together, create procedures which describe your quality system.

3.2 Implementation Planning: Respotting the Leopard

In changing the culture of an organisation to one of being quality driven it is necessary to creep up on the current management style rather than tackle it head on. - Roy Fox [68]

Purpose

To outline the resources and steps necessary for successful implementation of a quality management system.

The task ahead

If the last chapter didn't stop your quality system plans dead in their tracks, this one might. If you get past this chapter and still are a believer, you have an excellent chance of changing (for the better) the culture of your practice.

Meet the leopard. Get out your alchemy kit. This is it. [69]

We all grew up with the leopard metaphor. We now know that a few very gifted managers have made those spots look like decals, to be peeled off and replaced with the marks of a brand new species. These are the 're-engineering' experts.

Most of us are not 'very gifted', and the leopard hanging around in our office is very real, but as transparent and every bit as sneaky as Blake Edwards' enduring Pink Panther.

We can't peel off the decals, we have to try evolution, and
wait. Chapter 5.5: *Changing Your Calendar and Other
Strategies* looks at some ways to accelerate evolution, but
the best way to start one is so simple and obvious that
almost everyone misses it the first time around.

> # Treat Quality
> # Management
> # as a Project

This is the magic trick, the secret formula.

Do exactly with QM what you would do with any other project.

In the workshops that my firm runs, I take participants
through the exercise of listing each thing they do when
they get a new commission, then we apply those tasks to
QM. The result: suddenly the implementation of QM is
easily understood.

Everything else flows from this simple rule, and can be
readily understood by every practitioner. Understanding
the process doesn't make it easy to implement, however.
This may be the hardest project the practice ever carried
out.

Anticipating culture change

The introduction of a formal quality system to a firm will
mean increased documentation of its quality procedures. If
successful, in almost all cases such introduction will mean a
certain amount of change in the way the firm operates.

This anticipation of change is one of the most important
issues in contemplating adoption of quality management
systems. All corporate cultures are the way they are for
very powerful reasons - reflecting the vision, energy,
commitment and organizational style of the founders,
current management and general staff.

Just as the strengths of the people who make up the firm are
reflected in its operating style, so are the weaknesses -
biases, inefficiencies, lack of organization or chronic
inattention to detail.

Because of the durability of the forces that have shaped a firm's corporate culture, evolutionary change is possible, but wholesale, dramatic change is not, without severe disruption of the ability of the firm to operate.

What I find as I work with various firms is that all successful firms do most things right most of the time, but that the areas where firms could benefit by greater attention to procedure vary enormously.

To illustrate these differences, I use a little diagram, where each 'dot' represents some task the firm does. Three hypothetical examples are shown following. Note that it would be very difficult to actually chart any firm this way; the figures are to illustrate the concept only.

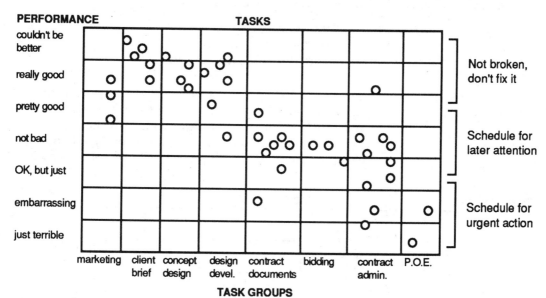

FIG. 3.1: PROFILE OF A STRONG DESIGN FIRM

A firm with this profile tends to over-value some aspects of its performance at the expense of others. It will win many awards and attract more than its share of lawsuits. After an initial period of correcting a few glaring weak links, a long term effort to improve documentation and contract administration skills to match the firm's design skills is recommended.

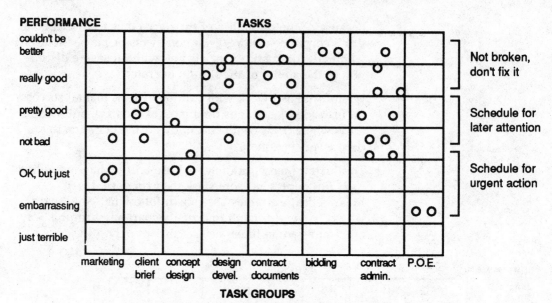

FIG. 3.2: PROFILE OF A STRONG TECHNICAL FIRM

This firm often finds it gets asked to do the documentation for the strong design firms. These firms are often reliable and efficient but their design skills may have declined after the founding director died a decade ago. Some new blood may be needed to improve the firm's design capacity.

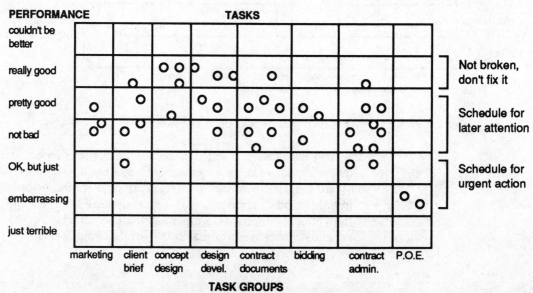

FIG. 3.3: PROFILE OF A WELL-BALANCED FIRM

The above firm is 'pretty good' at most things but rarely stars. Save for doing something right away about post-contract evaluation, the directors need to concentrate on a gradual lifting of performance across the organization, but probably in one area at a time.

In each of the above examples, what we see is that there are three general groupings of task performance: excellent, good, and needing improvement. This will be true for every firm. The point is to identify these groups for your firm; to know where to apply the focus for change. The analogy that seems most appropriate is that of the chain, with the chain being only as strong as its weakest link. The top group in each table contain the strongest links, the bottom group the weakest links.

Without regard to any other aspect of the firm's culture and performance, all firms have a common need to strengthen their weakest links, first to bring those to the level of the middle group and then to raise the middle group so the firm uniformly does its best in all ways.

As noted in Chapter 2.3, determining where the weak links are is an important purpose of the diagnostic audit. This permits priorities to be established which result in the most dramatic improvement at the least cost, which in turn tends to build overall staff confidence in the implementation of quality management.

Some expert thoughts on implementation

Many authorities have written on the problems of quality management implementation. In Chapter 1.2, I quoted Philip Crosby's statement that one reason he 'cheerfully' shared his knowledge was that many of those who read it would not be able to use it. Here are some samplings from other authorities. *Resources* at the end of Part 3 includes references for additional reading on implementation.

> *"Failures in the area of quality management are legion. I would consider that 90 per cent of TQM programs fail to achieve their full potential. Most of this is due to lack of persistence, the absence of positive hands-on leadership and failure to prepare and follow a sensible plan.*
>
> *"... implementation of TQM is a back-breaking, gut-wrenching business that requires constant attention, especially during the formative period."* - Roy Fox (70)

"The prime requirement ... is a thorough knowledge of the techniques of quality control ... But knowledge on its own is never enough; like the impotent Eastern potentate sitting forlornly in his harem, Kama Sutra in one hand and a promising pinch of powdered rhinoceros horn in the other, knowledge surrounded by opportunity needs something more if it is to enjoy fulfillment through action." - Frank Price [71]

"Invariably the introduction of the system will lead to change and most people are against change, even if it is manifestly for the better. Experience has shown that ... the most common reason for the failure of the project has been due to the obstructive attitudes of managers who resent change; although they may appear outwardly to be keen and committed, they are inwardly apprehensive and insecure." - Lionel Stebbing [72]

QM as a project

A client comes to you and says:

"I have this project I want you to do. It is a very hard project. It will take at least 10% of your time and of all senior people in your firm for at least 12 months, maybe up to 18 or 24 months, before you get enough of it done for me to pay you the first payment, which won't be set until we get to that point. Do you want to do the job?"

What is your response? Let's say that you really want to do this job; it's the Taj Mahal of Toledo. (Toledo, Spain.) You know what your profit margin is, and its not 10%, so to do this project, you - and your key staff - will have to make an investment of time, and some money. The payoff should be great, but much of it will be intangible, and hard to measure.

You know that if you don't give it adequate resources, a very careful schedule, and a realistic budget, you'll never get it done; never collect on the payoff.

You also know, from long experience, that if you do plan it properly, give it resources and a budget, and stick to the plan, you will finish the job, just like any other job.

This job is quality management.

If any group of people ever had the training and experience to successfully carry out the implementation of a QM program, it would be design professionals.

We do similar projects for our clients every day. It is our life.

There is one major flaw in the scenario posed above. What is this flaw? Being aware of it is key to success in this project. Here is the flaw:

> ... much of the payoff will be
> intangible, and hard to measure.

If your practice is like most, you will have assumed that the benefits will be intangible and hard to measure. That is because you have never measured the cost of quality in your practice. Somewhere in the world there must be design firms that log re-drawing on their time sheets, but I've yet to find them. And re-drawing is only one of the many costs of quality that are hidden in design firms.

In fact, if you are a typical practitioner, you probably would argue that because design is iterative, re-drawing is not waste, it is part of the necessary process. Maybe, but how much re-drawing? What sort of re-drawing? What is an acceptable level of re-drawing?

I will return to this most important question in Part 6 of this book. For now, assume that your acceptance of the idea that the benefits have to be intangible and hard to measure may be revised.

The practice as an auto body panel

Another metaphor! Even if you think it is silly, for a moment, think of your practice as an auto body panel, pressed into its smooth, unique shape by the force of hundreds of tons. Can you re-shape that panel? Not easily! What is the point? Your practice has been shaped by a force just as powerful, except that it happened over time, some-where between pressing-body-panels time and turning-leaves-into-coal time.

That force is the complex interaction of the personalities of the founders and current management of the firm, creating the unique shape it now has (not necessarily smooth).

It doesn't really matter if you are a sole practitioner or the CEO of a 1,000 person multi-disciplinary international practice. If you want to implement quality management, you will have to go back and do some redesign on those presses. That is the fundamental message that I read, and hear, and see, over and over.

There is nothing in the literature of QM that I have read to suggest any other answer. That is not to say that you can't pick up some hot tips on how to run your practice more efficiently, or with less risk, or more profitably. You can, and you can find a lot of good ideas for doing that in the literature of QM. Frank Stasiowski's guides are full of them. There are some good ones in this book, too.

I think that the issue of process re-design sits at the very core of quality management philosophy. The 'presses' of our practice urge us very powerfully to find some way - any way - to put in place a QM system which stays well away from the forces that have shaped the practice.

It's not the first time in this book I've come to this theme, nor will it be the last. I seem to come to it every day in my practice, advising clients on QM for their practices.

I am absolutely convinced that somewhere early in the QM implementation process you, personally, must make a clear and unequivocal choice: either you want QM for superficial reasons, or you want to change the culture of your practice. This is a point where the road, your path, divides, and you must make your choice. The 'road less traveled' is the road of changing the culture of your practice.

There are a lot of perfectly valid reasons why you might not pick that more difficult road:

◆   Your clients demand that you have 'QA'.

◆   You would just like to be 'more organized'.

◆   You would like to better control the risk of practice.

◆   You want to compete internationally.

There are plenty of examples of design practices which purport to have QM systems operating, but still manage to 'stuff up' the most routine operations as well as fail to provide an adequate level of professional service. When clients of those firms encounter failure to deliver, they become incensed; far angrier about the poor performance than if the firm said it didn't believe in all this 'QM baloney'. The firms hurt themselves greatly by pretending to have something they really haven't got.

There is a central tenet in quality management:

Never promise what you can't deliver.

This is a good place to draw the distinction between quality assurance (QA) and quality management (QM).

Quality assurance

QA is a promise, an *assurance*, to your client, and, by extension, to the public, that you have something special (quality) to offer them.

QM is the combination of systems that ensure you can deliver on the QA promise. Thus, what is QA from the client's perspective is, from your perspective, QM.

Planning for the Toledo Taj

Let's assume that you have decided to take on the QM project, this Taj Mahal of Toledo. This is a self-test. What are the key stages in the plan? Write them in the blanks below, in chronological order.

1 _____

2 _____

3 _____

4 _____

5 _____

6 _____

7 _____

8 _____

9 _____

10 _____

Turn the page, and see how your list compares to my list.

Key Stages: Implementation of QM as a Project

1 Decide whether you want QM to seep into the bones of your practice, or stay on the skin.

2 Work out a rough timetable for the implementation, with some milestones.

3 Review your human and financial resources, and decide if you can commit the necessary resources for at least one year - assume 10% of all senior management time and 5% of all other staff time.

4 Work out the financial cost of item 3 and put it into your next yearly budget.

5 Call a meeting of your entire staff to discuss this project and its implications. Listen carefully to their comments.

6 Educate yourself on the quality cost issues (see Chapter 6.2). You will need this to get through the next item.

7 Have a further meeting with your partners to decide if you are really going to do it, or not. Hear them out fully. Resolve the inevitable questions about who will pay for the time it will take, to your mutual satisfaction. This may take more than one meeting.

8 Revisit the implementation schedule with your key staff. Agree to the milestones, in both time and substance.

9 Establish time-sheet codes for the project and set target time commitments to the project for all staff.

10 Hire the best QM consultant you can find to expedite the process.

The importance of training

Virtually every guide to QM stresses the importance of training. Dr. Juran says that 'planning by amateurs' is a major obstacle to good planning [73]. For the design practitioner, your choices are to train yourself, or buy training from a consultant. Because the need for training is so well documented elsewhere, I won't dwell on it here, other than to endorse this point completely.

If you have plenty of time, train yourself. If you are busy, it will be much more cost-effective to buy the training you will need. Make sure that the pace of the training is one you can keep up with.

**Chapter 3.2
Summary Checklist**

✓ Treat quality management as you would any other project.

✓ Anticipate, and plan for, culture change.

✓ Your practice is the way it is for very powerful reasons, and will not change easily.

✓ Never promise what you can't deliver.

✓ Train yourself; train your staff.

Chapter epilogue

No other aspect of QM is so deeply thought-provoking as the issue of *commitment* to the process. Every book on quality contains anywhere from a few pages to whole chapters on the subject. Few people want to say they are unwilling to make a commitment, fewer still want to really make that commitment to 'redesign the presses'.

The matter is complicated by the paradoxical nature of commitment. If you do decide on the 'road less traveled', no great bolts of lightning will illuminate your way. Nothing overtly obvious, in fact, will change (but, see Chapter 5.5). The people around you may not be conscious of the change, at least at first.

If you met someone at a party, would her commitment to QM be obvious? Could you tell? Probably not. If she was noisy about it, you would doubt her commitment (who was she trying to convince?). Would she have arrived in a late model Porsche? Not necessarily. Would she seem contented, with a settled raison d'être? Not necessarily. I have to leave this question with you, to think about.

The one thing I am confident of is that if the person's commitment to quality is real, *and* founded in reality, the person will have an apparent, palpable aura of credibility. You could trust her, and not be disappointed.

3.3　Certification Pathways for Design Professionals

The estate of an auditor, or one who listens, is an honourable one of great antiquity. - BATALAS Training Guide.

Purpose

To provide an overview of, and identify the critical issues in, the ISO 9000 certification process.

A changing world

American architects and other design professionals are likely to consider the whole matter of certification irrelevant to practice. In 1985, British architects thought so, and in 1990, so did Australian architects. All that has changed, as the ISO 9000 movement is sweeping most of the developed world except North America.

Maybe it will never come to you - but that's what you said about 'going metric', isn't it? The truth is, we do live in a global community, and we do need common standards for international commerce. We should be glad that at least we can speak the international language of commerce; billions can't.

Client expectations

In almost every case, the client who expects certification to ISO 9000, or evidence of progress along the path to certification, will either have gone down that path or will be partway there.

Major corporations, especially those in areas where health and safety are important quality concerns (such as the automotive industry, health care, food and pharmaceuticals) will have spent thousands (or even millions) of dollars to achieve certification. They will have a very powerful commitment to the process, or they never would have achieved certification.

The earlier they began this process - headed down this 'path less traveled' - the more they had to find their own way, and the more powerful will be their commitment to a quality culture.

They will have conquered the obstacles, more or less, and will be believers. They will want their suppliers, contractors and consultants to do likewise.

Requirements of ISO 9000

In addition to this 'cultural' imperative, there is another powerful incentive built into ISO 9000 itself. It is the requirement that the supplier (of the goods and services your client provides to others; your client) consider the capability, including the QM system, of his subcontractor (that's you) into account when making the decision to purchase services.

The Standard does NOT say that the supplier of services to others (your client) has to require that *its* supplier (you) *have* a quality system in operation, only that the question must be considered.

In the usual case, this is interpreted to be one of case sensitivity: the question is: 'Does this project, and in particular the preferred consultant's role on this project, require that he have a quality system in operation?'

If the output of the consultant concerns health and or safety, the answer almost always is a resounding YES! If the answer affects the client's hip-pocket region, the answer is also usually yes.

Government drives the process...

In countries where ISO 9000 has become a reality of practice, it is usually government that drives the process. The pattern typically is that a federal or state agency responsible for design and construction, such as Department of Defense or a Public Works agency, decides to achieve certification.

There often is a sense of competition in this, to see who can do it first, and a tremendous departmental pride in achieving this station. I have sometimes wondered if this great sense of accomplishment might come from a latent sense of frustration at being a 'government architect'; not enjoying the freedom found in private practice. Whatever the reason, the pattern I have seen is that these agencies feel they cannot require the private firms they appoint to carry out work to have an ISO 9000-compliant quality system until they have achieved it themselves.

Once they do get certified, however, they immediately begin the process of phasing in requirements for outside consultants to 'have QA'.

This phase-in period is usually somewhere between one year and three years, with increasing levels of compliance required.

...and the big companies push

Companies large enough to be trading internationally usually find they have to have ISO 9000 systems to gain international acceptance of their products. This is particularly true in the automotive industry, petrochemicals, metals, and some other similar industries. To these companies, compliance with ISO 9001 or ISO 9002 has become a way of life, and they know how their profile has changed because of it.

Let's say that such a company wants to fit out a new office complex. If there is no general standard of QM in the country, the company wouldn't expect design consultants to have a QM system. If there is, however, the company *would* expect its consultants to have a QM system, and it will be an important factor in consultant selection.

What do clients want to see?

In all of the situations I have seen so far (essentially the experience in Australia), the typical pattern is that government clients will structure the phase-in period both in terms of a selection of system elements and a classification or rating scale within those elements.

There are various rating scales in use, all of which assess the level of implementation of specific system elements of the Standard.

With respect to which system elements are considered more important, again there will be differences, but in general, the following would receive priority:

4.1   Management responsibility
4.2   Quality system
4.3   Contract review
4.4   Design control
4.5   Document and data control
4.13   Control of nonconforming product

As an example, New South Wales Public Works has the following requirements for any appointment where fee value exceeds A $20,000 (about US $16,000):

◆ An assessment of *'documented, implemented and verified by external audit'* (the highest rating) for the following system elements:

4.1   Management responsibility
4.3   Contract review
4.4   Design control
4.5   Document and data control
4.13   Control of nonconforming product

◆ In addition, the following elements must be "fully documented/not implemented or partially documented/ partially implemented":

4.2   Quality system
4.6   Purchasing
4.13   Control of nonconforming product
4.14   Corrective and preventative action
4.16   Control of quality records
4.17   Internal quality audits
4.18   Training

In general, corporate clients will have less specific requirements, and will consider the level of quality system implementation relative to the importance of the project.

What does all this mean?

For the U.S. practice which is contemplating international work, it is important that you determine the requirements for ISO 9000 compliance in the country you want to work in - the details will vary considerably.

In general, from starting, it will take you 12 to 24 months of committed effort to achieve independent third-party certification of your system, but it might take half that to get your implementation to a point where it would be accepted.

If you have no such international aspirations, the only reason to actively pursue certification is that it will force you to focus attention on the development and implementation of your system. In the present climate in the U.S., there is not likely to be a marketing advantage in having certification, although it is possible that could change in the future.

What about audits?

For a discussion of the audit process, and what auditors expect to see, refer to Chapter 4.5.

What does certification cost?

The cost of certification has been a moving target, coming down as more firms become accredited to certify by the International Organization for Standardsization. With competition increasing, two things seem to be happening:

◆ Costs appear to be stabilizing with competition, and charges tend to be based on time at reasonable professional rates. In Australia, in 1995, these rates are around A $90 - 100 per hour (US $68 - 75).

◆ Certification providers are re-thinking their services and are a little less zealous in promoting the maximum services that might be needed (competition is a wonderful thing). The minimum standards of service are set by ISO and are quite stringent, but obviously there still is room for interpretation of the Standard on a case by case basis. The certifier decides how much or how little evidence it needs to see in order to make a determination.

In Australia, in 1995, certification costs between A $3,500 and A $6,000 (US $2,600 - 4,000) for a small practice (say 10 or less). There is usually an annual or quarterly maintenance fee, with re-certification required after three years.

Chapter 3.3
Summary Checklist

✓ Clients who expect you to have a quality system are those who have achieved ISO 9000 certification.

✓ Government clients tend to phase in QM requirements; corporate clients have variable standards.

✓ If you have a U.S. practice and do not intend to practice internationally, certification is not likely to be worth the cost.

✓ An increasing number of accredited providers are reducing the cost of certification.

3.4   The Continuous Improvement Pathway

Institute Never-ending Improvement - Roy Fox

Purpose

To discuss what 'continuous improvement' means in TQM and ISO 9000 systems, particularly as this concept relates to the small service business.

How is 'continuous improvement' different from what we now do?

Most, if not all, architects believe they practice some sort of continuous improvement: learning new technologies, striving to create better design, improving efficiency and profitability. What is the difference between this belief and the meaning of 'continuous improvement' as used in QM systems?

One way to answer this is to compare it with the AIA's recent decision to make professional development (PD) mandatory. That debate took a long, long time; but in the end the leaders of our profession decided that 'voluntary' improvement just wasn't good enough for the times we are in.

So, whether you like it or not, PD is no longer an option. Under either TQM theories or the ISO 9000 structure, the same is true: continuous improvement is not an option. It is central to the system.

In an earlier chapter, I discussed the fact that although we all value excellence very highly, we have a 'problem-solving' rather than a 'problem-prevention' approach to excellence (especially technical excellence). We ratchet forward in knee-jerk fashion, fixing whatever goes wrong.

In the previous chapter, we looked at some simple diagrams of profiling aspects of the practice, to see what needed to be fixed *before* it went wrong. Continuous improvement is a formalization of that process - a structured program where management collects information about the firm, reviews it to a plan, and makes decisions about the future.

TQM continuous improvement

In TQM parlance, continuous improvement is omnipresent and never-ceasing, as the term suggests. In discussing this point, Roy Fox notes that it is only the Japanese who have 20 or 25 years of TQM experience.

Observing that there are very few U.S. companies that have more than ten years, TQM experience, he says [74]:

> *"Reality is that we have to take the virtues of never-ending improvement very much on trust, with only the Japanese and a few others around the world to act as models."*

Fox also notes that in many American companies, the experience is that four or five years of effort produce relatively low changes in the corporate culture, and that the response is often to cut out the training and other key parts of the quality system, thus ensuring its demise. He sums up the problem thus [75]:

> *"Maintaining commitment to a long-term strategy where the pay-off can often only be measured ten years down the track in terms of prosperity and status in the marketplace is undoubtedly difficult when maintaining cashflow is a daily problem."*

This prospect may not sound very encouraging to you. It is one of the reasons why all members of the firm's management must have 100% commitment to the concept of continuous improvement if TQM is to succeed. Anything less will crumble when the going gets tough.

Dr. Deming's version of continuous improvement is his point 14: *Take Action to Accomplish the Transformation.* Deming recommends using the Shewhart (PDCA) cycle as the tool for this process (refer to Chapter 4.2 for a description).

He also says that this 'transformation' requires that everyone *'begin to think of his or her work as giving satisfaction to a customer'*.[76] This focus on the customer gives rise to the idea of the *internal* customer:

> *"Ask yourself, he says, who is the person who receives your work? Whom must you satisfy? Many people cannot identify their customers and therefore cannot determine precisely what their jobs are. Everyone has a customer and must know who it is."*

Since most of us work in (relatively) tiny businesses, we think we have a pretty clear idea of who our customers are. But you might be surprised. Consider this: You are the boss. You have a secretary. You provide your secretary with a service, called management, or, if he is lucky, leadership.

> If the wording of this and the previous paragraph confuses you, remember this is an even-numbered chapter, the boss is Hermione, and her secretary is male.

Your secretary is your customer in that transfer, and you owe it to him to provide a high level quality in your management or leadership.

Another important factor in planning for continuous improvement is the resistance of any culture to change. The technique often used to work on this change is called the Santayana review, after the Spanish-born U.S. philosopher George Santayana, who observed:

> *"Those who cannot remember the past are condemned to repeat it."*

Refer to Chapter 4.2 for more information on this technique.

This very brief discussion barely scratches the surface of the literature on continuous improvement as a requirement of TQM. Resources at the end of Part 3 give advice on further reading.

ISO 9000 continuous improvement

In ISO 9000, continuous improvement is a more finite and delineated process, which takes place to a pre-planned schedule, with specific inputs and outputs.

In many ways, the concept of continuous improvement under ISO 9000 is far easier to grasp and implement. For one thing, you will know if you have done what you were supposed to do.

Basically, continuous improvement is a combination of system elements 4.1: *Management responsibility*, 4.14: *Corrective and preventative action*, and 4:17: *Internal quality audits*. 4.14 and 4.17 provide structured feedback to management against specific tests, which tell you if the process is causing your objectives to be met. This information is considered in planned periodic meetings by management (4.1), and decisions are made to stay on or alter the course of the quality program.

Obviously, ISO 9000 can use any TQM tools that management thinks will be of value. The ISO 9000 path provides, in my view, a good way to make sense out of the idea of continuous improvement, and to keep it all in perspective without going crazy.

Chapter 3.4
Summary Checklist

✓ Continuous improvement is mandatory under both TQM and ISO 9000 systems.

✓ Continuous improvement means changing the culture of your practice to a culture you would like better, and that is hard work.

✓ If you have no desire to change the culture of your practice, QM is probably not for you.

✓ If you do set off on the path of culture change, do not expect much change very quickly.

✓ The ISO 9000 structure for continuous improvement is a good framework.

3.5 Restructuring Your System

Step 14: Do it over again. - Philip Crosby

Purpose

To develop a rational approach to 'continuous improvement' of a quality system once implemented.

OK, we will have 'continuous improvement' - what happens next?

It is clear that the old adage about a thing being 'never so good it can't be improved' is apt when extending the concept of continuous improvement back into system design.

However, the QM system has to be there to support the practice and help it become more efficient rather than the other way around.

How much time and energy should be spent on this activity? Experts will not agree; some insist that improvement must be happening every day in every sphere of activity; others hew to 'if it ain't broke, don't fix it'.

"Now that we've got it, what are we going to do with it?"

My experience is that the natural inventiveness of most creative people, if outlets are provided, leads to a natural, evolutionary system refinement. However, for various reasons, some system elements seem to get 'locked in', frozen in time, and are hard to dislodge even when it is clear they need fixing. These need a structured review approach.

In the previous chapter, I suggested that the ISO 9000 model was a good one. It provides for planned, directed reviews of system efficiency. Add to that some structuring to encourage refinement through spontaneous feedback, and you have a responsive, rational system for change.

My recommendation is that even if you have a TQM rather than an ISO 9000 orientation, your life will be easier if you borrow the ISO 9000 approach for evolutionary change. That is a personal preference; I prefer some order with my change; those with a predilection for chaos theory might be more comfortable without it!

Where are we in the process?

This chapter presumes that the practice has developed a quality system, scheduled its implementation, breathed a huge sigh of relief, and now feels very much like it is time to 'go back and get some work done'.

What? Go back? Go back to where? To where you were
before you started this odyssey?

Too late. If you were serious, there is no 'going back', and
going forward will be different than before. So how do we go
forward?

Readers with a 'people orientation' will have noticed by
now that this book has been fairly quiet about the role that
human interactions have in evolutionary change. Once
again, this issue is of such importance as to be worthy of a
fat book in its own right, and I can no more than touch on it
briefly in the scope of this volume. Some useful references
are provided at the end of Part 3.

The cultural imperative

I have emphasized earlier that the culture of a practice is
the way it is for very powerful reasons - all 'people' reasons.
But it is not just the founders and directors who shape the
practice, it is everybody in it, through an exceedingly
complex web of personal interactions.

Because we value the contribution of each member of the
practice, we keep some kind of truce with each of them, easy
or uneasy. We live with their demons, and they with ours;
so it has been from the dawn of time. Those who don't fit in
wander off or are ejected. The office is a little tribe, with
tribal customs; part of the bigger tribe of related design professionals (within which there is considerable mobility).

In this context, change - any change - is guaranteed to
threaten someone's sense of place and order in the tribe, and
a lot of activities follow: digging in of heels, maneuvering
for position, demanding assurances of stability, etc.

*The bedrock reason why the cultural change inherent in all
types of quality management is so difficult is because it can
potentially 'mess up' the tribal balance in the practice, and
every member of the tribe can smell it coming a mile away.
Even those who want it, and asked for it, can fear it.*

It is for this precise reason that I favor the prescription of
the ISO 9000 approach to evolutionary change. Because it is
so prescriptive, it is also relatively non-threatening, even to
the most vulnerable of our colleagues.

What is this useful and calming process?

It is for you to write! However, there are words in the Standard you must fit within. Copyright rules prevent me from quoting the guidelines verbatim, but sub-system element 4.14.3: *Preventative action* requires you to *'detect, analyze and eliminate potential causes of nonconformities'* with respect to any activities which are related to the quality of the service you provide. You also need to determine any steps needed to make sure this happens, ensure the steps are effective, and keep management advised of your actions.

I've tried to avoid definitions in this book, but it might be useful to define *nonconformities*. The term is defined in ISO 8402 as *non-fulfillment of specified requirements*. In this case, the 'specified requirements' are your quality procedures.

Read the clause again (or, better, get the Standard, and read *it*). That is a pretty sweeping order! *Detect, analyze and eliminate?* Good-bye, warm and fuzzy change! This sounds more like war, or espionage.

What else? Element 4.17 requires you to undertake internal quality audits which will determine whether or not your efforts to 'detect, analyze and eliminate' these *potential* causes of nonconformity are actually happening.

Why did I italicize 'potential'? Because of our prior knee-jerk approach to problems. ISO 9000 commands us to 'detect, analyze and eliminate' *potential* problems. We are not talking about a 'wait and see' attitude here. This is searching out the enemy, and I don't have to remind you who Pogo identified as the prime suspect.

This detection and analyzing function won't be so easy. Excellent TQM tools have been developed which make the process somewhat easier. See Chapter 4.2, especially pages 172-173.

Management review

Once we have got a handle on these potential problems, then what? The leaders of the practice are obliged to consider them on a planned, regular basis (even if only once a year) and ask themselves whether the findings are conducive to furthering the goals of the practice. If not, they are to make appropriate adjustments. This presumes that they have established those goals, of course.

This process is simple, clear, *relatively* unthreatening, and doesn't even have to take a lot of time. Nevertheless, it can be demanding of the practice. It 'regularizes' activities that should, but rarely do, happen in every practice.

Scheduling change

Fortunately, there are no restrictions on scheduling. Within reason, each practice can schedule its detection, analysis and elimination of potential problems in any way it wishes. Common sense tells us, of course, that unless this process is enough of a part of the regular business of the practice to be continuously felt, it will have little meaning.

We are at liberty to focus on any quality processes that we wish, in any order. This allows the practice to schedule its continuous improvement activities in a way which is compatible with its workload. However, the imposed regularity of self-audits and management reviews ensures that the workload does not permanently eclipse the improvement program.

Restructuring

The idea of restructuring is that, just as any practice can be improved, so can any system the practice develops to better itself. In a TQM-based system, this restructuring is seen as a continuous evolutionary process.

By contrast, in an ISO 9000-based system, there are scheduled review periods, which lead to change if that is the outcome of the review process. This does not prevent system change from taking place between scheduled reviews, but it provides a framework or prompting system for checking to see if the procedures are working as intended.

"Buying in"

Returning to the 'people' aspect of change, the best way to make people more comfortable with change is to get them to 'buy in'; to take some ownership of the process. This is not always so easy. Managers do not always know how to delegate authority, which is crucial to sharing ownership of change.

The idea that staff will acquire some ownership of change often sounds like they will have more responsibility and have to do more work, without being paid for any more hours. This is partly reality, and partly fear of being exploited.

The process has to begin with including all staff in the planning and implementation process. This means that they will have programmed time to work on their part of QM.

It is also of the utmost importance to make it clear that the system as developed is not 'cast in concrete', but fully intended to be improved over time.

This ability to motivate people to welcome change and participate in it actively is not something any of us were taught in design school. Few practitioners are skilled in this art.

Because the way the entire program is presented and managed is so crucial to its acceptance by staff, the directors of the practice either should get some training in these skills, or get the help of a consultant who has these skills. Without the enthusiastic support of the whole practice, the process of evolution really will not ever happen.

**Chapter 3.5
Summary Checklist**

✓ Some practice functions will evolve naturally; others will require planning and a structured commitment to change.

✓ We adapt to the idiosyncrasies of others in our practice because we value their contribution. This means we become bound, to some extent, to each other's fear of change.

✓ Openly planning the process of review for potential change makes it less threatening.

✓ Under ISO 9000, the requirement is to 'detect, analyze and eliminate potential causes' of your inability to meet your own standards.

✓ Management periodically reviews feedback from internal audits and project experience to determine the effectiveness of procedures and institute changes. This is restructuring your system.

3.6   Improving Communication

Establishing the culture is a leader's most important job. And right or wrong, deliberately or accidentally, the personal example of the leaders will set the culture. - Chuck Thomsen

Purpose

To emphasize again the need for better communication (introduced in Chapter 1.6) as a central strategy in QM system design, with a focus on internal communication.

Deaf and dumb

To open this chapter I must tell another story from my time as a design-builder in Boston. Our painting group was managed by Tony, who had a short fuse. Our painting foreman, George, was completely deaf from birth. George lip-read and had learned to speak quite sufficiently, so communication was no problem as long as you could get his attention.

One day Tony returned to the office, smoke coming from his ears, so upset that I sent him home for the rest of the day. He'd had a shouting match with George, which George won simply by refusing to look at Tony, thus, of course, being unable to 'hear' him. This infuriated Tony. I went over to the project to find out what all the fuss was about. George was up on the scaffold, painting away, and when I got his attention, asked what had happened. He looked at me for a while and finally said: *"He is both deaf and dumb!"*

Point to George.

Tony was, in fact, an expert at one-way communication, and did not improve his skill in two-way communication while in my employ. Once, we presented him with a device called the Maggio Self-Motivator (Maggio was his surname) which consisted of small funnels on both ends of a short piece of garden hose. The idea was that you put one end up to your ear, and talked into the other end, so you could hear yourself. He never did work out how to use it.

Hermione's hearing aid

The Maggio Self-Motivator seemed like a great idea at the time, but it never 'took off', and you won't find it listed in the 'TQM tools' section in the next part of this book.

Lessons

What can we learn from this story? Tony had a severe communication deficiency, which ultimately cost him his job. I, as Tony's leader, also had a communication problem, because I couldn't work out how to make him an effective communicator, and *he was my agent in communication.* So his problem was my problem. By comparison, George, who came to the problem of communication with a powerful handicap, was an effective communicator.

In truth, all of *your* employees are the communicators of the mission, resources, strengths, and weaknesses of *your* practice. Their skills are *your* skills, because they are *your* agents, with every letter or telephone call or any other personal interaction.

Let us consider what a few others have said on this topic. In *Lessons in Professional Liability*, by DPIC Companies, the comment is made that [77]:

> *"...when people feel that they understand one another perfectly, they are often actually operating by what psychologists call 'pseudo-communication'; that is, they think they have reached a common understanding when, in reality, they have not."*

This failure to communicate sufficiently is true both for our internal communication, within the practice, and with clients, other consultants, and others outside the practice. In Chapter 3.4 I discussed briefly the idea of the *internal* client; in Chapter 3.5 I noted the importance of involving the whole practice in ownership of the quality system. Both of these require excellent communication skills on the part of the directors to work successfully.

What is the official line?

International guideline Standards have weighed in on this point. ISO 9004.2 notes (clause 5.3.2.3):

> *"Service personnel, especially those directly involved with the customer, should have adequate knowledge and the necessary skills in communication. They should be capable of forming a natural work team able to interact appropriately with external organizations and representatives to provide a timely and smooth running service.*
>
> *"Team activities such as quality improvement forums, can be effective for improving communication between personnel and can provide an opportunity for supportive participation and cooperation in solving problems.*

"Regular communication within the service organization should be a feature at all levels of management."

The small practice

In the small design office, communication is taken for granted; it happens naturally. This is often the case, and it probably is true that architects are relatively egalitarian in the dealings with staff. Yet some practices have (to an outsider's eyes) almost unbelievable internal communication problems, and claim histories show that many practitioners have trouble communicating with their clients.

Many experts who do team-building consultation put much of this inability to communicate to personality differences; they use Myers Briggs testing to help people understand where each other is coming from.

Typical small-practice architects are not likely to engage professionals to help them communicate better, even though they would accept that whatever communicating skills they now have, probably could be improved.

What I think I heard you say...

Sometimes I get the feeling that you're not really listening to me.

Listening is a special skill, and often even people who understand how important it is aren't very good at it.

Norman Kaderlan says *"Perhaps the most critical communication skill you can develop is listening"*, and offers good advice on this skill, summarized below [78]. I've only given you the outline of his points; they are well worth reading in full.

◆ When someone is talking, first focus on what is said and then on what you think is really meant.

◆ When you are talking, watch the listener.

◆ Relax and clear your mind.

◆ Listen to everything the person says.

◆ You can listen much faster than a person can talk. Try to listen without analyzing, without interrupting.

◆ Don't pre-judge the person or the message.

◆ Take accurate notes to have an accurate memory of what was said.

◆ Listen for intent as well as content. If unsure of what was meant, ask for clarification.

Do you take communication for granted?

My experience is that a central problem in communication improvement is in taking that capacity for granted. As a result, the busy firm owner never does get sufficient time to either instruct or listen to his staff (it would appear that women are more sensitive to this need and more likely to make the time).

If you are too busy to properly instruct or listen to your staff, the only solution is to *change your calendar,* to use Tom Peters' concept [79]. This means, simply, for the person in charge to move communication improvement from the back of her mind to the front, and to keep it there, doing everything which can be done to make it work better. Of course this has to be balanced with all of the other things the practice leader has to do, but just an awareness and a commitment can make a tremendous difference in the outcome.

After this 'attitude change' at the top, there are a number of specific actions the practice can take which will significantly improve its communicating capability; these are presented and discussed below.

What else can the practice leader do to improve comunication?

Here is my own list. With a bit of thought, I am sure that you could create your own list, from your own experience. The hard part is to remember to follow your own advice.

◆ *Always remember that those around you have different priorities; different pressures, different agendas.* They may not believe in working a 14-hour day, even though they accept that you do. A lot of mis-communication results from 'the boss' thinking that all staff see the world the way she does.

◆ *Most people are reluctant to challenge their leader.* Even if you would prefer that they did sometimes. People survive peacefully by subordinating their own views. You might well have to stop and probe around a bit to get that brilliant idea out of a key staffer.

◆ *Ask questions.* Followed by more questions. When you know the answers to your own questions, bite your tongue.

◆ *Give people time to formulate answers.* Nobody wants to look foolish. Advance notice allows a person to think through an issue; do a bit of research.

◆ *Free up people's time to formulate answers.* Asking people under a lot of pressure to contribute meaningfully to a debate isn't doing them any favor, it is putting them in an impossible situation. Damned if they do, and damned if they don't. They won't respect you for it.

◆ *Having asked the question, don't demean the answer.* The best solutions have their negative aspects. They will become apparent in due course. What is your goal - better communication, or right answers? In the words of that old pop song, 'accentuate the positive'.

◆ *If an idea is full of problems, don't kill it yourself.* Ask someone else (a temperate person) what she thinks. If the idea gets a bucket of cold water, ask for another opinion from someone who will support anyone. What is your goal - better communication, or right answers? The person who missed it today may solve it tomorrow, and the last thing you need to do is gag her by criticism.

◆ *Bring in an outside opinion.* There is a saying, *familiarity breeds contempt*. Even if that is not the case in your office, people who know each other well will discount what their workmates say, based on past experience. They will listen more carefully to a stranger.

◆ *Reward good ideas.* Everybody secretly wants to be a hero. Appreciation is empowerment.

◆ Lastly: *DON'T ANSWER YOUR OWN QUESTIONS.* Unless the only reason for asking was to hear yourself talk. In which case, your staff might like to order a Maggio Self-Motivator for you. $29.95 plus shipping, anywhere in the world, fabricated to order.

**Chapter 3.6
Summary Checklist**

✓ Your staff communicate your vision and your practice to the world. Ensure that they know how to do it.

✓ Effective communication skills are a requirement of ISO 9000 QM.

✓ Practice your listening skills every chance you get.

Part 3 Resources

References

(59) Fox, Roy: *Making Quality Happen: Six Steps to Total Quality Management*, McGraw-Hill (Sydney) 1991, p 119.

(60) See p 20; the third of Deming's 14 points.

(61) Fox, p 44.

(62) Fox, p 69.

(63) Fox, p 77.

(64) Labeling in the quality industry is a bit like names for Chinese soup. New South Wales Public Works calls its system "Seven Gates". Giving these systems numbers is just a way of trying to organize diverse information.

(65) Stebbing, p 55 and Chapter 5.

(66) AS/NZS 3905.2 is available from Standards Australia, PO Box 1055, Strathfield NSW 2135 Australia. Fax (61-2) 746-8450. Cost: A $47.00 (about US $36.00) plus shipping.

(67) Fox, p 8.

(68) Fox, p 105.

(69) If your belief system permits it, a generous brandy is recommended to be taken with this chapter.

(70) Fox, pp 8, 99.

(71) Price, p 261.

(72) Stebbing, pp 49-50.

(73) Juran, p 3.

(74) Fox, p 196.

(75) Ibid., p 198.

(76) Walton, p 75.

(77) DPIC Companies, *Lessons in Professional Liability*, 1988, p 8.

(78) Kaderlan, pp 98-99.

(79) Peters, Tom, *Thriving on Chaos: Handbook for a Management Revolution*, Pan Books, 1987, pp 412-414. See also Chapter 5.5.

For more help on...

Writing ISO 9000 procedures: Lionel Stebbing's *Quality Management in the Service Industry* is excellent. Chapter 7 offers a thorough description of the audit process.

Implementation of quality systems: The last chapter in Stuart Rose's *Achieving Excellence in Your Design Practice* (refer to footnote 4, Part 1) is required reading. Entitled *Implementing Excellence*, this chapter consists of a set of 20 worksheets, which (quoting Rose, p 107) *"forces you to ask these questions:*

✓ *What is the action that needs to happen?*

✓ *How are we going to achieve the change we want?*

✓ *When should we expect results?*

✓ *Who should be responsible for seeing that the change takes place"?*

TQM generally:

◆ Of the many resources I have reviewed, one of the most readable and useful for the QM novice is by Roy Fox. See footnote 59.

◆ British readers would be interested in *Quality Management for Building Design,* by Tim Cornick (Butterworth Architecture Management Guides, 1991). It is a somewhat theoretical treatment of the subject, but Cornick offers useful information on structuring of ISO 9000 QM systems. The British have a penchant for inventing highly detailed and cumbersome classification systems. Cornick's QM model respects that tradition.

Establishing quality goals and objectives:

◆ Fox, pp 62-93.

◆ Juran (footnote 24), Chapter 2.

◆ Kaderlan (footnote 8), pp 9-31.

◆ Stasiowski (footnote 53), pp 6-23.

◆ Rose (footnote 4), Chapter 6.

Continuous improvement:

◆ Juran, Chapter 12.

◆ Fox, Chapter 6.

◆ Stasiowski and Burstein (footnote 11), Chapter 9.

For more help on...

People and 'ownership' of systems and ideas:

◆ *Managing Brainpower*, by Chuck Thomsen (AIA Press, 1989). All three of the small books in this set are worth your serious study, but on this topic, note especially Chapters 1 and 2 in *Book One: Organizing.*

◆ Rose, Chapter 5.

◆ Stebbing, pp 52-54.

◆ Fox, pp 83-87.

◆ *In Search of Excellence*, by Thomas Peters and Robert Waterman (Harper & Row, 1982), Chapter 8.

◆ Patching, Chapters VI and VII.

Communication skills:

◆ Rose, pp 66-69; 78-82.

◆ Patching, Chapters IX to XV inclusive. The author has done a very good job of pulling together the key points about communication in these 71 pages.

◆ Kaderlan, Chapters 6 and 7.

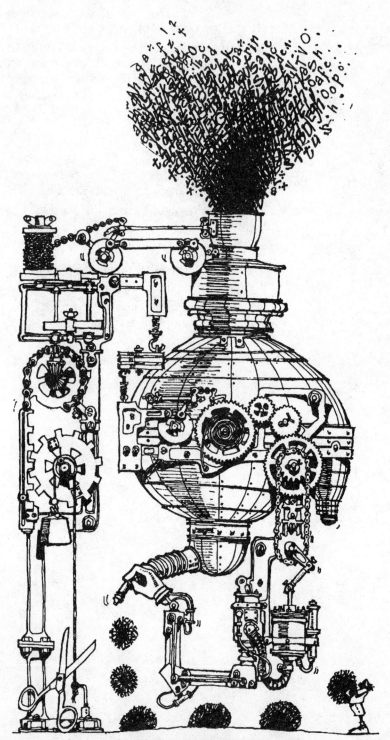

The Information Pelletizer

Part 4

TOOLS: Techniques for Managing Quality

4.1   Selecting the Right Tool for the Job

Only by creating its own route will a company have the greatest chance of achieving world-class quality products and services. - Stasiowski and Burstein

Purpose

To establish the validity of a 'toolkit' approach to quality management.

Tools to suit the tasks

How do you pick the right tool for the job? Is that even the right question? Alternatively, should you be designing your own (unique) tools? I suggest this process:

◆ Find out what the offerings are, and the purpose for which they were invented.

◆ Compare those purposes with your own situation, but keep your mind open to new possibilities.

◆ Adopt those tools which, at least on the surface, appear to address problems you experience. Give them time to start working.

◆ Try out other tools that look interesting, and see how they might be adapted to suit your practice.

TQM theorists have developed special sets of tools, which are catalogued in Chapter 4.2. Those I have judged most useful for designers are described in more detail.

These tools have their roots in industry rather than service organizations; developed for dealing effectively with the manufacture of objects.

Statistics and measuring things

A key to understanding many TQM tools is their reliance on statistical methods: if you want to fix something, first you must measure what you are doing now. Statistical methods have a role in architectural design, but this role is small compared to the importance of these methods in many other areas of industry.

TQM experts will argue against this view, maintaining that measurement is at the heart of any valid quality system. Certainly designers could do with more objective analysis of the way they practice.

I've yet to see the first practice that actually tracked the money it spent on re-working design and documentation. However, it is also obvious that the inherent differences in various industries change the benefits which can be gained from measuring performance.

I believe that there is a high positive correlation between the similarity of the products a firm makes, and the value of measuring performance. In the service industries, a fast-food chain such as Macdonalds is a classic example of a firm which can get very high value out of measuring (say) customer satisfaction, because its products are such a steady and reliable baseline against which to gauge success.

Most designers are in the 'one-off' business, where every project is special. The team at Macdonalds might argue that every hamburger is special, too, but there IS a difference.

Not a few TQM authorities would say that it's not the product (or service), it's the PEOPLE who matter - those on both sides of the counter. The fact is that very few design professionals regularly try to find out how people like using their buildings (or other designs), once they are completed.

As is probably obvious, I have some ambivalence about the extent to which measuring performance is key to quality management for the design professions. What I do know is that the argument won't go away, and that until we start to measure the things we really should be measuring, it will be difficult to determine how useful measuring can be for us.

Evolution of TQM

TQM has evolved considerably from its industrial roots, with Juran (in my view) leading the way. Juran's planning methodologies (The Juran Trilogy) are understandable to the design professional (good design is good design) and offer an interesting structure. Another valuable trend is the relatively recent focus on TQM in service industries.

Most of the QM examples still come from very large organizations, however, and warrant the most careful scrutiny in evaluating their direct application to 'small to medium' sized design practices e.g. 2 to 20 people.

One of the interesting outcomes of a comparison of ISO 9000 and TQM systems is that their areas of overlap in fact seem to offer the most promise for the design practice.

I have selected eight topics to study in more depth, in Chapters 4.3 to 4.10: The project brief, project quality plans, audits, design reviews, checking, performance specifications, partnering and document control.

Although these eight are specific quality 'strategies' or systems in their own right, they are all related to both TQM and/or ISO 9000 concepts, and they offer the design professional some powerful levers for improving practice.

In addition, Chapter 4.2 includes a summary description of 34 of the 37 TQM / ISO 9000 tools and techniques - those of the 90 reviewed which appear to offer 'high' or 'moderate' applicability to design practice, but which are not already generally used by the design professions. (The other three, design reviews, quality audits and ISO 9000, are covered under separate chapters.)

The next chapter also includes summary descriptions of 13 of the 14 tools/techniques classified 'Occasionally used' (the other one being partnering, which is covered in a separate chapter).

**Chapter 4.1
Summary Checklist**

✓ Review available tools pragmatically.

✓ Increasing the emphasis on design process measurement is a necessary improvement, but perhaps not to the degree appropriate to other industries.

✓ Many tools/techniques common to both TQM and ISO 9000 offer the design professional some powerful levers for improving practice.

4.2   The Designer's TQM Toolkit

*Lists of tools can never be complete. Most tools
exist in multiple forms and variations. New
variations are constantly being invented. Most of
the terminology has yet to be standardized.*
- J. M. Juran

Purpose

To outline the techniques that have evolved as standard
'tools' in the TQM world, and to explain them in simple
terms appropriate to architectural/design practice.

The whole toolkit: a wrench for every nut

This approach is reminiscent of the old full-page ads from the Sears Roebuck catalog, laying out the 497-piece master mechanics tool set. You may not need the 17-piece left-handed metric monkey wrench collection with chrome knurled micrometer calibration doodads.

and the tally:	
Frequently used	22
Occasionally used	14
High applicability	20
Moderate applicability	17
Low applicability	4
Not applicable	12

On the pages that follow is a set of comprehensive tables
which identify 90 TQM tools, techniques and systems. The
first 48 are those listed in Peter Mears' excellent book
Quality Improvement Tools & Techniques. The remainder
are identified by Deming, Juran, Crosby and Stasiowski and
Burstein. Where these relate to ISO 9000, the ISO 9000
system element is given.

For those who wish to read further on any of these tools, the
page numbers of the sources are given. It should be noted
that the referencing is not intended to be complete; only to
serve as a general guide to one place where more information
may be found.

In the fourth column of these tables I have made an attempt
to define whether the tool/technique was already being
used by design professionals, if so, how much, and if not,
how applicable it would be. This assignment of
applicability is personal and subjective; I expect others
would disagree with some of the assumptions made.

There are two reasons to make these assignments. The first
is to show that many design professionals are already using
many TQM tools; it isn't a totally new technology to us. The
second is to provide a way to focus; to discuss in more detail
those tools/techniques which are NOT in common use in our
industry, but which ARE likely to be of value to us.

Following the tables is a brief description and example of
those tools which I have given a 'High' or 'Moderate'
applicability rating, and those which are 'Occasionally
used'; and how they might be applicable to design practice.

The rest of Part 4 goes into some detail about a few of the tools and techniques which are of particular significance in a quality management system for design.

Tables of Tools Legend

Source data reference key		DMM	=	*The Deming Management Method*, Mary Walton
Refer to **Resources** at end of Part 4. Numbers are page numbers in text referenced		ISO	=	ISO 9000, system element as noted
		JQD	=	*Juran on Quality by Design*, J. M. Juran
		Q F	=	*Quality Is Free*, Philip Crosby
		S&B	=	*Total Quality Project Management*, Stasiowski and Burstein
Applicability key		FU	=	Frequently used by design professions
# = by the design professions		O U	=	Occasionally used by design professions
## = to the design professions		H	=	High applicability, rarely used #
		M	=	Moderate applicability, rarely used #
		L	=	Low applicability, rarely used #
		N A	=	Not generally applicable ##

Table 4.1:
The basic TQM tools

Items 1, 2 and 4-8 are considered to be the seven basic quality improvement tools. Mears adds checklists and run charts (items 3 and 9) to these as they are closely related.

Name of tool/technique		Source data		Applica-bility	Use, Notes
		Mears	Other		
1	Flowchart	14, 18-22	JQD 46-51 DMM 100-102	O U	Understanding situations
2	Check sheet	14, 23-28		H	Fact finding
3	Checklist	15, 29		FU	Fact finding
4	Histogram	16, 40-51	DMM 107-109	M	Identifying problems
5	Pareto diagram	15, 29-40	JQD 57-60 DMM 103-105 S&B 283-284	M	Identifying problems
6	Cause-and-effect (fishbone) diagram	16, 52-57	DMM 97-99 S&B 284-290	M	Generating ideas; showing relationships between events
7	Scatter diagram	17, 57-61	DMM 109-111	L	Visually gauging how a change in one thing affects another
8	Control chart	17, 67-90	DMM 111-116	N A	Implementation; statistically-based variation identification
9	Run chart (line graph)	17, 61-67	DMM 105-107	FU	Implementation; showing process output over time

Table 4.2:

More TQM tools

Items 10-31 are later developments; additional tools which represent a further development of the concepts of the core seven tools.

Name of tool/technique	Source data		Applica-	Use, Notes
	Mears	Other	bility	
10 Pie chart	91, 95-96		O U	Shows composition of whole
11 Bar chart	92, 97-99		F U	Compares differences in data
12 Stratification diagram	93, 102-107		F U	Organizes categories, shows structure
13 Frequency chart	93, 99-101		L	Compares differences in data
14 Single case boring	94, 107-109		N A	Depicts unusual data relationship
15 Likert scale	94, 108-109		O U	Measures subjective data
16 Radar chart	95, 109-114		M	Shows relative strengths of key activities
17 Plan-Do-Check-Act (Shewhart cycle)	119, 122-123	DMM 84-86	H	Outlines action/feedback process for simple activity structures
18 Personal quality checklist	119, 123-126		H	Structures to individually effect change (Mears calls it one of the most powerful quality improvement tools)
19 Vision or mission statement; quality goals	119, 127-131	JQD 27-43 ISO s/e 1	H	Establishes corporate goals (required by ISO 9000)
20 Deployment chart	120, 131-132		O U	Assigns resources (required by ISO 9000)
21 Kaizen	120, 132		N A (note 1)	TQM concept; extends continuous improvement throughout all aspects of employee's life; includes many other quality tools and techniques
22 Kanban	120, 133		N A	An empty box is authority to manufacture parts to fill it
23 Poka-yoke	120, 133-134	S&B 308-309	L	'Idiot-proofing'; design to prevent assembling defects
24 SMED	120, 135-137		N A	Means 'single minute exchange of dies' - for manufacturing only
25 Nominal grouping	121, 137-140		N A (note 2)	Idea generation and resolution for sensitive issues
26 Brainstorming	121, 137-140		F U	Idea generation
27 Multivoting	121, 139-140		M	Reduces list of ideas; used with brainstorming

28	Force field analysis, multivariable analysis	121, 140-142	S&B 302-307	M	Understanding of driving and restraining forces; change analysis
29	Classifying quality problems	122, 142-143		M (note 3)	Sorts problems; internal/external; large/small
30	Improving perceived quality	122, 144-145	JQD 159-217	H	Understanding client expectations; shaping marketing
31	Effective presentations	122, 145		FU	Analyze factors in presentation

Notes:

1 Kaizen, which means 'improvement', is not so much a technique as a philosophy of life. We can think of many brilliant designers who have approached their work with a commitment similar to Kaizen. Kaizen, however, includes many other quality techniques which do not have applicability to design.

2 Nominal grouping is a kind of structured brainstorming where everyone submits his or her ideas about an issue; then the ideas are organized and put up on a white board. The group votes on the ideas to arrive at a 'common' agreement. Idea generation and voting may be open or anonymous; the latter being used when the issue is sensitive (for example, if the question was to disband a department of the firm).

3 The technique of classifying quality problems forms the centerpiece of motivational guru Dr. Stephen Covey's time management system, which is illustrated in Chapter 5.5.

Are you a total quality person?

Scattered throughout Mears' text, with tick boxes to fill in, are questions that focus on the answer to the question at left. Here is Mears' aggregated list. What's your rating? .There is no evaluation scale; make up your own).

Seldom	Sometimes	Always	
☐	☐	☐	I treat others fairly.
☐	☐	☐	If I am dealt a lemon, I make lemonade.
☐	☐	☐	I feel good about myself.
☐	☐	☐	I am proud of my achievements.
☐	☐	☐	I take personal pride and ownership in my job.
☐	☐	☐	When in conversation, I make positive comments that move the discussion forward.
☐	☐	☐	I improve the quality of life for others.
☐	☐	☐	I attempt to improve the quality of my personal life.
☐	☐	☐	I set personal goals.
☐	☐	☐	I have specific plans to improve the quality of my personal life.
☐	☐	☐	I personally attempt to master something new, at least quarterly.
☐	☐	☐	I volunteer to help others in need.
☐	☐	☐	I have a healthy, positive outlook on life.
☐	☐	☐	I take control of my life and I do not rely on others to plan my future.
☐	☐	☐	I have developed realistic goals for my life, with achievable targets.
☐	☐	☐	I understand my values, which I follow in my personal life.

(continued on page 145)

Table 4.3
Advanced quality improvement techniques

Mears notes of this group (p 147) *"An application of any of (these) techniques ... requires both thought and careful planning."*

Name of tool/technique	Source data		Applica-	Use, Notes
	Mears	Other	bility	
32 Focus groups	147, 149-155		M	Structured brainstorming
33 Benchmarking	147, 155-159	S&B 300-302	H	Comparing your firm to others
34 Process ownership, team building	147, 159-163	QF 212-215 S&B 323 DMM 75-76	O U	Employees identifying with firm goals
35 Customer needs mapping	148, 163-165	JQD 72-115 S&B 235-259	O U	Organizes client needs; compares to processes
36 Quality functional deployment	148, 165-178		F U	Formal briefing; detailed program development
37 Hoshin planning techniques (the seven management tools)	148, 179-190		F U (note 4)	Divides planning into 3 stages, uses the 7 tools to resolve planning issues; see also items 84-90
38 Gap analysis	148, 190-196		H	Different views of providing service
39 Taguchi methods	148, 196-199		N A	Statistical extension of improvement concepts into design

Notes:

4   Hoshin is a planning technique involving a number of tools familiar to many design professionals, particularly those who work in facility management or interior design. Table 4.7 identifies the seven Hoshin techniques.

Seldom	Sometimes	Always	(Continuation of Mears' *'Are you a total quality person'* questions)
❑	❑	❑	I measure whether I am meeting my personal goals.
❑	❑	❑	I am open to changes in my life that will assist me to learn new things.
❑	❑	❑	I attempt to improve my home/family life.
❑	❑	❑	I admit my mistakes, and then move on with the goal of not making the same mistake again.
❑	❑	❑	I strive for continuous learning.
❑	❑	❑	I practice positive reinforcement.
❑	❑	❑	I actively listen to others.

Table 4.4:

Quality improvement systems

Items 40-48 are 'quality improvement systems' in Mears' structure, although I would suggest that ISO 9000 is more than 'quality improvement', and that the Baldridge Award, while certainly being a motivating device and structure for approaching TQM, is more of a standard by which quality achievements are gauged.

Name of tool/technique	Source data		Applica-	Use, Notes
	Mears	Other	bility	
40 Quality cost system	201, 203-205	QF 178-181	H/M (note 5)	Identifies cost of poor quality
41 The learning organization	201, 205-207		H (note 6)	Conceptualizes self-learning by the firm
42 Customer/supplier agreements	201, 207-209		O U (note 7)	Details client's requirements
43 Shojinka	202, 209-210	S&B 180-186	F U (note 8)	Moves workers to suit demand, used with Just-in-time
44 Just-in-time	202, 210-215	S&B 186-193	N A	Keeping inventory low; applicable only to manufacturing
45 Quality teams	202, 215-221	QF 152-169	M	Authority at production level; in design industry applicable only in very large firms
46 Quality council	202, 221-223	QF 220	M	Formalized executive level TQM focus; in design industry applicable only in very large firms
47 ISO Standards	203, 224-228, 263-272	Refer to Chapter 1.3	H	Mears lists it as a 'quality improvement system', but its application is almost as broad as is TQM
48 Baldridge Award	203, 253-262	S&B 317-320	N A	The pinnacle achievement in TQM, this award provides a rigorous structure for competing

Notes:

5   See Chapter 6.2.

6   See Chapters 5.1 and 5.2.

7   Design professionals very frequently use a low level of a 'customer-supplier agreement', the architect-client agreement or the equivalent for other areas of design. Usually these documents are not specific about the client's requirements. The process of developing the program (called 'brief' in Commonwealth countries) is of great importance in ISO 9000, and is the subject of the third system element.

8   Design professionals, of course, move workers around to suit demand all the time, and have never needed a Japanese word to describe the process.

Table 4.5:

More quality methods and techniques

Items 49-68 are tools, techniques or strategies not catalogued by Mears.

Name of tool/technique	Source data		Applica-	Use, Notes
	Mears	Other	bility	
49 Management commitment		QF 149-152 ISO s/e 1 S&B 320-326	H	Establishes management's role with respect to quality improvement
50 Identify customers		JQD 44-67 S&B 173-180	M (note 9)	Understanding who will be affected by achievement of quality goals, and how
51 Develop process features		JQD 218-273 ISO s/e 9 S&B 291-300	H	Modifying processes to respond to customer needs/wants
52 Quality audits		QF 66-67, ISO s/e 17 S&B 344-351	H	Determine whether firm is meeting its goals
53 Quality management maturity grid		QF 21-48	H	Charts quality 'maturity' of the firm
54 Process controls & inspections		JQD 274-298 ISO s/e 10, 11, 12	N A	Detect errors as they are made; prevention of defective products
55 Quality measurement		QF 169-178 ISO s/e 9 JQD 116-158	(note 10)	Objective analysis of nonconforming work
56 Corrective action		QF 191-198 ISO s/e 14 S&B 265-282	H	Permanently remove the causes of error
57 Zero-defects planning		QF 198-204	N A	Structures events leading up to Z D Day
58 Z D Day		QF 207-212	N A	Event to demonstrate change to quality
59 Training		JQD 438-461 QF 204-207 ISO s/e 18 S&B 206-211	FU	Structured training to improve skills
60 Error-cause removal		QF 215-218 ISO s/e 13	H (note 11)	Feedback loop from staff to management to identify causes of errors
61 Motivation & recognition		JQD 425-437 QF 218-220 S&B 335-344	H	Fostering belief and rewarding achievement in quality improvement
62 Make Certain program		QF 241-249	(note 12)	Structured elicitation of problems received by staff

63	Strategic quality planning		JQD 299-333	M	Structured process for defining mission and goals; selection of strategies for achieving them
64	Multifunctional quality planning		JQD 334-362	M (note 13)	Structuring the quality improvement process
65	Departmental quality planning		JQD 363-406	L (note 13)	Carrying out the quality improvement process
66	Database, Santayana review		JQD 407-425	M	Quality history in accessible format
67	Project quality plan		ISO s/e 2 S&B 59-60, 64	H (note 14)	Project-specific selection of applicable quality procedures
68	Design review		ISO s/e 6	H (note 15)	Structured, minuted check of design appropriateness
69	Recruitment		S&B 193-199	F U	Upgrading of ability to deliver higher quality services through hiring
70	Induction		S&B 199-200	O U	Entry training to ensure new staff understand quality systems and standards
71	Performance evaluations		S&B 200-206	O U	Structured interaction between staff and management where each benefits from the other's appraisal
72	Partnering		S&B 259-262	O U	Replacing the adversary relationship between client and builder with one that optimizes responsibilities and gains for both parties
73	Peer reviews		S&B 326-328	H	Structured evaluation of your firm's strengths and weaknesses by like professionals

Notes:

9   The term 'customers' here refers to stakeholders; <u>all</u> those who could be affected, including the public and 'internal' customers e.g. staff.

10 Quality measurement uses tools as appropriate for the industry. Generally, measuring actions is less rewarding in the design professions than using other TQM techniques.

11 Error-cause removal is part of the corrective action process.

12 Crosby's 'Make Certain" program would have good application for large practices; less for the small office.

13 Planning principles would find application in larger practices, especially in multi-office practices.

14 Project quality plans (PQPs) are a requirement under ISO 9000. See also p 174, pp 184-190 and pp 306-307.

15 Virtually all design firms do some kind of design review, but the vast majority of it is the 'desktop crit' informal review, where no record of the review is kept. Formal design review is a requirement under ISO 9000.

Table 4.6:

Design quality techniques

This group of tools is specific to design or the design phase of a project.

Name of tool/technique	Source data		Applica-bility	Use, Notes
	Mears	Other	bility	
74 Concept review		S&B 60	FU	Comparing design features to broad project requirements, including client brief, time and cost
75 Intradisciplinary review		S&B 60-61	FU	Ensures qualified person from each discipline checks output of that discipline
76 Interdisciplineary review		S&B 61	FU	Resolution of discrepancies between output of different disciplines
77 Drawing-specification crosscheck		S&B 61	FU	Resolution of discrepancies between graphic and written instructions
78 Multifacility crosscheck		S&B 61	FU	Resolution of discrepancies between parts of a large project designed by more than one team
79 Pre-tender check		S&B 75-83	FU (note 16)	Structured process for detecting mistakes at completion of documentation state
80 Vendor review		S&B 61-62	O U	Obtaining product manufacturers' review to detect inappropriate applications, out-of-date selections
81 Constructability review		S&B 62-63	O U	Ensuring that design does not include elements which are difficult or impossible to achieve on site
82 Operability review		S&B 63	H	Facility management review; ensuring design will be easy to operate
83 Record drawings		S&B 159-165	FU	Documenting changes between contract documents and built work

Notes:

16 All design firms believe in thorough pre-tender checking, but most experience difficulties in actually doing it regularly. Very few have the structured approach of REDICHECK, developed by William Nigro. See also pp 206-207.

Table 4.7:

Hoshin quality planning tools

Some of these quality planning tools have been long used by the design professions (refer to item 37).

Name of tool/technique	Source data		Applica-bility	Use, Notes
	Mears	Other		
84 Affinity diagram	179, 181		F U	Sorts related ideas into similar groups and identifies each group
85 Interrelationship diagram	179, 181		F U	Identifies cause and effect links between ideas/events
86 Tree diagram	180, 182-184		O U	Organizes detail groups of tasks to be accomplished
87 Matrix diagram	180, 185-186		O U	Shows relationships between activities
88 Matrix data analysis	180, 185-186		M	A specialized scatter diagram used to compare services you offer to services others offer
89 Process decision program chart (PDPC)	180, 186-187		M	Maps events together with countermeasures that may be required in case a problem occurs
90 Activity network (Gantt chart, PERT chart, CPM)	180, 187-189		F U	Relates events and time, establishes precedents for activities

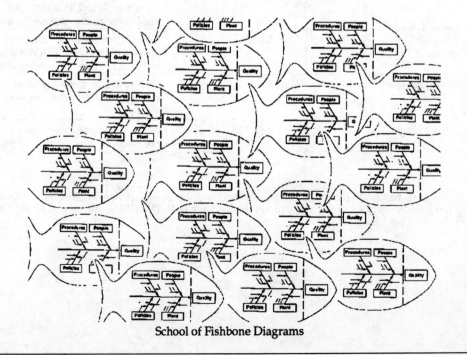

School of Fishbone Diagrams

In the preceding seven tables, the following 37 quality tools, techniques and systems were identified as being of 'high' or 'moderate' application to design practice, but were only rated as rarely used by design professionals:

✓ Checksheet (H)
✓ Histogram (M)
✓ Pareto diagram (M)
✓ Fishbone diagram (M)
✓ Radar chart (M)
✓ PDCA (Shewhart) cycle (H)
✓ Personal quality checklist (H)
✓ Mission statement; quality goals (H)
✓ Multivoting (M)
✓ Force field analysis (M)
✓ Classifying quality problems (M)
✓ Improving perceived quality (H)
✓ Focus groups (M)
✓ Benchmarking (H)
✓ Gap analysis (H)
✓ Quality cost system (H/M)
✓ The learning organization (H)
✓ Quality teams (M)
✓ Quality council (M)
✓ ISO Standards (H)
✓ Management commitment (H)
✓ Identify customers (M)
✓ Develop process features (H)
✓ Quality audits (H)
✓ Quality management maturity grid (H)
✓ Corrective action (H)
✓ Error-cause removal (H)
✓ Motivation and recognition (H)
✓ Strategic quality planning (M)
✓ Multifunctional quality planning (M)
✓ Database, Santayana review (M)
✓ Project quality plan (H)
✓ Design reviews (H) (refer to Chapter 4.5)
✓ Peer reviews (H)
✓ Operability reviews (H)
✓ Matrix data analysis (M)
✓ Process decision program chart (M)

The following 14 TQM tools and techniques are used occasionally by design professionals, sometimes without knowing the name given them by the quality experts:

- ✓ Flowchart
- ✓ Pie chart
- ✓ Likert scale
- ✓ Deployment chart
- ✓ Process ownership; team building
- ✓ Customer needs mapping
- ✓ Customer/supplier agreements
- ✓ Induction
- ✓ Performance evaluations
- ✓ Partnering
- ✓ Vendor review
- ✓ Constructability review
- ✓ Tree diagram
- ✓ Matrix diagram

What about the 22 TQM tools and techniques which ARE frequently used by designers already? Shouldn't they be described as well, so readers who don't use them will understand them? Part of the answer is that there isn't room enough in this book to cover every aspect of quality management in design; the other part is that other works already describe the use of many of these tools in our industry.

What this 'cataloguing' does is to highlight a key point, which is that architects and other designers are already using 40% of the tools of TQM, although they may never have thought of it in those terms. This use, however, tends to be isolated; that is, these tools are used to accomplish specific purposes rather than seen as part of an overall, coordinated practice management strategy.

Checksheet

Type: TQM basic tool
Applicability: High
More info reference: p 142/2

The purpose of checksheets is to facilitate and organize the collection of data. All design professionals must deal with a large quantity of data, which is usually highly diverse, comes from a wide variety of sources, and usually is poorly organized at source.

The purpose of having data is to make decisions - the right decisions, the first time. Poor data = poor decisions = re-work = lost time = lost money. Peter Mears notes: [80] *'Data, by itself, is seldom useful.'*

There are a number of reasons for data collection to 'go astray'. These vary in importance with the type of data being collected. In design, one problem that can occur (especially with less experienced staff) is that people collecting data have a 'perceptual' bias e.g. they see only what they are looking for.

In other words, they interpret what they see to fit the mindset they bring to the problem. In so doing, they may miss relevant data which, if known, would change the design. Obviously this amounts to a flawed 'design input' which increases the chances of flawed design.

Checksheets are purpose-designed, and it is always wise to think through the questions that you want answered before designing the checksheet, and then to get someone else to quickly review the questions for completeness.

Checksheets can be used to simply record the incidence of something happening e.g. traffic counting; or can be used to organize the collection of qualitative data e.g. room data sheets. Sometimes simple checksheets can be used to quickly graphically compare different options e.g. the facilities available in different CADD software, or the bids on a project per the example below.

	BIDDER	A	B	C	D
1	Was bid received on time?	✓	✓	✓	✓
2	Was bid properly completed?	✓	✓		✓
3	Was bid security included?	✓	✓	✓	
4	Was bid without exclusions or qualifications?	✓		✓	
5	Were all schedules and supporting documents attached?	✓		✓	

You can see that from the construction of this checksheet that a 'tick' is a positive. A quick glance tells you that bidder 'A' did everything right and bidder 'D' has a problem bid.

Now suppose question 4 was phrased the other way, which might seem more natural: 'Did bid include any exclusions or qualifications?' That change would make that tick answer negative, and would make the 'quick glance' assessment impossible. The checksheet would have been poorly designed, producing confusing results.

Flowchart

Type: TQM basic tool

Occasionally used by design professionals

More info reference: p 142/1

Flowcharts are one of the most popular and ubiquitous quality management tools. Their chief use is to graphically identify, organize and represent process steps.

There is no overall agreement among authorities on the meaning of symbols used in flowcharts, but there are similarities. For the purposes of this example, the symbols used by Juran are as follows:

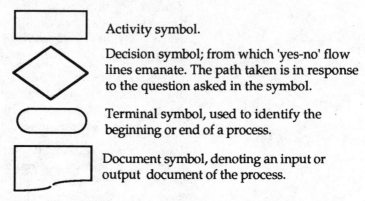

Activity symbol.

Decision symbol; from which 'yes-no' flow lines emanate. The path taken is in response to the question asked in the symbol.

Terminal symbol, used to identify the beginning or end of a process.

Document symbol, denoting an input or output document of the process.

A prototypical flowchart is shown opposite. This process is completely familiar, even instinctive, to all experienced design practitioners, even though few will ever have diagrammed the process.

Does the practice need this great TQM tool, flowcharting? Can we successfully manage the iterative process of design without it? If we use flowcharts, will we get back the time it takes to create them? The answer will depend on many factors, and will vary with firm size, project type, etc.

Obviously, a key factor is complexity of the project: if forgetting a step in the process could expose the firm to loss or risk, then using flowcharts may be good insurance.

Diagramming this process points out something that may not be so obvious from the 'experience' viewpoint: *there are a lot of reasons why a project goes back to be redesigned!* Obviously any failure along the way causes redesign after the design was thought to be complete. Quality management seeks to reduce this redesign; to save time and money.

What this flowchart shows is the absolute importance of ensuring that *as the design is developed*, it takes into account all of the requirements by which it will ultimately be evaluated. Design may be necessarily iterative, but should not be more iterative than necessary.

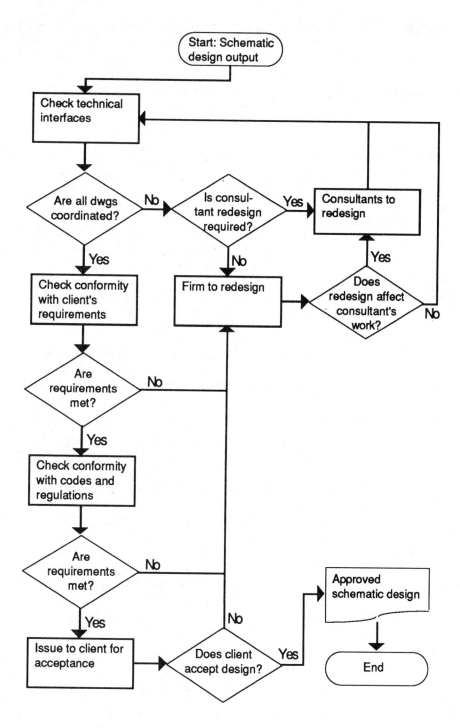

Schematic Design Review Flowchart

Pareto diagram

Type: TQM basic tool
Applicability: Moderate
More info reference: p 142/5

Back in Chapter 2.1 I made
the observation that
'problems facing practices
are ... those of which the
practice is unaware'. I don't
know how to test it, but my
hunch is that there would be
a high correlation between
the design situation not
previously encountered and
the resultant project
problems. That is why we
say 'experience is the best
teacher', and our more
experienced clients usually
opt for building type
experience in selection of a
designer.

Pareto diagrams [81] are used to identify problems. This tool explains data using Juran's discovery of the 'vital few / trivial many' principle; sometimes expressed as the '80-20 rule': 20% of the causes account for 80% of the problems. The idea of the Pareto diagram is that it identifies areas requiring further study, by separating the 'vital few' from the 'trivial many'.

I think we all have an instinctual awareness of this principle; as a farm kid I grew up with the idea of 'separating the wheat from the chaff'. The Pareto diagram replaces the hunch with the facts.

The validity of this principle was brought home to me sharply in 1994 when I was researching some data on construction cost and time growth for New South Wales Public Works, as preparation for their development of a strategy to reduce these factors in their building program. I found, in almost every set of construction reports, that 15% or less of projects were causing 85-90% of cost/time growth.

What this meant was that it would be foolish to develop 'across the board' remedies; what was needed was an 'early warning' program that could identify the problem projects before they turned into problems. These were the 'vital few' on which the spotlight needed to be aimed, if they could be identified.

How would we use a Pareto diagram in design? Let's say we wanted to identify the principal causes of cost overruns in construction. We would first collect data on a number of projects, say all the projects for one year. We would check all change orders issued, count them according to type, and group them in order of frequency. Such a chart might look like this:

COST OVERRUNS - 1995 Item	Number of Occurrences	Cumulative Occurrences	Cumulative Percent (%)
Client requested changes	56	56	37.1
Consultant coordination error	43	99	65.6
Specification error	27	126	83.4
Drawing error	16	142	94.0
All other errors	9	151	100.0

This data is then put into a Pareto diagram, as shown at right. Note that this method only tracks 'occurrences' rather than severity of the occurrence.

In TQM parlance, this is called 'discrete data'. What this data won't tell you is the relative value of the change orders. For that you need a different tool, although you could have charted cost of overruns, but not cost and frequency, both on the same diagram.

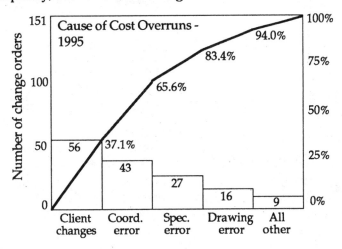

You may be thinking that this diagram isn't all that useful to you; you could get the same information just looking at the tabulation. True, but its real use is as a presentation device, to graphically demonstrate the facts. Obviously the purpose of the curve is to show the relative severity of the occurrence; the steeper the line, the more important the factor. If you thought this looks a lot like a bar chart, right again. As to interpretation of the above diagram, where you need to focus energy for improvement is obvious.

On the day I wrote this, I was at a meeting at an architect's office; he showed me a Pareto analysis of 62 objections to a planning application he had compiled for a client, using 25 complaint categories. Not only was he able to show quite graphically what the significant objections were, he could group them by their geographic source location.

Histogram

Type: TQM basic tool

Applicability: Moderate

More info reference: p 142/4

Mears has an excellent outline section on construction and interpretation of histograms.

A histogram looks like a Pareto diagram, without the curve. Unlike the Pareto diagram, which measures units of data, the histogram is used when the data is 'continuous' or 'variable'; for example, measurements or money. If, for example, we wanted to see the pattern of change order costs over many projects, we could use a histogram. The convention is to use as many categories of data as the square root of the number of events.

For example, if you had 150 change orders, you would round up from the square root (12.25) to 13 categories.

The construction of a histogram has many steps, can be time-consuming, and the discussion of interpretation of the diagram is involved, more than there is room for here.

If your work includes the interpretation of a lot of diverse data, such as ergonomic or sociological data, or measurements such as finding a pattern of discrepancies in floor slab heights, the histogram tool can be very useful. The average architectural/design office won't have much reason to use it.

Fishbone diagram

Type: TQM basic tool
Applicability: Moderate
More info reference: p 142/6

The fishbone diagram, one of the most used TQM tools, is also called a 'cause and effect' or Ishikawa diagram (after its inventor). It is used after a problem has been identified, to generate ideas for solution through identification of root causes of the problem. The general case is shown below.

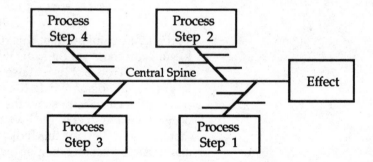

The steps to construct a simple fishbone diagram:

1   Identify the 'effect' - the head of the fish; the problem you want to solve. Draw the spine to the left.

2   Brainstorm causes; group them together as process headings (usually 4-6, but no rule); add them to the diagram.

3   Ask 'why?' 5 times to each of these headings; enter the answers off the main ribs of the fishbone.

4   Study and refine the results. Search for causes behind causes until you have the complete causal picture.

Example: Let's say that you have decided to get to the root of the problem with consultant coordination errors that you identified with the Pareto diagram above. Your diagram may end up looking something like this:

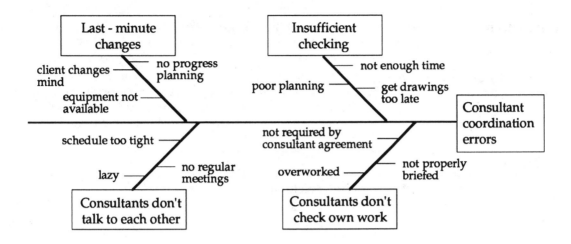

Pie chart

Type: TQM tool

Occasionally used by design professionals

More info reference: p 143/10

We see pie charts every day; they are widely used graphic means of 'at-a-glance' demonstration of quantifiable relationships.

Radar chart

Type: TQM tool

Applicability: Moderate

More info reference: p 143/16

Radar charts are a bit like pie charts, but show relative strengths and weaknesses of responses as a distance from the center of a circle out to the circumference. They are particularly good for getting an overall image of the results of using the Likert scale, and thus graphically showing areas where improvement is needed. This diagram serves the same purpose as a bar chart.

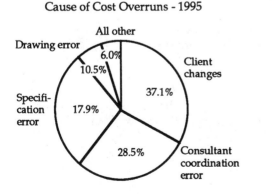

Pie Chart Example

Radar Chart Example

Likert scale

Type: TQM tool

Occasionally used by design professionals

More info reference: p 143/15

You have seen Likert scales many times, but probably didn't know that they were called that. Likert scales are used to gauge attitudes and perceptions, and usually have five or seven categories of agreement or satisfaction, as shown below. They are often used in program development and facilities management to determine user preferences and satisfaction; and can be used to test client satisfaction.

Likert Rating Scale						
◄── Disagree Neutral Agree ──►						
1	2	3	4	5	6	7
Disagree Very Strongly	Disagree Strongly	Disagree	Neither Agree Nor Disagree	Agree	Agree Strongly	Agree Very Strongly

PDCA (Shewhart) cycle

Type: TQM tool

Applicability: High

More info reference: p 143/17

The PDCA cycle is not to be confused with Herman's Sole Practitioners Ezypark Cycle (SPEC), shown at right. SPEC is not actually a QM tool, but it is unparalleled for assessing and navigating traffic congestion.

Suggested to Dr. Deming by Walter Shewhart, and developed by Deming as a key part of his quality strategy, the PDCA cycle is a very important item in the TQM toolbox. It is the fundamental technique for ensuring that we learn from our past actions.

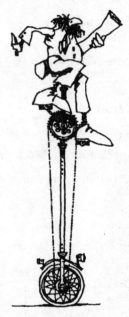

The details of the PDCA cycle and its application to design practice are discussed in more detail in Chapter 5.1.

Personal quality checklist

Type: TQM tool

Applicability: High

More info reference: p 143/18

This tool takes your QM program directly to each person in your practice, starting with yourself and your partners if any. If you think about the 'weak links / strong links' idea of improving your quality delivery, it follows that each person in the firm will 'own' some of the strong and some of the weak links - each will have a different set.

I think the 4 pages Mears gives to this topic are worth the price of his book. He notes that the hardest part of using this tool is identifying what belongs on it.

It further follows that each of us will need a different checklist - tailored to his or her own 'improvement' needs. If you are a person who can't keep a timesheet, please go on to the next item; you are wasting your time reading this. Keeping a personal quality checklist will be much more demanding than simply recording how you spend your day.

Below is Peter Mears' own checklist, from his book (Sorry, I haven't got one of my own to show you).

Personal Quality Checklist: Peter Mears							Week of:	
Defect category	Mon	Tue	Wed	Thu	Fri	Sat	Sun	Total
Excessive handling of paperwork								
Delayed return of forms								
Not prepared for meeting								
Office not clean at end of day								
Not answering phone within two rings								
Typos in correspondence								

Mission statement; quality goals

Type: TQM/ISO 9000 tool

Applicability: High

More info reference: p 143/19; also pp 91-94

Defining the purpose of your practice is a requirement of all versions of TQM and of ISO 9000, and is emphasized by every writer about these systems that I have read. In quality management theory, the core purpose of procedures is to help the firm achieve its mission, and therefore that mission must be defined if the procedures are to have any connective meaning. Mears differentiates between vision and mission statements thus: [82]

> "Vision *defines what we want to be.* Mission *defines the accomplishments needed that will result in realization of the vision.*"

Your mission and vision statements should be shorter rather than longer; reduced to be as concise as possible. This makes them easier to remember. Many companies put their mission statement on the backs of the calling cards of all staff; thus both reinforcing the message throughout the organization, and using it as part of the marketing message of the firm.

Deployment chart

Type: TQM tool

A deployment chart is simply a graphical way of assigning responsibility for key actions to get something accomplished. Example:

Deployment chart
(cont.)

Occasionally used by design professionals

More info reference: p 143/20

■ = Primary responsibility

■ = Helper/assist

TASKS	Hermione	Frank	Fred
Write goals and objectives	■		■
Standardize office forms		■	
Work out electronic file coding			■
Work out paper file coding	■		
Organize library		■	■
Organize samples room	■	■	

Multivoting

Type: TQM tool
Applicability: Moderate
More info reference: p 143/27

Multivoting is a technique for focusing - sifting out the 'vital few'. Brainstorming, with which we are all familiar, generates a lot of ideas. Multivoting reduces them down to a short list which most agree are the most important. How it works:

1   Check list for duplications; combine and eliminate.

2   Number items to facilitate voting.

3   Each person votes for the most important items. All vote for same number of items, which should be about 1/3 of total on list.

4   Tabulate votes. Eliminate all with one or no votes.

5   Repeat steps 3 and 4. The result is your list.

Force field analysis

Type: TQM tool
Applicability: Moderate
More info reference: p 144/28

Force field analysis is a method for identifying forces that shape a situation, to better understand things that needed to change, and what is required to make the change. The theory is that if the 'restraining' forces are stronger, change won't happen; if the 'driving' forces are stronger, change will occur. Change can be effected by reducing restraining forces or strengthening driving forces. Here's an example:

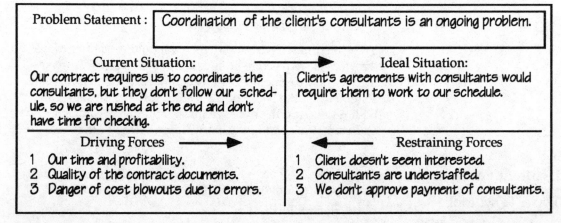

Problem Statement :	Coordination of the client's consultants is an ongoing problem.

Current Situation: ⟶ Ideal Situation:

Our contract requires us to coordinate the consultants, but they don't follow our schedule, so we are rushed at the end and don't have time for checking.

Client's agreements with consultants would require them to work to our schedule.

Driving Forces ⟶

1   Our time and profitability.
2   Quality of the contract documents.
3   Danger of cost blowouts due to errors.

⟵ Restraining Forces

1   Client doesn't seem interested.
2   Consultants are understaffed.
3   We don't approve payment of consultants.

Classifying quality problems

Type: TQM tool
Applicability: Moderate
More info reference: p 144/29

Motivational guru Dr. Stephen Covey advocates the use of this method to help you better manage your time. See Chapter 5.5.

As soon as a business starts to focus on quality issues, so many 'problems' are identified that the whole idea seems unmanageable. It is important to conserve the firm's resources; to work on only as many items as can be accommodated without compromising the ability to earn money. One way is to profile your delivery strengths (see pages 106-107). Another way is to 'classify' found problems: Are they 'big' or 'small', and are they internal or external to the practice? Example:

	Internal	External
Small Problem	Our filing system is a mess.	We have had a claim filed on a project but we aren't at fault.
Large Problem	The person responsible for site administration has resigned; no one else in the office has much site experience.	Price cutting by our competition is hurting our market share.

Improving perceived quality

Type: TQM/ISO 9000 tool
Applicability: High
More info reference: p 144/30

Here we come back to the idea of 'meeting and exceeding the client's expectations'. Mears defines three aspects of the client's view as follows [83]:

"Perceived quality *is the customer's opinion regarding what they received.*

"Actual quality *is what the customer feels they received.*

"Expected quality *is what the consumer expects upon use of the product or service.*"

Perceived quality is measured by the ratio of the actual quality to the expected quality: If 'more than 1', then the clients are satisfied; their expectations exceeded. Earlier I stated that you should *never promise more than you can deliver.* If you do, the perceived quality of your service will be 'less than 1', and the client will be unhappy, no matter how good the service was.

Sometimes practices promise too much to get work. Even if they then work very hard at pleasing the client, it may be impossible to meet the ultra-high expectation created. Improving perceived quality involves two parts: Promise less, and do more.

Focus groups

Type: TQM technique

Applicability: Moderate

More info reference: p 145/32

Mears has an excellent section on focus groups - refer to pages 149-154 in his book. In particular, his steps for developing the questions to be asked are recommended reading.

Focus groups are widely used in market research to determine how people feel about a new product or service, or a new idea. On a recent project, my colleagues used focus groups to find out what people of different ages and ethnic backgrounds felt should be the key issues in establishing a museum of immigration for Australia.

Some design practices have used this technique to learn more about how target groups evaluate the performance of the practice, and how the services of our industry are perceived by other groups. In the former case, one might invite a number of former clients in to discuss the service they got; in the latter case, one might organize a group of hospital administrators to discuss their views of what they expected from a health-care architect.

Focus groups require a trained facilitator, and must 'focus' on a specific question. Constructing a good focus group takes care and significant advance preparation. My advice is to utilize the services of a firm that has these skills, until you have developed the skills yourself through participation.

Benchmarking

Type: TQM/ISO 9000 technique

Applicability: High

More info reference: p 145/33

Benchmarking is the art of imitating others who are the best at something you do. Mears identifies five types of benchmarking: Internal, competitive, shadow, functional, and world-class. [84] The middle three of these have the most application to the design industries, because of the relative size of typical practices.

Competitive benchmarking involves studying your competitors carefully to see how they perform their services, and comparing yours to theirs on a point by point basis.

Shadow benchmarking means keeping a close watch on what industry leaders are doing, and watching how they change: offering new services, for example.

Functional benchmarking compares indices of your firm to industry standard; for example the salaries and perquisites you give your employees, or your overhead multiple compared to other design practices.

There are two stages to benchmarking : needs assessment and the benchmarking process itself. Needs assessment focuses the effort, by identifying clients' needs, and asking if your practice is meeting those needs, meeting them but not as well as the clients would like, and whether others are meeting them better than you.

Example: Let's say that you have learned (perhaps through a focus group) that clients would prefer that their engineers had better project management skills. How would your firm rate? The needs assessment process identifies the *critical success factors*; those of strategic importance to the practice.

These factors must be known to do the benchmarking; they will determine what it is you study about the industry or your competition. This process defines these factors, establishes your own performance against them, identifies those who perform the best in respect to these factors, collects data on their performance (which may not be easy), analyzes the data, and finally develops strategies for improving your performance against these higher standards.

Process ownership, team building

Type: TQM/ISO 9000 technique

Occasionally used by design professionals

More info reference: p 145/34; also see Chapter 5.4.

Most designers would understand the importance of having their employees feel a sense of ownership about the practice. Some practice leaders have succeeded in this admirably; many have not. What is the right technique?

In TQM, the process ownership technique is fairly involved, requiring that all employees identify the processes in their work, their 'suppliers' (those who precede them in the process flow) and their 'customers' (those who follow them in the process flow).

The needs of these 'customers' are then analyzed to see what their needs are, and these are compared to the parts of the process over which the employee has control. Finally, the employee is invited to work out how she can modify her 'part' of the process so the people downstream can have more of their needs fulfilled.

This formal process wouldn't be applicable to the great majority of design practices, because of the small size of most of them, and the fact that in the average design practice, there is very little specialization of work.

In ISO 9000, the need for process ownership is acknowledged, but there are no formal processes other than a requirement to have accurate role descriptions for all staff members.

There are a number of process ownership steps that are applicable to even very small practices, including the following:

◆   Ask staff to write up their own job descriptions; discuss the results with them until you both agree on their role.

◆ Reinforce the concept of the 'internal client' - every person who receives and uses the work of another. Be sure to set the example.

◆ Encourage staff to 'invest' in their own roles, by studying to see how they can make their own contributions to the practice more valuable, thus making themselves more valuable.

◆ Reward and immediately enact good suggestions.

Paul Laseau has studied the application of systems to design. He rcommends using bar charts and simple PERT charts as a tool for improving working relationships at the project level. [85]

Customer needs mapping

Type: TQM/ISO 9000 technique

Occasionally used by design professionals

More info reference: p 145/35

This technique continues the idea of the 'internal client'. It is a method for identifying external and internal clients' wants, and then checking to see how the practice satisfies those wants. Identifying the needs of external clients can come from sources such as focus groups or project briefing documents. Identifying the needs of internal 'clients' can come from sources such as process ownership development.

The 'map' is a simple chart like the one shown below. The second column rates the needs, with (1) being lowest and (5) being highest. The effectiveness of the practice in meeting these needs is shown by the H-M-L letters in the boxes, where H = high, M = medium and L = low. These ratings are not made up by the practice's leaders, but are the result of surveys of clients, external and internal.

CLIENT WANTS		Internal Processes	Importance Rating	Client Meetings	Returning Calls	Program	Schematic Design	Design Document	Contract Documents	Site Administration
	SERVICE	Availability	2	L	M	-	M	M	M	L
		Responsive	5	M	M	H	H	H	M	L
		Knowledgable	4	M	-	-	M	M	M	L
	DESIGN	Creative	5	H	-	M	H	H	M	-
		Flexible	2	M	-	H	H	M	L	M
		Control Changes	3	L		L	M	M	L	L
		Keep Cost Down	4	L	-	L	M	M	L	L

External Client Needs Map

Gap analysis

Type: TQM technique
Applicability: High
More info reference: p 145/38

Gap analysis is a technique for understanding the differences in perceptions about the services offered by the firm. These differences may be internal or external. Mears identifies five such gaps: [86]

1   Client Expectation / Management Perception Gap.
2   Management Perception / Service Quality Specifications Gap.
3   Service Quality Specifications / Service Delivery Gap.
4   Service Delivery / External Communications Gap.
5   Expected Service / Perceived Service Gap.

As you can see, there is a sequential nature to these 'gaps' in the service delivery process, and it could be that each gap is partly responsible for creating the next gap. This structure is particularly applicable to design practice. As earlier discussed, there frequently is a difference between what the client thinks is important (cost, time) and what the designer thinks is important (design). That's Gap 1.

Gap 2 usually occurs because there *is no service quality specification* - it has never been 'specified'. Who knows what it is? If staff are not 100% confident of management's service delivery perceptions, they are not likely to meet them: Gap 3. Gap 4 means that what we tell the client she will get is different from what the client gets (or thinks she got). This creates Gap 5, where the client's expectations exceed her perception of the value of what we deliver.

The gaps are usually measured with Likert scales constructed to test the extent of the gaps.

Quality cost system

Type: TQM/ISO 9000 quality improvement system
Applicability: High/moderate
More info reference: p 146/40

A quality cost system identifies, measures and controls quality costs. Crosby defines the *cost of quality* as *"the expense of doing things wrong"*. [87] This cost, for designers, is not only the payment of errors and omissions insurance and the deductibles when there is a claim, it is the wasted person-hours of drawing that get thrown away because of poor design planning, it is the necessity of putting the best people out on the job site to find the mistakes before the contractor does, it is the loss of reputation, and much more.

There is a concern among professional design institutes that the cost of quality includes a lack of public confidence in the design professions generally. (Pogo was right.)

The cost of quality is discussed in Chapter 6.2.

The learning organization

Type: TQM/ISO 9000 quality improvement system

Applicability: High

More info reference: p 146/41

Peter Mears says that *"TQM systems often fail because organizations have failed to deal with a current truth: continuous improvement requires continuous learning"*. [88]

He describes the learning organization as one which has moved from *adaptive* learning to *generative* learning: [89]

> *"Adaptive learning concerns itself with reacting to the changing business environment and coping with current situations. Generative learning expands an organization's capabilities and creates new opportunities. Generative learning requires new ways of looking at the world. Generative learning sees the systems that control events and focuses on the systems rather than on the results or the event itself."*

Peter Senge has researched and written about the learning organization. [90] Mears quotes Senge with respect to the five disciplines of a learning organization: Personal mastery, mental models, shared vision, team learning and system thinking. [91] I wish I had space here to include Mears' summary of Senge's work, but I don't - I urge you to read further on this. Senge's *The Fifth Discipline: The Art & Practice of The Learning Organization* is good stuff for design professionals.

Thinking about the quotation above reminds me of a talk by Wayne Schmidt FAIA, at the AIA's *Service Delivery in Architecture* workshop in Seattle in March, 1995; where Schmidt quotes Wayne Gretzky as answering a question about his success with *"Others go toward the puck, I go to where the puck is going to be."* That's a learning organization!

Customer/supplier agreements

Type: TQM/ISO 9000 quality improvement system

Occasionally used by design professionals

More info reference: p 146/42

We are quite used to the idea of a contract between the client and ourselves; most of us have got past relying on a handshake as a legal document. But what about that other client, the *internal* kind? At the simplest level, a jointly agreed job description is a client/supplier agreement (especially if we remember that both of us are both supplier and client). In TQM companies, there is an increasing focus on written agreements between departments; as a way of clarifying needs and defining expectations.

ISO 9000 requires customer/supplier agreements; that is the whole purpose of system elements 4.3 and 4.6.

Quality teams

Type: TQM quality
improvement system

Applicability: Moderate

More info reference: p 146/45

*One of my clients, a star
design firm of about 35, has a
quality team of six people
representing all "corners" of
the practice, which meets
every two weeks. They are
seeking certification under
ISO 9000 to mark the 20th
anniversary of the founding
of the practice, and they've
given themselves 16 months
to get there.*

A quality team is two or more people who meet regularly to
discuss and resolve quality issues. A sole practitioner could
conceivably be a quality team by talking to herself, but my
advice would be to find another sole practitioner and talk to
each other. Given the size of many of our practices, it makes
sense to think of the quality team as spanning several firms.

That is what happens in the quality workshops I run: Six to
ten practices form a working group, and each practice sends
one or two key people; this 'quality group' becomes an informal forum for shared learning about quality systems. All but
the smallest of these practices, however, will have an
internal quality team.

As we have already seen, there are diverse, very real
pressures that mitigate against the development of quality
systems and cultural change in the practice. As a practical
matter, no firm will achieve its quality goals unless it
formalizes the effort and the responsibility in a quality
team. It is essential. For this team to be effective, however,
there are some absolute ground rules:

◆ All functions of the practice must be represented,
  including secretarial/bookkeeping.

◆ Meetings must be to a regular schedule, with a program
  of actions to be accomplished and dates for results.

◆ The time spent (including appropriate preparation
  time) must be budgeted and chargeable to an overheads
  account.

◆ Management must give its absolute commitment to the
  process, as well as its enthusiastic support.

If the practice is large or multi-office, there will need to be
a central coordinating quality committee, as well as working
task groups with particular problems to research and make
recommendations on (see next system).

Quality council

Type: TQM quality
improvement system

Applicability: Moderate

More info reference: p 146/46

The central coordinating quality committee noted above is
called the Quality Council in TQM-speak. It must include
senior management. Mears comments [92]:

*"It is not unusual to find organizations that have a
quality council, but what is unusual is to find a
council that is successful in implementing and
directing their TQM program."*

Mears says that the chief reason for this lack of success is that councils are often composed of executives who are used to operating autonomously. Obviously management's real commitment to the quality program is required for the system to be a success!

Management commitment

Type: TQM/ISO 9000 strategy

Applicability: High

More info reference: p 147/49

In an ISO 9000 system, the chief quality function of management is called management review, and is the subject of clause 4.1.3. This clause requires that management with 'executive responsibility' review the quality system at 'defined' intervals sufficient to ensure its continual suitability and effectiveness in satisfying the standard and the company's quality policy and objectives.

'Defined' is key here: the firm must schedule these reviews and do them as scheduled.

Management commitment is step 1 in Philip Crosby's 14-step approach to quality.

Identify customers

Type: TQM strategy

Applicability: Moderate

More info reference: p 147/50

You might think this 'TQM strategy' is a bit silly, until you realize that it means 'identify all customers', including the internal ones. As we have already seen, TQM theory puts great emphasis on this change in thinking, and this 'strategy' is more of the same.

Juran devotes some 23 pages to the subject. Stasiowski and Burstein state that when a design firm grows, there is increasing rivalry between administrative managers and technical staff, and this *"leads to an adversarial relationship that increases overhead costs, hurts morale, and encourages destructive office politics"*.[93]

The key to this strategy is to understand how all 'customers' - internal and external - will be affected by achievement of quality goals. This understanding is essential if boycotting of the system is to be avoided.

Develop process features

Type: TQM/ISO 9000 strategy

Applicability: High

More info reference: p 147/51

The essence of this strategy is to modify how you do things such that the results are more likely to enhance progress toward the quality goals. As pointed out in Chapters 3.1 and 3.2, it is first necessary to document the processes you now have, and then look at how much modification they will need to meet your quality goals and, if you go the ISO 9000 route, to comply with the standard.

Quality management maturity grid

Type: TQM tool

Applicability: High

This TQM tool is the invention of Philip Crosby, who says there are five stages to quality maturity. The purpose of the grid, shown below [94] is to figure out where you are now, and to see what changes you need to make to get to the next stage of maturity.

More info reference: p 147/53

QUALITY MANAGEMENT MATURITY GRID					
Measurement Categories	Stage 1: Uncertainty	Stage II: Awakening	Stage III: Enlightenment	Stage IV: Wisdom	Stage V: Certainty
Management understanding and attitude	No comprehension of quality as a management tool. Tend to blame quality department for "quality problems."	Recognizing that quality management may be of value but not willing to provide money or time to make it all happen.	While going through quality improvement program learn more about quality management; becom-ing supportive and helpful.	Participating. Understand absolutes of quality management. Recognize their personal role in continuing emphasis.	Consider quality management an essential part of company system.
Quality organization status	Quality is hidden in manufacturing or engineering departments. Inspection probably not part of organization. Emphasis on appraisal and sorting.	A stronger quality leader is appointed but main em-phasis is still on appraisal and moving the product. Still part of manu-facturing or other.	Quality department reports to top management, all appraisal is incorporated and manager has role in management of company.	Quality mana-ger is an officer of company; effective status reporting and preventive action. Invol-ved with con-sumer affairs and special assignments.	Quality manager on board of directors. Prevention is main concern. Quality is a thought leader.
Problem handling	Problems are fought as they occur; no reso-lution; inade-quate definition; lots of yelling and accusations.	Teams are set up to attach major problems. Long-range solutions are not solicited.	Corrective action communication established. Problems are faced openly and resolved in an orderly way.	Problems are identified early in their devel-opment. All functions are open to sugges-tion and improvement.	Except in the most unusual cases, problems are prevented.
Cost of quality as % of sales	Reported: unknown Actual: 20%	Reported: 3% Actual: 18%	Reported: 8% Actual: 12%	Reported: 6.5% Actual: 8%	Reported: 2.5% Actual: 2.5%
Quality improvement actions	No organized activities. No understanding of such activities.	Trying obvious "motivational" short-range efforts.	Implementation of the 14-step program with thorough under-standing and establishment of each step.	Continuing the 14-step program and starting Make Certain.	Quality improvement is a normal and continued activity.
Summation of company quality posture	"We don't know why we have problems with quality."	"Is it absolutely necessary to always have problems with quality?"	"Through man-agement commit-ment and quality improvement we are identifying and resolving our problems."	"Defect prevention is a routine part of our operation."	"We know why we do not have problems with quality."

Corrective action

Type: TQM/ISO 9000
strategy

Applicability: High

More info reference: p 147/56

Corrective action is a requirement of both TQM systems and ISO 9000. It is step 6 in Crosby's 14 step quality system, and is the subject of system element 4.14 of ISO 9001. The Standard has four requirements for corrective action:

◆ Effective handling of client complaints and reports of service nonconformities.

◆ Investigation of causes of nonconforming service, and recording results of investigation.

◆ Determine corrective action to eliminate causes of nonconformities.

◆ Apply controls to ensure that corrective action is taken and is effective.

Crosby says that corrective action is most successful when the biggest problems are attacked first, next biggest next, and so on. [95] Stasiowski and Burstein have developed a design office version of Dr. Juran's 11-step process for corrective action: [96]

1   Assign priority to projects

2   Pareto analysis of symptoms

3   Theorize on causes of symptoms

4   Test theories; collect and analyze data

5   Narrow list of theories

6   Design experiments

7   Approve design; provide authority

8   Conduct experiment; establish proof of cause

9   Propose remedies

10 Test remedies

11 Action to institute remedy; control at new level

Error-cause removal

Type: TQM/ISO 9000
strategy

Applicability: High

More info reference: p 147/60

This strategy is also common to TQM and ISO 9000 systems. In ISO 9001, it is called 'preventative action' and is the other topic covered by system element 4.14, which requires the following:

◆ Using 'appropriate sources of information' to 'detect, analyze, and eliminate potential causes of nonconformities'. Here the key word is 'potential'. Preventative action means fixing a problem before it happens.

◆ Determining steps needed to deal with problems requiring preventative action.

◆ Initiating preventative action; applying controls to ensure effectiveness.

◆ Management review.

Crosby's step 11 is error-cause removal, which he says gives employees a method of communicating to management the situations that make it difficult for them to meet quality objectives.[97]

Motivation and recognition

Type: TQM/ISO 9000 strategy

Applicability: High

More info reference: p 147/61

The force-field analysis tool states that driving forces must be greater than restraining forces if change is to occur. Recognition of the contribution of employees motivates them to further contribution, which ensures that the driving forces outweigh the restraining forces in your team.

To be effective, rewards must be specific to the contribution and the person. The yearly bonus may be thought of as recognition by management, but is thought of as part of the pay packet by staff. Recognition also increases your chances of retaining corporate memory - see Chapter 5.2 for my recommendation.

Strategic quality planning

Type: TQM/ISO 9000 technique

Applicability: Moderate

More info reference: p 148/63

Strategic quality planning is a key component of Dr. Juran's TQM system and the subject of Chapter 9 in the referenced book. In this system, strategic quality planning consists of a structured process for defining the mission and strategic goals for the firm, and then determining the means required to reach those goals. This includes establishing the Quality Council, development of goals, and deployment of goals, and deployment of the goals throughout the firm, as well as developing strategies to overcome resistance.

This process would be a separate activity in a large practice, but in the average design practice, these functions would be integral with the general management commitment.

Multifunctional quality planning

Type: TQM strategy

Applicability: Moderate

More info reference: p 148/64

This is the second tier in Dr. Juran's quality planning philosophy, described in detail in Chapter 10 in the referenced work. Large, multi-office practices will find his analysis and recommendations of interest and applicable; average practitioners are not likely to.

Database, Santayana review

Type: TQM tool

Applicability: Moderate

More info reference: p 148/66

In Dr. Juran's TQM approach, this process is structured; a job for the 'historians'. It includes five steps: [98]

◆ Identification of the critical variables

◆ Establishment of cause-effect relationships

◆ The data bank (facilitates information retrieval and decision making)

◆ The checklist (what to do, what not to do)

◆ The countdown (ordered list of things to be done)

My version of the 'data bank' is called 'corporate memory'. See Chapter 5.2.

Project quality plan (PQP)

Type: ISO 9000 tool

Applicability: High

More info reference: p 148/67, pp 184-190 and pp 306-307

The PQP is emerging as one of the most important tools in an ISO 9000 quality system, particularly for the design professions. One of the reasons for this is that procedures are not public documents and not available to the client, whereas the PQP is available for the client's review. More importantly, however, the fact that every project is different means that every PQP is also different; indeed unique.

ISO 9000 requires the preparation of project quality plans 'as appropriate', but the test of that is left to the practice to decide.

A PQP is essentially a subset of the firm's quality system. It can be as short as a few pages or; for large, complex projects, a substantial document. The PQP normally has the following elements:

◆ The firm's quality goals and objectives.

◆ A description of the project.

◆ Quality requirements, if any, of the project.

◆ Project team and assignment of key positions of responsibility.

◆ A listing of applicable procedures, which is usually by reference rather than including them.

◆ Any other information required by the client.

This PQP then becomes a 'road map' for carrying out the project. See Chapter 4.4 for an emerging view of the importance of the PQP, and Chapter 6.6 for a brief discussion of how clients are using the PQP to reduce their risk of time and cost growth due to design.

Induction

Type: TQM/ISO 9000 tool

Occasionally used by design professionals

More info reference: p 148/70

Induction is a formalized orientation process for new employees. In most design firms that have an induction process, it takes place either on a twice-annual basis, or when a certain number of new employees have been put on.

The induction is an intensive training process, where top management is on hand and not interrupted by telephone calls or meetings. The training involves all aspects of the practice, from vision and mission, to housekeeping rules and details.

Performance evaluations

Type: TQM/ISO 9000 tool

Occasionally used by design professionals

More info reference: p 148/71

There are substantial differences of opinion about the value of performance evaluations. A prominent Boston firm has long used twice-yearly performance reviews as a way to understand how the staff see management, and to share expectations of each other. This firm spends about 12 days per year of partner level time on performance reviews (3 partners x 2 days twice a year), and an equal amount of other senior staff time, so the overhead is a significant item.

If performance reviews are done in the spirit this firm uses, they can be a very worthwhile motivator as well as a tool for uncovering problems before they happen - a true TQM tool. If, on the other hand, reviews are simply forums for management to judge staff in, the results are more likely to be negative than positive.

Mears advocates using performance reviews as a place to establish specific quality goals with staff.[99] Stasiowski and Burstein recommend that staff evaluate management as well as management evaluating staff.[100]

Peer reviews

Type: TQM tool

Applicability: High

More info reference: p 148/73

Although identified as a TQM tool, peer review is also a good augmentation of the management review process required under ISO 9000. In QM-speak, the peer review *validates* management's own review. Refer to pages 62-64 for a brief outline of the peer review process.

Vendor review

Type: TQM/ISO 9000 tool

Occasionally used by design professionals

More info reference: p 149/80

In ISO 9000, vendors are called suppliers, and review of suppliers' quality systems is required under system element 4.6: *Purchasing* to ensure that purchased products/services conform to requirements. This includes (Clause 4.6.2) the evaluation of subconsultants. This vendor review is of the vendor by the purchaser.

In TQM, the term has a different meaning; where the vendor reviews your documents, to identify equipment incompatibility, obsolete specifications and models, and inappropriate use of materials. In certain areas of design, such as hardware selection, such review is essential because of the complexity of products available and the rate with which they change.

Constructability review

Type: TQM/ISO 9000 tool

Occasionally used by design professionals

More info reference: p 149/81

In my early years, I worked for a stretch with the Detroit firm of Smith, Hinchman & Grylls. The chief draftsman there had the ability to age a building a hundred years in ten minutes, as you watched your lovely details rot, leak and decompose to nothing. Unrolling your drawings in front of him was a pretty sobering experience, one I will never forget.

That review might better be termed a 'destructibility review'; but that would be the reverse of a constructability review. A constructability review is more than just checking the durability aspects; it is also checking the ease of construction. This can - and should - be both from the macro level to the micro level.

For example, what size cranes, and how many, are needed to reach all parts of the project? Where can they be located, and how can they be removed? These are design issues, or ought to be.

At the micro level, it seems that architects have a penchant for designing joinery details that literally cannot be fabricated as drawn. Having spent big chunks of my life writing specifications, I've seen the drawings from many practices, and one recurring nasty detail is the reveal around door frames, deeper than it is wide, impossible to paint and keep free from joint compound. I've seen it on jobs where the screws from the hinges stuck through into the reveal. Our forefathers invented casings for very good reasons!

Operability reviews

Type: TQM tool
Applicability: High
More info reference: p 149/82

No part of our industry is evolving as rapidly as mechanical and electrical systems, which have reached levels of sophistication beyond most architects and some engineers.

This evolution includes the rapid change toward integrated systems and performance specifications, the latter of which move the designer one step further away from control of project quality. Add to this the increasing requirements for functional recycling of structures within their first-cost lifetime, and you have all the makings for systemic operability problems in the future.

Operability reviews must look at the ability of a structure to respond to changing use as well as to keeping its first inhabitants comfortable and at the lowest possible cost.

Tree diagram

Type: TQM Hoshin tool

Occasionally used by design professionals

More info reference: p 150/86

Tree diagrams are simple graphic tools used to map out detailed groups of tasks to be accomplished. The general structure is shown below, together with a sample tree diagram as it might be used in a design office.

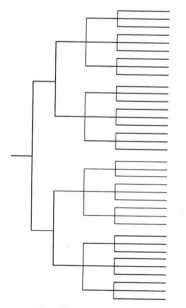

Tree Diagram format

		Interviews
Function	Select & Appoint Consultants	Interviews
		Request fee proposals
		Prepare & execute agreements
	Start-up	Briefing
		Agree to program schedule
		Agree to formats & media
	Quality Monitoring	Arch. / Consult. coord. check
		Verify consult. cross-checks
	Completion	REDICHECK
		Spec./drawing coord. check
Time & Cost	Design	Check progress to schedule
		Resolve any delays
	Construction	Check estimates to cost plan
		Check long lead equipment
		Resolve any discrepancies

Consultant Coordination Plan

Matrix diagram

Type: TQM Hoshin tool

Occasionally used by design professionals

More info reference: p 150/87

The matrix diagram is used to show graphically relationships between activities; it is particularly useful where the impact of demands needs to be identified on system capabilities and priorities developed. In the example below, I have extended the tree diagram from the previous page, to add responsibilities to the actions.

Consultant Coordination Responsibility Matrix

■ = Primary responsibility
O = Support responsibility

			Partner	Project director	Project architect	Spec. writer	Site administ'r
Function	Select & Appoint Consultants	Interviews	O	■			
		Request fee proposals		■			
		Prepare & execute agreements	■		O		
	Start-up	Briefing		■	O		
		Agree to program schedule			■		
		Agree to formats & media			■		
	Quality Monitoring	Arch. / Consult. coord. check			■		
		Verify consult. cross-checks			■		
	Completion	REDICHECK			■	O	O
		Spec./drawing coord. check				■	
Time & Cost	Design	Check progress to schedule			■		
		Resolve any delays		O	■		
	Construction	Check estimates to cost plan			O		■
		Check long lead equipment			O		■
		Resolve any discrepancies		O			■

Matrix data analysis

Type: TQM Hoshin tool
Applicability: Moderate
More info reference: p 150/88

This is another simple graphic device to show the intensity or strength of relationships, thus adding a dimension to the information in a matrix diagram. These 'intensity' ratings are provided by some other TQM tool, such as a Likert scale or multivoting. Example:

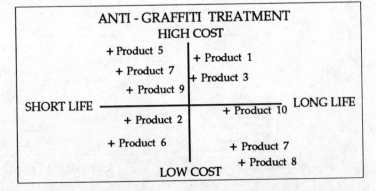

ANTI - GRAFFITI TREATMENT
HIGH COST

+ Product 5   + Product 1
+ Product 7   + Product 3
+ Product 9

SHORT LIFE ———————————— LONG LIFE
+ Product 2   + Product 10
+ Product 6   + Product 7
                 + Product 8
LOW COST

Process decision program chart (PDPC)

Type: TQM Hoshin tool
Applicability: Moderate
More info reference: p 150/89

This TQM tool graphically shows relationships in a tree-type structure, but its purpose is to predict where problems can occur, and to suggest solutions. Thus, it is a 'preventative action' tool. Code for the 'boxes', and example below:

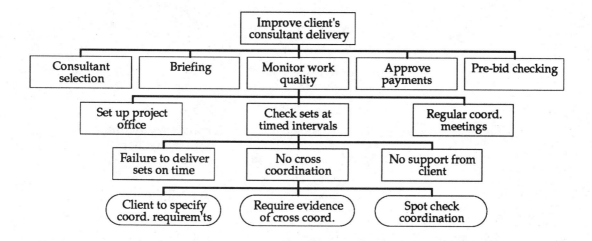

Chapter 4.2 Summary Checklist

We can draw a number of conclusions from this very quick overview of nearly four dozen TQM tools which have some application to design practice.

✓ TQM is a lot about theory and a lot about tools. These tools make the theory real. The theory will be slightly different in our industry; and so will the tools.

✓ About half of the TQM tools have some equivalent in ISO 9000.

✓ Most of the tools were developed in response to specific needs in large manufacturing companies. The needs are not the same in small design firms.

✓ Some of these tools have high applicability. The rest would only be useful in large, multi-office practices.

4.3 The Project Brief

A brief is everything an architect needs to know about the building a client needs. The client's yearnings, ideas and vision should be clearly expressed in it, together with every activity and important piece of equipment or treasured possession to be accommodated. - Frank Salisbury

Purpose

To highlight the crucial, central importance of getting the brief established, getting it right, and living by it.

Terminology

In this chapter I will use the Commonwealth countries' terms - just a slight cultural shift for U.S. readers!

U.S. terminology:		Commonwealth countries' terminology
Program	=	Project Brief
Schedule	=	Program/Programme

Starting off on the right foot

If TQM or any other QM program is to 'get it right the first time', agreement on what the job is about is undeniably a crucial issue.

However, with all but the most experienced clients, the process of brief creation goes on well into schematic design and design development, and is usually more the responsibility of the architect than the client. This situation is well known and accepted. What is not so well known or accepted is that this process creates some of the particular problems which cause risk for the architect. If the architect, in helping the client develop the brief, gets the brief wrong, the design will also be wrong.

Failure to get the client to formally accept (sign off on) the brief is endemic among architects, a failure which ultimately imperils them.

For architects, one of the most powerful benefits of an ISO 9000 QM system is the *requirement* to ensure that the brief is agreed to by the parties. This forces a necessity to clarify contractual terms both between architect and client and between architect and subconsultants.

It forces the client to come to terms with suggestions put forward by the architect, rather than to tacitly permit them but criticize them later.

The necessity for resolution of the brief also can act to force the architect's attention on the details of the project, and chase away woolly thinking and (perhaps) inappropriate dreams of making the project an award-winner.

The brief as 'driver' of the design review process

The thoughts of the client tend to come in over the course of the project, sometimes by telephone and sometimes in scribbled notes or more formal correspondence. These 'instructions' from the client all form part of the brief.

The project brief is an important document against which the design must be tested in design review. The reviewer must refer to the project brief in order to review the design.

Practically speaking, the only way the design review can function so as to meet the intent of ISO 9000 is to have access to a concise and complete project brief. Hence all communications from the client regarding the design must be collected together and readily accessible.

What happens more often is that this information is scattered throughout the project files; virtually unretrievable as a unified document. Therefore we need a regularized way of channeling this data into such a unified document.

One of my clients, a high-profile practice in Western Australia, has developed a way of doing this that is a quality auditor's dream. For selected projects (most large ones), on all design documents up through the completion of design development, they put the entire project brief right on the design drawings, in a space reserved on the right-hand fourth or third of the drawings. This technique is illustrated in Chapter 5.6.

Another simple way to accomplish this is to have the project brief (program in the U.S.) as a heading in your project filing system. Then all documents forming part of the client's instructions, or copies of them, are filed there, and that file comprises the complete project brief.

Another good way to help properly develop the brief is to begin the data collection in a formalized way. An example is the *Project Data Record*, shown overleaf.

ABC ARCHITECTS PTY LTD		Project Data Record

| Form approved by _____ Date: | Refer Actions K1b and M4a in filling out this document. | Date opened: _____ Project No. _____ Project name (office) _____ Dates revised: _____ _____ |

PROJECT DATA

Complete project title: _____
_____
_____

Location / address: _____
_____
_____

CLIENT DATA

Client Information:
Name: _____
Address: _____
_____
_____
Contact: _____
Tele: _____ FAX: _____

Owner Information (if different from client):
Name: _____
Address: _____
_____
_____
Contact: _____
Tele: _____ FAX: _____

PROJECT RESPONSIBILITY

Director in charge: _____
Project director: _____
Project architect: _____
Independent reviewer: _____
Contract admin. _____
Specifications: _____
_____
_____

SUBCONSULTANTS

Structural engineer: _____
Mechanical engineer: _____
Electrical engineer: _____
Hydraulics: _____
Civil engineer: _____
Landscape architect: _____

PROJECT SET UP

BRIEF: Is project brief: ☐ Client's responsibility ☐ Architect's responsibility ☐ Joint responsibility

QA: Does client have QA requirements for the project? ☐ YES ☐ NO

If YES, describe requirements: _____
_____
_____
_____

The following items are required for this project (Tick as appropriate):

☐ Project Quality Plan ☐ Formal design reviews ☐ External audit by client ☐ Staged development

☐ Work program ☐ Internal project audit ☐ External independent audit ☐ Trade packages / fast tracking

Describe timing for reviews and/or audits _____
_____
_____

CONTROLLED DOCUMENT DISTRIBUTION

For each type of record, indicate number of controlled documents to be distributed to each party, in the boxes below the letter designating each role.

	A	B	C	D	E	F	G	H	I	J	K	L
Project quality plan												
Project brief												
Approved design drawings												
Contract drawings & revisions												
Contract specification & revisions												

A Directors
B Quality manager
C Project director
D Project architect

E Contract administrator
F Client
G Builder
H Project manager

I _____
J _____
K _____
L _____

Many firms have developed and use forms such as the one at left - they all have the benefit of beginning to organize information about the project.

This particular one picks up some other requirements of ISO 9000, such as the assignment of project responsibilities, defining whether preparation of the project brief is the client's or the consultant's responsibility or both, defining quality management parameters for the project, and setting up the distribution schedule for controlled project documents.

Chapter 4.3
Summary Checklist

✓ An ISO 9000 QM system includes the requirement to ensure that the brief is agreed to by the parties. This benefits the architect and the project, and protects the client.

✓ Design review requirements necessitate a complete and readily accessible project brief.

4.4   The Evolving Importance of the PQP

The introduction of quality assurance into the Building and Construction industry has been frustrated by a variety of circumstances, not the least of which has been a failure to adequately adapt the requirements of the ISO 9000 series of Standards to suit the realities of the building project environment. - Adrian Renouf

Purpose

To gaze into the crystal ball of the future of quality management for our industry, and come away with some useful direction-markers.

The swell that signals a sea-change

I've noted several times in this book that QM, especially the ISO 9000 variety, is very much in its infancy, and is going through a maturational and evolutionary development. ISO 9000 is the child of the world-wide TQM movement. There is no doubt in my mind that the offspring of such a powerful lineage will persevere and change the course of our destiny. There is also no doubt that this toddler will become more useful as it grows up and learns some new skills.

I imagine that Deming, Juran and Crosby disciples might in turn think this view childish, but they haven't tried to make the theories work in the design and construction industries, so far as I have read. Adrian Renouf, who was responsible for developing the ISO 9000 system used by the Client Service Division of NSW Department of Public Works, is one who has. In early 1995 he wrote a 17-page paper, unpublished at this writing, which outlines his vision of the evolution of ISO 9000 in our industry. Excerpts are included in this chapter, with his permission.

I've been completely immersed in the evolution of ISO 9000 systems for design and construction for the last five years, and read many thousands of pages of learned words in preparing to write this book. Maybe I had to go through that to appreciate Renouf's arguments, but nothing I have read seems to me as important as his conclusions. I see them as that almost imperceptible swell that signals the sea-change that will irrevocably alter our direction.

Renouf's thesis

Adrian Renouf asserts that the answer to making quality management work in our industry is to begin with what he calls a 'bottom up' approach rather than a 'top down' approach.

By 'top down' he means the theory and structure of formal quality systems. By 'bottom up' he means developing project-specific quality plans (PQPs), which answer project-specific quality requirements.

To appreciate why this is such a revolutionary idea, you need to remember that we design professionals live in a much more project-specific world than do most people.

The 1987 version of ISO 9000 barely mentioned PQPs - they were no more than a footnote suggestion as one of seven possible ways of meeting the requirements of system element 4.2.3. The 1994 version goes a bit further; it raises the PQP out of the 'note' status and makes it one of eight 'activities' that must be considered in choosing how to meet the quality requirements.

Renouf states *"the project environment requires systems which can expand, contract and evolve to suit the needs of each project"*. He says that project-based QA systems must have the following features:

◆ *The scope of the system must reflect the differing functions which may be required to perform under different procurement methods.*

◆ *The system must be flexible enough to allow users to re-define who does what and how on each project or contract, depending on the type of service or asset the client wishes to procure or construct.*

◆ *The system must be flexible enough to interface with the systems of other contractors, consultants and clients whenever responsibilities are shared, or functions overlap.*

Renouf sees the need for quality systems as being similar to insurance coverage, and points out that this 'quality coverage' could be managed by a single, all-in QM system operated by a primary consultant/contractor e.g. under a design-build structure. Alternatively, this 'quality coverage' could be met by a number of consultant firms, each putting in their respective parts, but avoiding overlaps.

In his model, he suggests that if a project manager takes responsibility for, say, audits and design reviews, then it is not necessary for other consultants to perform these functions.

In other words, Renouf advocates a *team*-specific QM structure rather than a *practice*-specific structure. The contributions that individual members make would vary from project to project. What this implies is that success of the quality system would be measured across the whole team in order to have any meaning.

Two conclusions flow from this line of thinking:

◆ The applicable QM standards must be part of the project brief; established by the client.

◆ The principal member of the team carries the responsibility for interface and coordination of the quality contributions of all other participants.

You are probably thinking that this isn't much different from what happens now, and you will be right. The architect is usually responsible for the coordination of all consultants' documents, whether or not the other consultants are engaged by the architect or the client. This is the core of Renouf's point, which is that implementation of quality systems must be flexible enough to fit the way an industry functions best.

Coalface QM

Coalface is a good word, which Australians use to describe the taking of an active rather than administrative role in a project; something like 'getting one's hands dirty'. It seems an appropriate term to encapsulate Renouf's views.

What I've written above is hardly earth-shattering stuff. It's the conclusions that come from it that matter: It follows that the PQP - the project quality plan - is the most important document in the system, not the Quality Manual, not the Procedures. What's more, it is a different document on every project. This poses a powerful challenge for those in the audit and certification game: how can you certify such an elastic system?

More importantly for us, how do you develop such a system? Here is Renouf's response:

"The answer lies first in developing a minimum system which can then be modified as the firm's familiarity with implementing QA grows with each project. Such a minimum system should be based on project specific Quality Plans which document the unique requirements of each project or contract and how they are going to be achieved. Over time, as the company develops its own 'corporate' quality manual, procedures, checklists and forms, these can gradually be referenced to Quality Plans to provide greater guidance and controls for critical processes or tasks."

Unless you have worked for a while in the ISO 9000 system structure, it is impossible to appreciate how revolutionary an idea this is, even though it may seem to be eminently reasonable.

One way of looking at this approach is that it is somewhere between ISO 9000 and TQM philosophy. All mainstream TQM thinking has highly pragmatic roots: strategies developed in response to specific found problems in industry, which in maturity took on the patina and cult worship status of the system founders. ISO 9000 is no more than a common denominator of those systems, with the personal identities and unique aspects of the systems stripped away.

A client's view of the PQP

Renouf's view of quality management is that of the governmental client, as he sees the process from the point of view of Australia's largest purchaser of design consultant services. He notes that the PQP is of particular interest to the client, because it is an accessible document (whereas the firm's procedures usually are not). He identifies the following issues which *"need to be addressed before deciding on a particular format or structure, otherwise the PQP may undergo an unnecessary number of major revisions during its development".*

1   *The need for PQPs to reflect the requirements or expectations of specific clients which may vary from project to project.*

2   *How PQPs relate to other company systems such as project management systems, time/costing systems and management information systems.*

3   *The need to arrive at a format which is easy to prepare, modify and update if necessary.*

4   The need for 'user friendliness' so that PQPs do not unduly frustrate those who are expected to prepare, maintain, review, approve and audit them.

5   What information should reside in PQPs, and what information can be referenced from elsewhere in the QA system to minimise duplication.

6   How PQPs are distributed, updated and maintained.

With respect to user friendliness (item 4), Renouf notes:

"It is surprising how many firms place a higher priority on expediency than user friendliness when developing their QA documentation."

Observing that often clients and service providers have differing expectations, Renouf says it is important that inspection and test plans (ITP's), activity checklists or task plans included within PQP's include the following:

◆   The sequence of each task,

◆   Its description,

◆   Who is responsible for its completion, either by name or position title,

◆   What procedures, standards or references staff should follow in completing the task,

◆   What records need to be produced to verify that the task has been completed acceptably,

◆   When the task was completed, and

◆   Where the required records can be located for verification or audit purposes.

PQP contents

To complete this overview outline of Adrian Renouf's views on the role of the PQP, below are his suggestions for the contents of a typical PQP. Remember, this is the client speaking! He says the first 8 are suggested for projects of any size, and that 9 and 10 may be required for major projects or contracts, or where specifically required by the client.

1   A summary of the project particulars, including the name of the client, the scope of works, budget, delivery method and project role which the company has been commissioned to play.

2   *A project organisational chart which shows the key participants by position title and name, including the "management representative" and verification personnel for the project. For primary consultants and contractors, the chart should also show key subconsultants or subcontractors.*

3   *Position descriptions for all key project personnel shown on the organisational chart. Alternately, these descriptions could be directly referenced to the firm's quality manual or elsewhere in the QA system.*

4   *A program for the project which identifies each major phase or trade and key milestones including document submissions, project reviews, internal audits, client approvals, inspections and/or verification activities. This program could typically take the form of a Gantt chart, critical path diagram, or a simple table listing phases or milestones with their planned and actual completion dates.*

5   *Detailed inspection and test plans, activity checklists or task plans for each major phase or trade.*

6   *A list of all relevant QA system procedures, instructions and checklists to be used. including their document number, title and revision status.*

7   *A contact list of all key personnel, including clients, contractors, subcontractors and consultants.*

8   *A document control system to record the PQPs approval, distribution and amendment as the project progresses.*

9   *An internal audit and surveillance plan which covers the activities of the company, as well as those of any subconsultants or subcontractors.*

10 *Procedure outlines for each applicable requirement or system element from the specified QA standard. These outlines should summarise how the company's standard procedures will be varied to suit the specific requirements of the project or precis the standard procedures to be used.*

A cautionary summary

If you are like 99% of the design professionals I work with, by now you will be shaking your head in dismay, and wondering how you will ever get your fees up enough to cover the cost of providing this kind of service.

I can only say that if a client came to you and offered you a fee to design some templates so *they* could accomplish the above for *their* clients, you probably could rise to the occasion and develop cost-effective ways of adequately addressing the problem. In this case, you may need to do it for yourself.

Renouf and his agency are not unique. Increasingly, major corporate and governmental clients are requiring this kind of documentation.

One final quote from his paper, which should give you something to think about. I've heard this sentiment from more than one source. Whether you like it or not, I suspect it predicts the future. Will you be ready for this future?

"As the concept of PQP's continues to gain increasing acceptance, it is also likely that clients will begin to use PQP's as their primary performance monitoring tool. Some public sector clients have already pre-empted this possibility by requiring their consultants to submit updated copies of their PQP's with every major document submission as evidence that the necessary internal reviews and verification activities have been completed.

"In the near future, the submission of updated PQP's and associated quality records will also become a pre-condition for payment, thereby ensuring the QA systems are properly implemented and maintained for each major commission."

Chapter 4.4
Summary Checklist

> ✓ The PQP is emerging as the key document in QM systems for design and construction.
>
> ✓ A 'bottom up' approach to QM starts at the project level, with master documents evolving through use and experience.
>
> ✓ Expect that some of your major clients will in the future require you to prepare comprehensive PQPs as a condition of engagement, and will use them to monitor your performance.
>
> ✓ Be ready.

4.5   Audits and the Audit Process

It is relatively easy to identify what is wrong with an organisation. It is a completely different thing to put it right. - Roy Fox [101]

Purpose

To present an overview description of what certification to ISO 9000 requires with respect to the audit process.

What is a quality audit?

ISO 8402 [102] defines a quality audit as *"A systematic and independent examination to determine whether quality activities and related results comply with planned arrangements and whether these arrangements are implemented effectively and are suitable to achieve objectives."*

As defined then, an audit is an information gathering activity so that the need for improvement or corrective action may be evaluated. There is no element of a witch hunt or apportioning blame for problems. It is important to establish this fact among auditees because defensiveness is not conducive to information flow.

In Chapter 2.3 I discussed the *diagnostic audit* as a preliminary evaluative tool, noting that the diagnostic audit could be fairly informal. ISO 9000 audits, by contrast, are formal affairs.

Quality audits may be internal or external and do not necessarily have to cover the whole system at once but may cover elements of it. Independence is ensured by the auditors having no direct responsibility in the audited area but preferably working in cooperation with the relevant personnel.

Although audits, auditing and auditors are synonymous with assessments, assessing and assessors it may be considered that an audit is an examination of a single activity, element, department etc., whereas an assessment is a collection of such audits.

Audit types

There are two main types of audits, called system audits and compliance audits:

The system audit:

The *system audit* is also known as an adequacy or management audit and is an office exercise which determines the extent to which the documented system represented by the quality manual and the associated procedures, work instructions and forms, adequately meets the requirements of ISO 9000, and if it provides objective evidence that the system has been designed to do so.

A project audit may be considered a vertical audit, i.e. looking at all the systems that went into the production of a specific project or service.

The compliance audit:

The *compliance audit* seeks to establish the extent to which the documented system is implemented and observed by the workforce. Compliance audits may be either of company-wide activities or project audits.

Company-wide audits are usually restricted to specific system elements e.g. two to four closely related system elements. Regardless of which systems were being audited, it would be usual to also look at the quality records generated by that system.

The auditing party

Audits are also classified according to who performs them: They can be first party (self-audits), second party, or third party.

Internal audit (self-audit):

The self-audit process is a keystone of any ISO 9000-compliant quality system. This is the most important of all audits, which requires a company to look in on its own systems, procedures and activities in order to ascertain whether they are adequate and being complied with.

Internal audits provide management with information on whether or not its policies are being met, if the system is as efficient and as effective as it should be, and whether changes are needed.

Internal audits may be undertaken by trained members of an organization's own staff or by hired, professional auditors. There are advantages in both options; the main consideration is which approach provides the more cost-effective information.

It is usual for internal audits to be performed by the firm's Quality Manager, who may be any senior member of the practice, with delegated responsibility for maintenance of the quality system.

Typically, an audit either covers general administrative functions or specific projects.

A question often asked is whether a specialist's knowledge of the area or activity to be audited is required. In theory the answer is "no" because the auditor should be looking for objective evidence based on the requirements of the standard and provided by the documented system and conformity to it.

In practice some general knowledge is probably preferable to assist in the analysis of the acquired data and in the formation of a judgment. However, the auditor must be independent and not have *direct* responsibility in the area of any audit undertaken.

Second party audits:

There are two types of second party audits, called 'external' and 'extrinsic'.

- **External audit:** An audit that is performed by a company on its own suppliers, subcontractors or subconsultants. It may be an adequacy and/or a compliance audit.

- **Extrinsic audit:** The reciprocal of an external audit. It comprises an independent third party or a client coming in to look at your firm. The audit may be an adequacy and/or compliance audit. The extrinsic audit may be either second-party or third-party. If the client sends out his or her own auditor to audit your system, that is a second party audit.

The third-party audit:

The third-party audit is an independent certification of your quality system and your compliance to it by an organization accredited by the International Organization for Standardsization (ISO), or a national standards body accredited by it.

Third-party certification is accepted internationally as evidence of a complying quality system.

Certification is usually for a period of three years, after which it must be renewed through re-audit.

However, during this period, periodic reviews are required (usually half-yearly or quarterly), and a charge is made for this review.

The auditor

What does the internal audit involve?

The process of internal audits begins with the implementation of a TQM or ISO 9000 quality management system (it is a requirement of the latter). It has two main functions:

◆ To find out how well implementation of the quality system is progressing, and

◆ To find out if the firm is ready for an external certification audit (if an ISO 9000 system).

It usually works best to either audit a few elements of the quality system across the whole office or to audit all relevant quality systems for a single project. To audit all elements across the practice would be like a stock-taking in a department store; you would have to shut down the practice for a few days!

The use of standard forms simplifies and greatly speeds up the audit process, as well as ensuring consistency.

A sample audit form is shown opposite, in this case the Management Responsibility audit form from the *ABC Architects* model design quality system which my firm provides to Australian architectural practices. Note the use of a rating scale for assessment. Also, note that AS 3901 is the Australian equivalent of ISO 9001-1987.

Different client groups working to ISO 9000 have developed different (but similar) rating scales; the one used here is a combination of the rating scales developed by New South Wales Public Works (NSW PW) and Australian Capital Territory Capital Works (ACT CW) organizations.

It should be noted that the whole issue of assessment ratings is still being debated by standards associations and client groups.

ABC ARCHITECTS PTY LTD	Internal Audit Report

Form approved by	Refer to Procedure C in completing this document	Audit of: _____ Page ___ of ___
Date:		Auditor: _____ Audit date: _____

AS 3901 AUDIT OF: 4.1 MANAGEMENT RESPONSIBILITY

SUMMARY OF AUDIT FINDINGS:

_____

_____

_____

_____

_____

	Total	No. items	Average
A: System audit	☐	÷ [9] =	☐
B: Project audit	☐	÷ [1] =	☐
C: Consultant audit	☐	÷ [10] =	☐

Auditor's signature: _____ Date: _____

IMPLEMENTATION RATING SCALE:	0 Not documented 1 Partially documented 2 Significantly documented and partially implemented	3 Fully documented and significantly implemented 4 Fully documented and fully implemented	5 Documented, implemented and verified by internal audit 6 Documented, implemented and verified by external audit

No.	Audit item Code: [AS 3901 cl.] [System ref.]	Use	Assess-ment	Auditor's comments:	Refer instructions on cover sheet.
1	Does the firm have documented quality policies and objectives? [4.1.1] [QM 1]	A C	☐		_____
2	Has the managing director / managing partner signed the quality policy? [4.1.1] [QM 1.2]	A C	☐		_____
3	Is information about the quality system easily accessible by all members of the firm? Is there general awareness of the quality system? [4.1.1] [B2]	A C	☐		_____
4	Have all staff, current as of the audit, signed a statement that they understand the firm's policies and objectives? [4.1.1] [B2d]	A C	☐		_____
5	Have roles, responsibilities and authority for all personnel been defined, particularly with regard to cl. 4.1.2.1? [A Appendices]	A C	☐		_____
6	Have project verification (checking) requirements been defined, and an independent reviewer assigned? [4.1.2.2] [A2a, O5]	B C	☐		_____
7	Has a quality manager been appointed, with defined responsibility as required? [4.1.2.3] [A3, B2a]	A C	☐		_____
8	Has management adopted a program for the management review of the quality system, including documentation of the review process? [4.1.3] [A4]	A C	☐		_____
9	Have any management reviews been completed? If so, were they as scheduled? [4.1.2.4] [A4]	A C	☐		_____
10	If management reviews were carried out, were they in compliance with documented procedures? Were results communicated to staff? [4.1.2.4] [A4]	A C	☐		_____

■ ABC IAR 4.1	■ Ver. 2.5	■ Date: 22.6.94	■ Rev:	■ Appr.	■ Page 1/1

We can expect continuing evolution of the preferred method of assessment methods and scales.

Audit planning

System audits should focus on specific system elements, for example to look at the way design verification is working across a number of projects. Project audits should consider all system functions for a single project or phase of a project.

ISO 10011, the Standard governing audits, recommends the following items for inclusion in an audit plan:

◆ Audit objectives and scope.

◆ Identification of individuals having direct responsibilities regarding the objectives and scope.

◆ Identification of applicable reference documents.

◆ Identification of audit team members.

◆ Date and place of audit.

◆ Identification of aspects of the practice to be audited.

◆ Expected time and duration of audit.

◆ The schedule of meetings to be held with the auditee (in this case, others in the firm who have to participate in the audit).

◆ Confidentiality requirements.

◆ Audit report distribution and expected date of report.

As you can see, not all of these items are needed for an internal audit in a small firm. It is important, however, that your audit plan describe briefly those items from this list that are applicable.

You can expect that your audit plans will be examined as part of an external audit of your firm.

Discrepancies: major or minor?

A convention has grown up in the audit industry which assigns a 'major' or 'minor' status to nonconformities; the former obviously being more important than the latter. The idea generally is that major nonconformities prevent certification and minor ones are noted for follow-up but do not prevent certification. Several international certifying groups use this classification.

There is no requirement to use these designations; indeed they are not even mentioned in ISO 10011.

For purposes of internal audits (especially in small companies), the distinction is not considered essential, and has not been included as part of the audit system in this model.

Discrepancies vs. nonconformity

The audit process results in a list of discrepancies. Depending on the nature of the discrepancy, it may be cause for raising a notice of nonconformity.

A nonconformity (also called a nonconformance) is defined in ISO 8402 as *"the nonfulfillment of specified requirements"*. The 'specified' requirements can be internal (the firm's quality procedures) or external (the project brief, codes, standards and other regulations).

Some auditors do not use the term 'discrepancy', referring instead to all inconsistencies as nonconformances.

Audit follow-up

The audit process doesn't end with the audit report: Management must act on the findings of the audit, and this action will be considered in an external audit of this system element. Therefore management's follow-up actions must be documented (refer to Chapter 4.10).

The results of audits must be considered in management's review of the quality system, and should be an agenda item for those review meetings.

Chapter 4.5 Summary Checklist

✓ Audits are information gathering activities which identify need for improvement or corrective action.

✓ System audits compare your quality system to ISO 9000. Compliance audits compare your actual performance to your quality system.

✓ Internal (self) audits are the most important type - they are your own objective look at your own performance.

4.6   Design Reviews

*Design review is the most critical aspect of a
quality management system for a building design
practice.* - Tim Cornick

Purpose

To outline the difference between the traditional 'desktop
crit' and the formal design review, verification and
validation process required under ISO 9000.

**The 'desktop crit'
vs. ISO 9000 design
review**

All architects and other designers do design review: usually
informally, as a 'desktop crit', and usually without keeping
any records of the review. These reviews usually look only
at the design itself, at its internal cohesion.

Design review is a requirement of ISO 9000. ISO 8402 defines
the term as *"a formal, documented, comprehensive and
systematic examination of a design to evaluate the design
requirements and the capability of the design to meet these
requirements and to identify problems and propose
solutions"*. We see from this that there are four key parts to
design review:

◆   Evaluate requirements

◆   Evaluate capability of design to meet requirements

◆   Identify problems

◆   Propose solutions

The 1994 revision of ISO 9000 extended and clarified the
design review process significantly. This revision breaks the
process into three steps, called design review, design verification, and design validation.

The design review process must include each of these factors,
which I will consider separately.

Design review

Design review is covered by clause 4.4.6 of ISO 9001. The
requirements are:

◆   The reviews are planned (scheduled).

◆   Participants shall include representatives from all
functions concerned with that stage of the design, and
any other specialists needed.

◆   Records are maintained.

ISO 8402 notes under the definition of 'design review':

"The capacity of the design encompasses such things as fitness for purpose, feasibility, manufacturability, measurability, performance, reliability, maintainability, safety, environmental aspects, time scale and life cycle cost."

To the extent that these factors are important in a design, they need to be considered in the design review.

A design review checklist is an excellent prompt for the review process, which can also serve as the planning and recording tool. An example is shown opposite.

Design verification

Verification is covered by clause 4.4.7 of ISO 9001, which requires that design stage output meet design stage input requirements, and results are recorded.

There are several acceptable methods of design verification, but the one most applicable to architecture is design review. Thus, the design review will satisfy the verification requirement. For engineers, the most applicable method is usually performing alternate calculations.

Design validation

Described under clause 4.4.8 of ISO 9001, the chief requirement of design validation is to determine whether or not the design satisfies the client's requirements.

You can see that if the client's requirements, expressed as the program (project brief), are made part of the design input requirements at each stage, then a design review can satisfy all three of these requirements.

ABC ARCHITECTS PTY LTD		Design Review Checklist

Form approved by: _____ Date:	Refer Work Instruction O5b in filling out this document.	Project. name: _____ Project No: _____ Prep. by: _____ Date _____

Type of review: **INPUTS to be considered in review (Check appropriate boxes):** Other (list):

- ☐ Internal
- ☐ Client
- ☐ Consultant

- ☐ Quality Manual
- ☐ Project Quality Plan
- ☐ Project brief

- ☐ Codes/regulations
- ☐ Approved schematic design
- ☐ Approved design development

☐ _____
☐ _____
☐ _____

MATTERS FOR REVIEW (Check appropriate boxes):   Other (list):

1 ☐ Design inputs
2 ☐ Project brief
3 ☐ List of significant restraints
4 ☐ Acceptance criteria
5 ☐ Design changes
6 ☐ Schematic design output
7 ☐ Design development output

8 ☐ Contract documentation
9 ☐ Subconsultant coordination
10 ☐ Consultant coordination
11 ☐ Specifications
12 ☐ Design calculations
13 ☐ Marketing/tenanting
14 ☐ Environmental impact

15 ☐ Site data
16 ☐ Initial cost
17 ☐ Life cycle cost
18 ☐ Value engineering
19 ☐ Buildability
20 ☐ Safety
21 ☐ Performance

22 ☐ _____
23 ☐ _____
24 ☐ _____
25 ☐ _____
26 ☐ _____
27 ☐ _____
28 ☐ _____

Items 1 - 7 correspond to Items of review in Work Instruction O5b 01. Refer to referenced Standards for other items.

ATTENDEES
(Enter names and project role under "Code".)

DR = Director	QM = Quality manager	SC = Subconsultant	CL = Client
PD = Project director	IR = Independent reviewer	OT = Other	CO = Consultant
PA = Project architect	PS = Project staff		PM = Project manager

Name	Firm	Code
_____	_____	☐
_____	_____	☐
_____	_____	☐
_____	_____	☐
_____	_____	☐
_____	_____	☐
_____	_____	☐
_____	_____	☐

RESULTS of design review: Identify by number in front of matters reviewed, as above. Use reverse side if extra room is needed.

_____
_____
_____
_____
_____
_____
_____
_____
_____
_____
_____
_____
_____
_____
_____
_____

Were minutes kept of the review? ☐YES ☐NO	Does the design comply generally with the input requirements? If YES, note any exceptions on reverse side. ☐YES ☐NO	Are any nonconformance notices recommended to be issued? If YES, list on reverse side. ☐YES ☐NO

Signed as a true record of the design review:

Client: _____
Independent reviewer: _____

Project architect: _____
Project director: _____

Costs and benefits

If a well-designed form is used to plan, prompt and record the design review, the cost of this formal review process would be no greater than an informal review. The benefits of this formal review, however, could be very significant. One of the problems with the traditional review is that it is 'ad hoc': It happens when there is time for it to happen, and when everyone gets busy, the reviews either don't happen, or they are not thorough enough.

A problem with the desk-top crit is that it tends to focus on the design itself, rather than focusing on whether the design is actually complying with all of the requirements.

The planning and reporting requirements of the ISO 9000 design review process force the practice to think ahead, schedule reviews at the right time, make sure that everybody is in attendance who should be there, and ensure that the design is checked against all of the relevant criteria.

This process is likely to have prevented the 'disaster scenario' described in Chapter 4.8, and might very well have prevented the collapse of the walkways in the Kansas City Hyatt Hotel, had the engineers and fabricators been working under ISO 9000 systems.

**Chapter 4.6
Summary Checklist**

✓ ISO 9000 design review evaluates design requirements, asks if the design meets those requirements, identifies problems, and proposes solutions.

✓ Design reviews are planned, include everybody with relevant inputs, and are recorded.

✓ Design verification asks if the design output meets the design input requirements.

✓ Design validation asks if the design meets the client's needs.

✓ The traditional 'desktop crit', without the rigor of the formal process, may not adequately serve its purpose.

4.7   Checking and Checklists

Many architects and engineers do not devote enough time to a final coordination review. Those who know how to coordinate documents tend to be very experienced. Ironically, those experienced in the process are often thought to be too valuable for such work. Result: the least experienced person in an office frequently makes the final coordination review. Sometimes designers wait until the last minute to consolidate drawings for other disciplines. Result: no coordination review at all. - DPIC Companies

Purpose

To delineate the role of the checking process in quality management: its importance and its limitations.

Is checking a quality management function?

Checking is not quality management or quality assurance, it is quality control. It seeks to fix mistakes, not prevent mistakes, much less eradicate cultures that tolerate mistakes. Because of this 'end-of-chain-fix' that drives checklist logic, checklists are clearly in the 'little Q' category of Juran's seminal thinking on the subject.

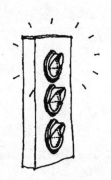

But is the relegation to 'plumber' status justified? What happens if the checklists become a key part of the feedback system, even become part of the 'early warning' system that predicts and can help control systemic failure?

At their best, checklists are warning indicators that start flashing red lights when systems aren't working, or when conditions are different from those anticipated.

William Nigro was the first person to develop a system of validating the usefulness of checklists, and his controlled experiments will stand a long time as having established the worth of checking. His REDICHECK system is described briefly on pp 206-207.

Checklist theory: memory-jogger vs. process-based

For all their popularity, checklists are not easy to get right. Most checklist system developers use the 'memory jogger' approach, which tends to eventuate into such massive structures as to be practically useless.

The memory-jogger checklist is simply a long list of items - nouns - that should be considered in evaluating a set of documents or a situation. The problem with the memory-jogger checklist is that it doesn't actually tell you what to look for or what to do when you find it.

For that you need a process-based checklist, designed so that if you do what the checklist tells you to do, you will have satisfied the quality requirements.

The CHECKIT system

The CHECKIT system, which I developed for the National Practice Division of The Royal Australian Institute of Architects (RAIA), is similar to Nigro's pioneering efforts, in that it is process-based rather than a memory-jogger, but it covers the entire process design, documentation and contract administration rather than just validation of contract documents. Part of one of these checklists is shown on page 204, to illustrate the arrangement.

At the risk of being seen to be blowing my own horn, I will discuss what we learned from a decade of working on these checklist systems - the experience may be useful to you if you are developing your own checklists.

Prior to publishing the first of the series, we did some research that established that a major reason why architects did not use checklists was that they were too long and took too much time. At that time, the only checklists that RAIA members had were the British RIBA checklists, which were very comprehensive. Too comprehensive, in fact, for Australian users.

So we worked on the 85% theory - that it was better to have an easy-to-use system that got 85% of things right most of the time than to have a system that would get 100% of things right, but be too lengthy to use.

We decided that the checklist for each checking function should be limited to what would fit on one A4 page, which, by allowing two lines of standard typing on a matching fill-in form, turned out to be 28 items. We used an alphabetical system, so we ended up with the 'vital few' being 26 functions x 28 items - which, being process items, represented the '85%' of quality checking an architect had to do. (On the example, the bottom 3 items have been removed to permit less of a reduction from the original.)

RAIA SITE ADMINISTRATION REPORT

Site Administration Setup

No.		Check box
01	Obtain and become familiar with complete set of construction drawings. Note any reference to "details to follow" or the like. Request schedule for completion of details from project leader.	
02	Obtain and read complete project specification. Highlight all items indicating compliance required of builder, such as submissions, tests, prototypes, etc. (Refer CHECKIT 1: Section W)	
03	Obtain and read copy of architect/client agreement. Note particularly any alterations to standard text affecting site administration responsibilities.	
04	Check contract documents generally. Check that these are consistent with construction documents. Cross check all revision numbers and dates of issue. Resolve any discrepancies.	
05	Review Project Quality Report V "Tendering". Note and resolve any outstanding items. Confirm that tender nonconformities and exclusions have been resolved and that resolution is reflected in contract documents.	
06	Check all requests for clarification by tenderers and ensure that the documents have been modified to remove any uncertainties.	
07	Cross-check all schedules with specification and BOQ (if any).	
08	Cross-check all monetary allowances with specification and BOQ (if any). Confirm that language is consistent in describing allowances.	
09	Cross-check all unit prices with specification and BOQ (if any). Confirm that language is consistent in describing unit prices. (Refer CHECKIT 1: K27)	
10	Check list of drawings against drawings set for numbers, dates and revision numbers and dates.	
11	Ensure that instructions are issued with regard to any discrepancies found in A01-A10.	
12	Review project filing system for adequacy for site administration filing. Extend or set up separate site administration filing system if required.	
13	Confirm site administration responsibilities for all consultants.	
14	Prepare and distribute contact list of all authorized site personnel and representatives of all consultants. Ensure list contains contact telephone number, facsimile number and address.	
15	Obtain, review and forward to Proprietor any performance bonds required from the builder.	
16	Check certificates of insurance with contract requirements. Ensure project leader forwards report to client and obtains confirmation that insurances are acceptable to his insurance advisors.	
17	Check and confirm status of all authority permits and approvals. Clarify responsibility for obtaining outstanding approvals and assess any impact on building program. Ensure project leader advises client of any delays.	
18	Obtain and review builder's schedule of required shop drawings.	
19	Obtain, review and obtain approval, if appropriate, of builder's progress schedule.	
20	Provide builder with required copies of contract documents.	
21	Ensure client has submitted applications for permanent gas, electricity, water, telephone and other services if required. Schedule any outstanding action required.	
22	Ensure client is regularly informed through the project leader of potential delays and/or cost variations.	
23	Check that all nominated subcontracts have been nominated to the builder. Confirm that nominated and main contract conditions are consistent. Clarify any inconsistencies and advise builder.	
24	Refer to existing conditions survey and become aware of any easements and covenants and the location of any public services crossing the site. (Refer CHECKIT 1: B06).	
25	Check existing conditions drawings of all existing structures on the site. (Refer CHECKIT 1: D23).	

The initial issue of CHECKIT was sent to all subscribers of the RAIA's Practice Notes; some 2500 copies. Subsequently we developed CHECKIT 2 in two versions, contract administration checklists for the two main forms of contract the RAIA produces.

At this writing, the CHECKIT system has been used throughout Australia for eight years, and reactions from users are a valuable test as to what does and doesn't work in checklist system development.

From this experience, some very important findings have emerged:

◆ Checklists must be easily practice-definable; e.g. able to be customized to suit the practice.

◆ Checklists must be project-definable.

◆ Checklists must be easy to complete, without too much thinking or writing.

◆ Project checklists should not include non-applicable items (to the specific project).

◆ One set of checklist forms should work for multiple checking periods, rather than being re-cast for each checking period.

This experience has caused us to re-evaluate the whole design of our checklists, because what those findings *really* mean is that the checklist has to be an interactive database to work the way users want it to work.

Fortunately, computer systems have progressed to the point where that is now feasible, and in our latest design, we have the entire CHECKIT system as an integral part of the *'ABC Architects'* quality management system, running as a database with FileMaker Pro as the engine. This allows fast and easy customization of the checklist system to the practice, fast and easy customization of the firm's own version to suit any project, and even allows task printouts specific to each staff person.

Some of our clients prefer the checklist version of the QM system, and so run their quality management system as a set of checklists.

The REDICHECK system

Enough on CHECKIT - let's look briefly at the REDICHECK system, which is very good and (unlike CHECKIT) is currently available to U.S. designers.

William T. Nigro is an architect who was a Lt. Commander with the U.S. Navy, responsible for construction of naval facilities during the 70's and early 80's. Appalled at the number of change orders and cost blowouts on these projects, he developed a system of pre-bid checking that would pick up coordination errors. Through analyzing thousands of change orders, he had discovered that about half of all changes were due to avoidable coordination error.

In a 1984 paper, Nigro noted: [103]

> *"During the last nine fiscal years (FY-76 through FY-85) NAVFAC constructed approximately $13 billion in military construction (MILCON) and operation and maintenance contracts, of which approximately $1 billion was change orders. This amounts to an average change order rate of 7.7% for the nine fiscal years.*

> *"During the coordination review of an average ten million dollar project with 100 drawings, almost 500 errors are typically found."*

At the time that paper was written, a number of NAVFAC divisions were using REDICHECK, with varying approaches and results. One of the more dramatic turn-arounds was with the Pacific Division, headquartered in Pearl Harbor, Hawaii. From 1976 to 1982 their change order costs ranged from a low of 5.5% of cost of construction per year to a high of 17%, with the average about 10%. After the introduction of REDICHECK in 1983, the costs of change orders dropped to a steady 3%. This division used independent consultants to do the checking, at an average cost of $3000 per project.

In the Atlantic Division, Norfolk, VA, checking began in May 1985, with a team of four in-house checkers. By February 1986, the team had checked 52 projects, and found an estimated $703,850 in avoided variations, which worked out to $1300 in savings for each hour of checking.

Nigro's conclusion from having tracked the results of pre-bid checking on hundreds of NAVFAC projects is that savings are typically 3% of cost of construction.

Against that needs to be subtracted the cost of checking, which in Navy experience ranged from 1/8 of 1% to 1% of cost of construction; also any recovery that may have been made under professional liability insurance.

If Nigro's assertion that half of change order costs are due to coordination problems, and using the average change order figure of 7.7%; then a 3% reduction due to using the checking system results in a high efficiency of error detection:

Costs of coordination errors = 7.7 + 2 = 3.85%

Errors found (3%) + errors existing (3.85%) = 78%

Nigro's method includes the use of spot checks, final checks and comparing plans drawn by various disciplines, overlaying them on a light-table. I won't review the details here; they are readily available from Nigro. Refer to *Resources* at the end of Part 4.

Other checklist and checking systems

The Heery International model: 'Red-Green-Yellow' method of checking is a well developed, fairly rigorous, 9-step checking process. It identifies 'potential' changes in green pen, signaling other checkers that there is a problem which must be solved through coordination. 'Definite' changes are marked in red. Green items are reviewed and gradually converted to red as interdisciplinary solutions are found. Finally, an independent review checks the changes and marks corrections in yellow. [104]

Fred Stitt of Guidelines, Orinda CA, is the world's most prolific checklist generator. Some of his checklists are superb. However, the majority of them tend toward the 'memory-jogger' model, which I find less useful than the process-based model. See *Resources* at the end of Part 4.

As I noted in the Introduction to this book, Frank Stasiowski is a master at the art of writing checklists, most of which are very good. You will find them throughout any of his many books.

Chapter 4.7
Summary Checklist

✓ All checklists are either of the 'memory-jogger' or 'process' type. Generally, the latter are more useful.

✓ The Pareto principle applies to checklists. Being mostly right most of the time is better than trying to be 100% right and never getting there.

✓ Checklists should be easily practice-definable; e.g. customized to suit the practice.

✓ Checklists should be project-definable.

✓ Checklists should be easy to complete, without too much thinking or writing.

✓ Project checklists should not include non-applicable items (to the specific project).

✓ Use REDICHECK. Your client, your insurance company, and William Nigro will thank you.

4.8   Performance Specifications

Today, the prime reason for litigation against architects is 'failure of function'. Behind that worrying wide classification usually lies either poor control over workmanship or an inadequate specification. And there is a direct, inverse relationship between the rise in specification-linked litigation and the profession's tendency to off-load this vital area of design control. - Louise Rogers, Deputy Editor, RIBA Journal

Purpose

To focus on a particular issue of significant concern to architects contemplating TQM or any other QM system; which is the special consequence of moving design responsibility downstream, while still retaining accountability for the outcome of the design result.

The allure and the peril

The performance specification method describes the results a building component must achieve in use, rather than describing what it is built from. Performance specifying can have great advantages for certain building systems. That is its allure. However, it also presents the possibility of heightened risk to all parties involved in a project. That is the peril.

Why use performance specifying?

Performance specifying is being used increasingly for the following reasons:

◆ To optimize value. The specialist subcontractor has the freedom to design systems as competitively as possible as long as the performance is met.

◆ To transfer risk. By centralizing the responsibility for the design and execution, the design risk passes to the subcontractor.

◆ To reduce construction time. The subcontractor can choose from components most immediately available.

◆ To resolve the problem of the designer not understanding the system sufficiently to be able to write a good proprietary specification.

When a little bit of knowledge is dangerous

The first three reasons are valid, the last is not. If this last reason is part of why performance specifying is used - whether or not admitted by the designer - then all parties are put to increased risk, including the client.

If the designer does not understand a building system well enough to write a proprietary specification, it is not likely that she will understand how to determine whether or not the system as proposed by the specialist subcontractor is going to meet the performance requirements.

You might argue: What difference does that make? If the specialist subcontractor, backed up by the builder, has taken responsibility for the performance of the system, it isn't the designer's problem.

Research into design risk shows that it is *not* possible to transfer *all* of the risk to some other party; that at the very least designers must understand the workings of a building system well enough so they can reliably advise the client as to whether a proposed solution will in fact meet the performance requirements.

It is my view that the design professional needs to know more about the way the system works than he would if writing a proprietary specification. When the specification is performance based, you do not know what you will get back, but you must understand it. The designer who does not is putting the client at risk, regardless of the language of the contract.

Most performance specifications are not solely performance based, but some mixture of proprietary and performance requirements. This can pose a particular problem for the inexperienced specifier. In a mixed specification there is always the possibility that some of the performance requirements could be mutually exclusive with the proprietary requirements.

This is a formula for trouble for all concerned. It also can create particular legal problems, as we will see below.

A prototypical nightmare

To take a simple example, let's say that a facade was specified to have certain conductivity and reflectivity performance requirements, but the drawings called up a type of colored glass which could not meet those requirements.

Let's say the client had selected the glass from samples shown by the architect, and the engineer had designed the air conditioning system based on the performance characteristics. Let's also assume that the project was fast-tracked, and the columns were going in before the air conditioning subcontractor was selected.

A narrative poem in American folklore describes how, for the want of a horseshoe nail, a decisive battle was lost. This is the situation here: a failure to check the performance characteristics of a selected (proprietary) component has set the scene for delay, cost blowout, frustration to all parties, and a loss of money or reputation or both to the architect.

Let's assume the client insists on having the glass which was originally selected, and tells the architect that any resulting problems are up to the architect to resolve. The engineer says, terribly sorry, but the air conditioning system will have to be re-designed, and someone will have to pay for it. Without agreeing to pay for it, the architect tells the engineer to redesign the system.

The redesign shows that the ducts have to be made larger to handle the increased heat gain of the building. This means raising the floor-to-floor height by 2" (50 mm) as it was designed right to the limit in the first place.

All of the pre-made column forms are now too short, and the builder submits a claim for delay and extra cost. Then it is discovered that the main return air plenum in the core will also have to be increased, which will either require relocating some existing footings and columns, or putting in a big, expensive transfer beam which in turn will require a re-routing of main trunk ducts on the ground floor level, which have already been fabricated.

It is about now that our architect starts to think that he should have taken out a professional indemnity policy.

You may be thinking that no architect would be so stupid as to overlook such a simple matter as to make sure the selected glass met the performance requirements specified.

True, most petty oversights do not end up as horror stories. Nevertheless, in every case where one part of the instructions conflicts with another part of the instructions, risk to all parties increases.

Architects and engineers know this. Many specifications contain elaborate statements which say, in effect, "Mr. Builder, by tendering on this project, you are certifying that you have understood everything in the contract documents, that you agree that it all will fit together the way the architect intended, and if it doesn't, it's your job to make it right at your own expense." Such 'murder clauses' are a waste of words, and cannot be counted on to exonerate the designer who failed to check the contract documents.

A real example

Let us consider another, more complex case, which occurred on a major Melbourne office tower a few years ago. The architect carefully researched facade systems. The specification was scrutinized by all involved. The system was designed as a proprietary system of the "stick-built" type: e.g. the erection of a metal framework into which would be set the vision and spandrel glazing sheets.

The builder could propose alternative systems. The winning bid included such an alternative system; on which was based on a 'panelized' system: e.g. the glazing sheets factory fitted to metal frames which were then fixed to the structure. This system represented the cutting edge of technology and offered significant advantages. However, few firms had the technology to produce this kind of system, so it was not suitable as a base bid design.

The specification provided for a joint width of 15 mm (5/8"), with tolerance limits.

Well into the facade contractor's design, it developed that in certain locations, building deflections would require a 20 mm (3/4") joint. This set the width of the joints for the entire facade at 20 mm. The architect accepted this change. However, the 20 mm joints were significantly more expensive than the 15 mm joints, and the facade contractor sought a large claim for the increased cost.

The architect was able to demonstrate that the 15 mm joint would have sufficed quite well in the original stick-built design, and pointed out that the facade contractoring firm had failed to advise in its proposal that the way the panels moved under deflection loading was different than the way a stick-built system moved.

In this case, the architects had done their homework and it was the facade contractor who had to absorb all of the risk of the alternative system.

The point of these examples is that the ability to change some aspect of a building system - a central concept in performance specifying - can trigger a whole set of consequential changes which may be hard to appreciate at the outset.

This is not to warn you away from performance specifying - but to warn you to be careful when considering doing it!

Performance specifications and ISO 9000

It is important to remember that ISO 9000 was developed for the manufacturing industries. It presumes a seamless responsibility between design and production. In this model, the designer has an obligation to track **all** changes in design, and verify that they comply with design input requirements.

What happens when responsibility for the *completion* of design is transferred to some other party? No one knows, and it hasn't been tested in court to my knowledge, but I can readily imagine that the courts would find that the 'master' designer had a responsibility to the end-users to ensure that the secondary designer also complied with all design input requirements.

The only way around this, in my view, would be an agreement, not unlike a deed of trust, where the secondary designer accepted this responsibility and agreed to hold the first designer harmless from any downstream problems. I've not yet seen such a clause in my travels.

If you consider that the people to whom this secondary design responsibility gets passed on to - mostly building services subcontractors - have no control or sometimes even knowledge of how their design inter-relates to other building systems, then the matter of responsibility gets murky indeed.

The situation in Europe

Information in this section is abstracted from an article by Louise Rogers in the November 1993 RIBA Journal.

Under present European legislation, the architect is banned from thwarting free competition by demanding that a named brand is used. So traditional, prescriptive specification is difficult. The answer is to recommend one specific, preferred product accompanied by the option for the contractor to allow an alternative only as long as it meets the detailed performance specification.

A well-written performance specification will ensure that substitutions later on will have to stand up to the criteria set by the architect.

Current guidance on the writing of adequate performance in design specifications is hard to come by. An unpublished report by John Veal, RIBA Assistant Director for Practice, points to the distinct lack of information in this area. The report, which monitors the available design and performance specification guidance says:

> *"It requires patience, but without certainty, to locate design standard information, a commodity which is in short supply in the majority of design offices, especially if a quality management system is not in operation."*

What happens if the contractor changes the specification without getting permission from the architect? The news from the U.K. is not encouraging. An industry-wide survey by Barbour Index found that only about half of specifiers are aware of changes made to their specifications. The RIBA says that many architects labor under the illusion that if the end product fails and is not the one specified, the blame will fall elsewhere, but that the truth can be very different.

> *"From the many cases of specification law in court across the country, the message is clear. The architect's design duty continues right up to practical completion and that includes detecting and putting right any diversion from the specification of design. It may not be fair, but architects should take note.*

> *"The key judgment in this area, Richard Roberts Holdings Ltd v. Douglas Smith Stimson Partnership, took place in 1989. The case involved the switching of a specification made by the architect. The judge in the case found the architect to be at fault when the substitute specification failed despite the fact that the architect had not recommended it. The judge decided that the architect, as the expert in the process, had a duty of discovery."* [105]

The situation in the U.S.

An aspect of the new Federal procurement reform law that affects design professionals is the call for greater use of performance specifications, in contrast to design specifications.

The Schinnerer *Liability Update* newsletter notes: [106]

> *"It will be important for architects and engineers to be aware of how the courts have been defining the differences in terms of how contractor claims are handled when it is alleged that the contractor failed to comply with the different specification approach.*
>
> *"Whether the specifications are ruled to be either performance or design is critical in resolving contractor claims because under an old and still-prevailing doctrine known as the 'Spearing Doctrine', if the specification is deemed to be a design specification there is an implied warranty from the owner that if the specification is followed an acceptable result will be produced."*

The designer who mixes prescriptive and performance criteria in the same specification will thus significantly complicate the resolution of claims. This may be primarily a risk management issue, but it has ramifications for quality management as well, especially when coupled with the ISO 9000 implied responsibility for ensuring that design complies with design input requirements.

Chapter 4.8
Summary Checklist

✓ The use of performance specifications has untested implications under an ISO 9000 QM system.

✓ Reliance on performance specifications does not take away the responsibility to ensure that the completed design meets the design requirements.

✓ Mixing proprietary and performance clauses in one specification can cause legal problems of assignment of responsibility.

✓ In a proprietary specification, the contractor cannot be held responsible for fitness for purpose.

4.9 Partnering

Our distant forebears moved slowly from trial by battle and other barbaric means of resolving conflicts and disputes, and we must move away from total reliance on the adversary contest for resolving all disputes. For some disputes, trials by the adversarial contest must, in time, go the way of ancient trial by battle and blood. Our system is too costly, too painful, too destructive, too inefficient for a truly diversified people. To rely on the adversarial process as the principal means of resolving conflicting claims is a mistake that must be corrected. - Warren E. Burger, Chief Justice of the United States, in 1984

Purpose

To present an overview and key elements of the partnering process and the design professional's role in partnering.

Why partnering?

Finding ways to run building projects which minimize disputes is a high priority for everyone in the building industry. Most of the attention has been on how to *resolve* disputes. Partnering is about how to *prevent* disputes.

In the last few decades, major strides have been made in developing arbitration, mediation, and other forms of non-litigation procedures as more acceptable methods of dispute resolution.

Partnering goes a step further by attempting to structure a mechanism to deal with potential problems, as well as actual problems, before they reach the dispute stage.

Is partnering really a new idea?

Partnering is a new word for a very old idea; one which has been used by architects for centuries and which is still used on small projects, especially in the residential arena.

The essence of partnering is to agree to solve problems without fighting; without claims, without litigation. This idea has got lost somehow in the dog-eat-dog world of both commercial and public building.

However, partnering does bring some important new elements to the old common-sense idea, which largely are to formalize what was once informal and understood without the need for agreements.

This formalization is not just a new gimmick, it is a very important part of the process of turning around the litigation juggernaut; of reversing the debilitating cycle of fear and self-protection which characterizes so much of late 20th century building.

Workshop strategies

One of the techniques which can be used in a partnering workshop is to get participants to put their biases, or prejudices, to paper. This is best done in an open (public) way, say with flip charts.

One good way is to use role-playing. If everybody has to change roles e.g. the builder pretends to be the architect, the architect pretends to be the client, and the client pretends to be the builder, they can be more candid about their perceptions of the 'secret agendas' of the others. Once these secret agendas, no matter how derived, are up on the white board or flip chart, they can be discussed; generally at first, and then in terms of the specific project.

Fears can be identified and talked about in the project context.

If you think your way through this process, it becomes apparent that the exposure of a secret agenda of any party could destroy the viability of the project for that party, if the party relied on its secret agenda to protect its position.

For example, if the builder had perfected a strategy of 'low-balling' the bid and not only counted on making a profit but recovering costs from change orders, a program of early identification of 'errors' could destroy the viability of the project for him. This very real possibility clearly demonstrates how important it is that the partnering process begin as early as possible.

It is entirely possible that a successful outcome to a partnering workshop (with the above premise) would be that the builder stated finally that because the drawings were sufficiently vague and inconclusive that he had purposely bid the job 5% below real costs, and could not undertake the work if the underbid couldn't be made up through change orders.

The courage that such a statement would require would be stunning.

The point is that partnering agreements, like any partner arrangement, must be built on a baseline of mutual trust, and (like any partner arrangement) it is always possible to enter the partnering agreement in bad faith, and exploit one's partners.

This possibility is one of the strongest reasons for the partners to retain an experienced facilitator - to 'keep the partners honest', and to help the partnership identify and resolve any latent fears that could encourage such exploitation.

Strategies in action

Let's look at a practical situation. You are in the partnering meeting, and potential problems are being discussed:

Builder: *"What happens if the engineer makes a mistake? Who is going to pay for it?"*

Client: *"Not me."*

What is your response here? Do you firmly fold your arms across your chest and make a speech about never making any mistakes?

This is a speech you know nobody in the room will believe, so you unfold your arms and think fast. What are your options?

Suppose you say: *"It depends when the mistake is discovered."*

This will make the others start thinking - thinking of the circumstances of time, and how that might affect the cost of 'fixing' a mistake.

Suppose you then said *"It also depends on what you mean by a 'mistake'."*

Whether or not the above things are the right answer in the circumstances is not the point; the point is that you are doing some very important things:

◆ Suggesting that the question is more complex than the black/white way it was posed.

◆ Signaling your willingness to be flexible.

◆ Suggesting that some definitions of terms are needed.

'A mistake is a mistake'

Now we have the basis for a meaningful discussion, rather than a stand-off.

Now the other parties have many options. They may ask questions of you; *"What do you mean - what is a mistake to you?"*

The builder may attempt to keep the simplicity of the original construct, by saying *"I've seen thousands of mistakes. A mistake is a mistake, and it always costs money and takes time to fix."* This is a belligerent response.

Or he might play the good guy and say: *"On every job, we take care of hundreds of little mistakes, we just fix them at our own expense to keep the job going. It's the big ones that we can't do for nothing."*

Depending on the personalities involved, this is where the progress of the meeting could begin to deteriorate, and a watchful facilitator will at this point enter the discussion, moving everyone back into their corners, and re-direct the discussion to the points made by the engineer.

On the issue of time: On the facilitator's prompting, the engineer might say: *"Well, if I did make a mistake, and anybody on the team discovered the mistake before any wrong materials were ordered or installed, then it wouldn't cost anything or take any extra time to fix it. Nobody would have to pay anything."*

Now, this is may not be an answer the builder likes much, if *his* secret agenda is to make his profit on change orders. For change orders he needs to find 'mistakes' - if at all possible after he has bought the materials and at least started to install them.

However, the engineer's logic here will appeal to the client, who will quickly appreciate that the best way to avoid change orders is to find mistakes before materials are ordered, which is the beginning of a specific 'goal' for the goal statement.

The facilitator will be watching the builder closely here, and will begin to craft a strategy to get the builder to start thinking of other ways to make profits besides finding mistakes.

The facilitator, recognizing that the builder needs some time to think about the next tack to take, may suggest that the definition of a 'mistake' should be discussed.

The builder, who is expert on mistakes, would be invited to define the term. Here the definition is not important, the discussion is. For it will develop in the course of the discussion that a lot of 'mistakes' are no more than differences of interpretation in the meaning of the contract documents: the engineer meant one thing and the builder took it for another; a problem in communication.

Now a thousand scenarios are possible. An obvious one might be that the client views this interchange with some smugness: the communication problem is obviously between the builder and the engineer; not his to worry about. However, in attempting to save money on fees, the client has only bought a brief 1/2 day visit per month to the site, and it begins to be apparent that a 1/2 day a month is not enough to ensure that the builder and engineer understand each other perfectly.

If both the builder and engineer agree that communication would be dramatically improved by twice-weekly, full-day site visits, and the result of this would be to catch mistakes before materials were ordered, as well as ensure that the builder understood the engineer's intent, the client would start thinking about how much this extra service would cost, and how it would compare with his fear-based secret allowance for a cost blowout.

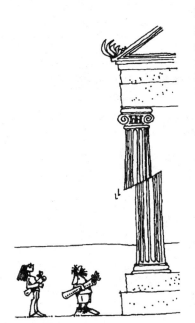

'Let's consider the remote possibility of a 'mistake' by the engineer.'

This story could be a full length movie; it is not important to continue exploring the myriad possibilities. What is the key issue?

The key issue is that the engineer, without actually admitting she ever made any mistakes, was willing to put the *possibility* on the table. The possible results that could have flowed from this willingness include:

◆   Identification of a key goal in the project (early identification of any possible errors).

◆   A clearer concept of terms (is this problem a 'mistake' or only a 'miscommunication'?).

◆   A perception on both the client's and the builder's part that the engineer is a responsible person who is 'not afraid to admit a mistake'.

◆   A re-focusing of the builder's need to make a profit.

◆   An increased role and fee for the engineer.

Not a bad result!

Hidden agendas

In the imaginary partnering exchange above, the issue of hidden, or secret, agendas comes up a number of times.

Hidden agendas occur because people have learned how to survive in the corporate jungle by playing games, and like many games (especially card games), skill at playing is not measured by luck but by concealing the 'cards' they hold.

We use the expression 'playing your hand' to cover a very wide set of human activities. Playing the game successfully requires that the 'opponents' be kept guessing.

This entire concept is built on a 'win-lose' mentality; that the only way to win is at somebody else's expense.

It is here that the very concept of partnering must be examined. One cannot play 'win-lose' with one's own partner, because if your partner loses, you lose.

Partnering is 'win-win' or it is not partnering.

Partnering means that the partners can, and do, put their cards on the table; no secret agendas.

Accomplishing this is NOT easy, which is one of the reasons why the use of a trained facilitator is so important in starting up the partnering process.

What about errors and omissions?

The first time a design professional hears of the concept of partnering, invariably one of her first questions is - what happens if we have to admit we made a mistake? Aren't we putting ourselves at risk? Could this be a reason for our insurer to cancel our professional liability policy?

The predictability of that response is a powerful indicator of how enshrined the atmosphere of litigation is in our professional life, and how fearful of exposure we have become.

We know about the 'reasonable person' test, but don't trust it as we don't know what a judge or jury will decide was 'reasonable' in the circumstances.

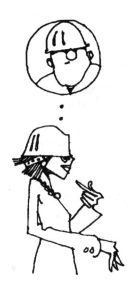

Above we considered the problem of hidden agendas in partnering. Partnering can work only if the hidden agendas are put on the table by all parties to the partnering agreement. In the architect/engineer's case, the 'hidden agenda' is to successfully conceal any error or omission material to the project.

This need to conceal is based on experience: from the builder who has learned how to survive by 'low-balling' the bid and making up for it with change orders by exploiting any possible discrepancies in the contract documents, and from the client who will not listen to the argument that if the 'omission' had not been omitted, it would have been included in the bid, and the client would have paid for it anyway.

Here we have an all-too-familiar cycle of fear: The design professional fearful that the builder will blame her for the extras, the builder fearful that the designer will retaliate by demanding impossible standards of workmanship, the client fearful that costs will blow out, etc.

The reality is that no single party to this vicious cycle can reverse the process - it takes all parties to do it, and they can only do it together.

How does partnering start?

Partnering comes into a project when one of the parties to a contract convinces the rest it is the way to go. Typically this party is one with prior experience in partnering or knows someone who is very positive about it.

In most cases, it is the contractor or owner who initiates the move to partnering, but it can just as easily be the design professional.

The partnering workshop

Partnering workshops can take a great variety of forms, all the way from retreats featuring hot tubs and inspirational counseling to business-like negotiating meetings. It depends on who runs them, and what the participants want.

Trappings aside, there are some crucial issues that make for a successful partnering workshop:

✔ Full attention, without interruption, of the most senior people in all parties to the partnering agreement.

Actually, that is probably <u>the</u> crucial issue; all the other issues flow from that one. However, they are important and need discussion:

✔ A re-alignment of priorities of all parties, such that success of the whole project is seen by all parties as the surest way to optimize their financial and personal rewards.

✔ Identification of the most likely problems to come up, and agreement on a strategy for resolving them.

✔ The establishment of a 'charter'; a non-binding "heads of agreement" which sits alongside the formal contract as blueprint for problem resolution.

✔ As an underpinning part of the charter, a mutually agreed set of quantifiable, measurable, achievable goals that can be referred back to when tensions rise.

The facilitator's role

To understand why the right facilitator is so important in partnering, one must consider the forces at work. My metaphor is that of a giant wheel, moving very slowly but of overwhelming mass; the whole legal functioning of Western society. As this system has moved out from dealing with criminal problems into the civil arena, it has all too often bogged down, while the lawyers argue and the whole show stops.

We architects study the art of self-protection; the kung-fu of 'CYA' letter-writing. We start with our feet in a psychological tar-pit, based on a lot of history.

What a good facilitator can bring to this situation is experience in some skills we never were taught in school; such as team-building, conflict resolution, and group dynamics.

The better ones have a smorgasbord of useful tools as well, such as the ability to administer and interpret personality tests. Equally importantly, they bring something else: detachment. And with it, objectivity.

**Chapter 4.9
Summary Checklist**

✓ Partnering is about how to *prevent* disputes, rather than how to resolve them.

✓ Partnering is 'win-win' or it is not partnering.

✓ Partnering can work only if the hidden agendas are put on the table by all parties to the partnering agreement.

✓ Partnering requires the full attention of the most senior people in all parties to the partnering agreement.

Successful partnering - an artist's impression

4.10 Document Control

There is no department which does not come under the umbrella of document control. In the author's experience, this is the most neglected of activities and many of the problems which arise are due to inadequate control in this area. - Lionel Stebbing

Purpose

To communicate what is meant by 'document control' in quality management, and describe ISO 9000 requirements for document control.

The importance of document control

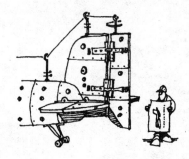

Imagine that you are a workman assembling the rudder controls for a light plane. The design has been changed - not much, but just enough so the parts go together just a little differently. For some unknown reason, you were never given the revised drawing. You do what you would have done before, with the new parts.

The plane crashes and kills the four occupants, due to the improper assembly.

In this situation, the need for absolutely foolproof document control is obvious. It is to prevent this kind of occurrence that system element 4.5 of ISO 9001 was created.

Does this have any direct application to architecture? Where health and safety are concerned, it certainly does.

The error which caused a bridge over the Hyatt Regency Hotel lobby in Kansas City to fall and kill 114 people wasn't one of issuing the wrong documents, but the error was close to that and it could just as easily have been a document control problem.

Document control is regarded by third-party certifiers as the most difficult of all procedures for most firms to get right.

In an era of rapidly increasing reliance on electronic transfer of project documents, and the relative difficulty in catching errors in electronic media, document control of our CADD and other electronic files is becoming strikingly more important.

A related problem is the security of electronic media; also a crucial document control problem.

ISO 9000 requirements

Document and data control is the subject of system element 4.5 of ISO 9001. The basic requirements are:

◆ All documents and data that 'relate to the requirements' of the standard are subject to control.

◆ Such documents and data shall be reviewed and approved by 'authorized personnel' prior to issue.

◆ A 'master list' or 'equivalent document control procedure', which identifies the current revision status of all such documents must be maintained and available, to preclude the use of obsolete versions.

◆ Documents must be available where 'operations essential to the effective functioning of the quality system' are carried out.

◆ Obsolete or invalid documents must be removed from points of use. If retained for legal or records purposes, they must be marked as obsolete.

◆ Changes to such documents are to be reviewed and approved by the same person or function as reviewed and approved the original documents, if possible. Reviewers shall have access to appropriate background data to facilitate their review.

◆ The nature of the changes shall be identified where practicable.

Those requirements seem quite logical, and not far off what we do, or think we should do, as design professionals. In practice, however, it is not easy to demonstrate the consistency of that doing.

There is another ISO 9001 system element, 4.16: *Control of quality records*, which affects all such documents. Its requirements are as follows:

◆ Documented procedures are required for the 'identification, collection, indexing, access, filing, storage, maintenance and disposition' of 'quality' records.

◆ Records must show that the system is working as
   planned.

◆ Storage must provide for easy retrieval, and prevent
   damage, deterioration and loss.

◆ Retention periods shall be established and recorded.

Those requirements also seem reasonable enough. However,
when you think about it, you quickly realize that there are
literally thousands of pieces of paper in your files which do
NOT meet the above requirements. The idea of having to
record all of them on a list would alone create a monstrous
overhead task, of dubious value.

How has document control been interpreted in the design field?

It turns out that the real question of document control in an
ISO 9000 system is WHAT IS A QUALITY RECORD? This is
not so easy as it might appear, and there is little agreement
among authorities about it.

At one end of the spectrum, the argument is that because
design control is regulated by the standard, and the business
of the design practice is design, then all design documents
are to be controlled. That is just about every piece of paper in
your files!

At the other end of the spectrum, there are those who argue
that management can properly decide which documents it
will control and which it won't, with the quality manual
and quality procedures alone being the only ones where
control is mandated by the standard.

The first group to tackle this question was the Royal
Institute of British Architects (RIBA). In 1990 the RIBA
published *Quality Management: Guidance for an Office
Manual.* [107] This guide states that control procedures are
required with respect to:

◆ Incoming mail, telexes and facsimiles

◆ Handling, filing and storage

◆ Records of telephone calls

◆ Records of meetings and site visits

◆ Outgoing letters

◆ Internal issue and distribution of internally and
   externally produced documentation

◆ Packaging, posting and delivery arrangements

◆ Withdrawn documents

The RIBA defines quality records as including, in addition to quality system documentation and review records, the following information for each project:

◆ Statutory and other approvals received
◆ The basis used for the design
◆ Product information
◆ Evidence of records of reviews
◆ Evidence of performance (calculations, tests) demonstrating compliance with records
◆ Output documents and the project documents index
◆ The project brief
◆ Codes and standards used in satisfying the client's brief
◆ Records of actions taken in verifying design solutions and in contract administration
◆ Records of time and expenses incurred on the project

That is a fairly sweeping list, but notably it *excludes* all drawings and sketches up to the 'output' documents.

The second organization to tackle this subject (as far as I know) was Standards Australia (SA). In response to extensive queries, SA and Standards New Zealand established a joint committee representing 16 relevant organizations to develop a guide standard for ISO 9000 for the construction industry. This resulted in the publication, in January 1993, of AS/NZS 3905.2. [108]

This guide lists the following items as 'normally' subject to document quality control (notes in parentheses added):

◆ Quality manual and quality procedures
◆ Project quality plans
◆ Design documents and drawings, both internally and externally produced
◆ Specifications
◆ Conditions of contract
◆ Inspection and test plans (applicable to builders only)
◆ Computer input and output relevant to quality
◆ Technical procedures and instructions
◆ Quality records (refer to list below)
◆ Client's instructions
◆ Project brief
◆ Design statements

◆ Architect/engineer instructions
◆ Variation approvals (variations are change orders)

This guide further identifies a long list of typical quality records, including the following relevant to design:

◆ Management reviews
◆ Tender (bid) reviews, contract reviews and design reviews
◆ Acceptable subconsultant records
◆ Inspection and test records and certificates; records of inspection authorities
◆ Personnel training
◆ Audit reports
◆ Corrective actions

You can see from this that the coverage is quite extensive. AS/NZS 3905.2 notes:

> "Records are ... the objective evidence of the operation of a quality system at all stages and are required to be kept to prove the effectiveness of the implemented system."

In practice, government agencies requiring compliance with ISO 9000 have put out their own lists of documents subject to document control, which vary, but have tended to be more onerous than the guide lists.

What does all this really mean?

What this experience means is that there is no international agreement on the interpretation of the ISO 9000 requirements for quality records and document control. From a purely pragmatic point of view, the fewer records you define as quality records, subject to document control, the less of a headache you will have trying to implement your procedures.

If you are developing an ISO 9000 - based system where there is a current client requirement, find out what the client groups want and tailor your list accordingly.

If you are developing an ISO 9000 - based system where there is no current client requirement, define these narrowly. You can always add more items to the list later, when the system is up and running. I would suggest the following as a *minimum* list. These items are either specifically noted in ISO 9000 as required, or are reasonably inferred as being required.

- Quality manual and quality procedures
- Audit reports
- Management review records
- Contract reviews (of the designer/client agreement)
- Project quality plans, including design planning records
- Design review, design verification and design validation records (refer to Chapter 4.5 for definitions of these terms)
- Master list of current quality documents
- List of acceptable subconsultants, including information about their quality systems if any
- Records of any client-supplied materials which are lost, damaged or unsuitable for use (applies mostly to interior design practices)
- Records of changes to procedures as a result of corrective or preventative action
- Records of implementation and effectiveness of corrective actions
- Training records

I am sure you will agree that the above list is extensive enough!

What are some of the problems of document control?

In my experience, document control in the average design office ranges from bad to abysmal. The ground rules for good document control are very simple: If you took the contents of the project files for three different projects and dumped them all in a box, could an untrained assistant figure out how to reconstruct the files? If the answer is *NO*, then you have got a document control *PROBLEM*.

One example from my experience: I was carrying out a diagnostic audit for a large, prestigious architectural firm in Brisbane, Australia. As usual, I asked to review the project files for three random projects. I also asked for a copy of the firm's standard project filing code. The answer was that each project director could make up his or her own, on a project-by-project basis.

Already the red lights were flashing, but I thought I should see how this approach functioned in practice, so I began reviewing the records for the first job, a large and important project which had won numerous design awards.

For U.S. designers who have never seen a lever-arch binder, this is a clever British 2-hole hardback binder with a lever clamp that hold the papers tightly. One of these will hold about twice as much paper as a 2" 3-ring binder.

The records consisted of 18 lever-arch binders, crammed full of paper. The first two of these binders contained the custom-designed filing system, with some material filed therein. The other 16 binders were full of literally thousands of documents, all under 'general' and in no order other than in order of filing.

Here was a system where meaningful 'retrieval' was virtually impossible; where filing was truly out of control. Any uniform filing system this firm put in place would be a dramatic improvement. Needless to say, there was no way of finding out how many untold hours of profes-ional time had been wasted hunting for lost documents, but it must have been a very significant part of overheads.

The photocopier as a dangerous tool

Let us consider another all-too-typical case of poor document control. The invention of the photocopier has made it very easy to advise others of design changes: Just slap that working drawing down on the platen in the right place, print as many prints as needed, put transmittal notes on top and send them off.

What happens when this package arrives at its destina-tion? The transmittal note goes in the rubbish and the frag-ment of drawing gets put in a file or stapled to another drawing. It has no date, no provenance, no nothing. It is information without an anchor. And it violates every rule of good document control. If this process happens even occasionally in your practice, then you need the brilliant, 15-cent invention of architect Barry Cameron in Canberra. You'll find it described in Chapter 5.6.

What are the benefits of document control?

Without respect to any other consideration, instituting any level of document control in your practice will force you to look into files and find out what is actually happening. Unless your practice is in the minority, it is not likely to be what you think should be happening. Most people hate filing, putting it lower in interest than washing dishes. They do it as a way of getting rid of piles of paper, rather than as a way to find them again.

If your filing system isn't working well for you, it probably means that it isn't very well designed, *and* that staff don't really believe that it is very important to you to have good records. Improvements are almost guaranteed to have the following benefits:

♦ Finding things quickly; when, for example, the client is on the telephone, and wants to know the status of something.

♦ Finding things, at any speed: Reduction of lost records.

♦ Lower overheads; money saved.

♦ Being prepared for meetings.

♦ Being prepared for claims against the practice.

Someone should write a book just on document control; it is such a pervasive problem, and so important to good practice. I haven't touched on the very real problems with controlling electronic documents, especially after they leave the office, and of many other crucial issues of document control, such as the degradation of thermal fax paper documents.

But this isn't that book. It can be argued that the rigor of formal quality control places an unreasonable demand on small firms with respect to document control, but that doesn't change the fact that most of us need to improve the document control we've got; some of us dramatically so.

Chapter 4.10
Summary Checklist

✔ Document control is regarded by third-party certifiers as the most difficult of all procedures for most firms to get right.

✔ Defining the scope of quality records is crucial to success in setting up an ISO 9000 QM system.

✔ If you are developing an ISO 9000 - based system where there is a current client requirement, find out what the client groups want and tailor your list accordingly.

✔ If you are developing an ISO 9000 - based system where there is no current client requirement, define quality documents narrowly.

✔ Instituting any level of document control in your practice will bring your firm direct and immediate benefits.

Part 4 Resources

References

(80)	Mears, p 23.
(81)	If you are a trivia lover, borrow a copy of the referenced Juran book and read his account of how he came to incorrectly ascribe the term 'Pareto' to the situation, and then discovered the error after everybody else made it common usage. Appendix to Chapter 3, page 68.
(82)	Mears, pp 127-128.
(83)	Ibid., p 144.
(84)	Ibid,. p 155.
(85)	Laseau, Paul, *Graphic Thinking for Architects and Designers*, Van Nostrand Reinhold, 1980, pp 184-185.
(86)	Mears, pp 190-196.
(87)	Crosby, p 11.
(88)	Mears, p 205.
(89)	Ibid.
(90)	Senge, Peter M., *The Fifth Discipline*, Doubleday, 1990; Random House, 1992.
(91)	Mears, p 205.
(92)	Ibid., p 222.
(93)	Stasiowski and Burstein, p 174.
(94)	Crosby, pp 32-33.
(95)	Ibid., p 192.
(96)	Stasiowski & Burstein, pp 271-278.
(97)	Crosby, p 215.
(98)	Juran, pp 409-425.
(99)	Mears, p 221.
(100)	Stasiowski & Burstein, pp 200-206.
(101)	Fox, p 70.
(102)	ISO 8402-1986: *Quality - Vocabulary*.
(103)	Nigro, LCDR William T., *REDICHECK: A System of Interdisciplinary Coordination*, DPIC Communiqué newsletter, April 1984, DPIC Companies Inc., PO Box DPIC, 2959 Monterey-Salinas Highway, Monterey CA 93940.
(104)	For a more complete description of the Heery International system, see Stasiowski and Burstein, pp 81-83.

(105)   Rogers, Louise, from an article in the RIBA Journal, November, 1993.

(106)   Schinnerer *Liability Update* newsletter, October 1994.

(107)   Royal Institute of British Architects, *Quality Management: Guidance for an Office Manual*, pp 2K and 3J.

(108)   AS/NZS 3905.2-1993: *Guide to quality system Standards AS 3901/NZS 9001, AS 3902/NZS 9002 and AS 3903/NZS 9003 for construction*. See pp 54-55, 74-75.

For more help on...

TQM tools generally:

Peter Mears' book (footnote 19) is the best source of general information on a broad range of TQM tools. It is recommended as a reference guide for quality managers in design practices who want to know more about specific tools not covered in this book, and for more detail on tools which are covered. It contains references to other works which are good examples of detail about these tools and techniques.

For more information on any of these tools, refer to the readings listed under the Source Data column in Tables 4.1 to 4.7. Cross references are provided at each tool outlined.

The project brief:

◆ Frank Salisbury, *Architect's Handbook for Client Briefing*, Butterworth Architecture, London, 1990. The best book in print on this subject. Although written to the client, it is a superb resource for any architect.

◆ William Peña, CRSS *Problem Seeking: An Architectural Programming Primer* (3rd Edition, AIA Press, 1987).

◆ Henry Sanoff, *Methods of Architectural Programming*, Dowden, Hutchinson & Ross Inc., 1977.

◆ Cornick (page 134) has a chapter on briefing, pp 47-60.

Audits:

◆ There is a useful international standard which describes the audit process: ISO/DIN 10011: *Guidelines for auditing quality systems, Part 1: Auditing*.

◆ Stebbing (footnote 36) includes a good chapter on audits; pp 106-134.

Design reviews:

◆ Cornick, pp 177-182.

◆ For an excellent discussion of the best way to do the 'desk-top crit', read Franklin (see page 82), pp 3.24- 3.26.

For more help on...

Design reviews (cont.):

◆ ISO 9004.1: *Quality management and quality system elements, Part 1: Guidelines* contains a lengthy section (pp 10-11) on design review, design verification and design validation.

Checking and checklists:

◆ Stasiowski and Burstein, pp 74 and 367-382, for design review checklists.

◆ For information on the REDICHECK system, contact William T. Nigro, The REDICHECK Firm, 109 Greensway, Peachtree City, GA 30269; tele (404) 631-4430.

◆ For information on CHECKIT, contact Building Technology Pty. Ltd., 126 Russell Street, Melbourne Australia 3000; tele (61-3) 9650-3846, fax (61-3) 9650-3848.

◆ Fred Stitt can be reached at Guidelines, PO Box 456, Orinda CA 94563; tele (415) 254-9393.

Performance specifications: Cornick, pp 87-93.

Partnering: Guides and resources include:

◆ Stasiowski and Burstein, pp 259-262.

◆ *Partnering News*, a newsletter published by Venture Consulting Group Inc., 674 County Square Drive, Suite 105, Ventura CA 93003; tele (805) 650-8040, fax (805) 644-0790.

◆ *TQM and Partnering*, August, 1993; published by the AIA.

◆ *Partnering: A Tool for Managing Change*, by Jim Eisenhart and James R. Franklin; available from the AIA.

◆ *A Project Partnering Guide for Design Professionals*, published by the American Consulting Engineers Council (ACEC) and The American Institute of Architects, 1993. Available from the AIA or ACEC.

◆ *Design Firm Management & Administration Report*, a newsletter which includes partnering news, 29 West 35th Street, New York NY 10011; tele (212) 244-0360.

◆ *Partnering: A Better Way of Doing Business*, by Richard M. Miller PE, Compass Consulting Group Inc., 515 South Main Street, Springboro, Ohio 45066.

For more help on...

Consultancies specializing in facilitation of partnering workshops include:

◆ Gathering Pace, Inc., 28 Gould Road, Bedford MA 01730. Contact: William Ronco, tele and fax: (617) 275-2424.

◆ FMI Corporation, Suite 600, 90 Madison Street, Denver CO 80206. Contact: William Spragins, tele (303) 377-4740, fax (303) 377-3535.

◆ Flynn-Heapes Kogan, Suite 301, 218 North Lee Street, Alexandria VA 22314. Contact: Ellen Flynn-Heapes, tele (703) 838-8080, fax (703) 838-8082.

Partnering, for readers in Australia:

◆ Alan Patching's *Partnering and Personal Skills for Project Management Mastery* (see page 83).

◆ *Partnering: A Strategy for Excellence*, published by the Construction Industry Development Agency (CIDA) and Master Builders Australia Inc., available from CIDA, 9th Floor, 50 Margaret Street, Sydney NSW 2001.

◆ Partnering Consulting Group, a consultancy specializing in facilitation of partnering workshops, 246 Bridge Road, Richmond VIC 3121; tele (03) 9428-6352, fax (03) 9428-6897.

Document control: Stebbing, pp 65-70.

Part 5

RESULTS: Making It Work / Keeping It Simple

5.1   Going in Circles vs. Feedback Loops

And then, all of a sudden, Winnie-the-Pooh stopped again, and licked the tip of his nose in a cooling manner, for he was feeling more hot and anxious than ever in his life before. There were four animals in front of them!

'Do you see, Piglet? Look at their tracks! Three, as it were, Woozles, and one, as it was, Wizzle. Another Woozle has joined them!'

- A. A. Milne, *Winnie-the-Pooh*.

Purpose

To describe feedback systems in TQM and ISO 9000 QM, and discuss how these can improve design practice.

Going in circles

'Going in circles' is a universal metaphor for working hard and getting nowhere, rendered with consummate charm in the story of Pooh and Piglet following their own tracks around the Spiney Wood, filled with anticipation and trepidation as to what they were following.

'Going in circles' seems such a common experience that we have many names for this activity:

◆   Running in place

◆   Being in the squirrel cage

◆   Chasing our tail

and so on.

They all mean the same thing: we go through a cycle of work; start and complete a project, and we do not appear to have learned anything from the process; we are back where we started.

The iterative process

To be sure, 'going in circles' can be a very positive - perhaps even vital - aspect of the design process. We call this 'iterative'; it *is* the way we design. James Franklin has captured this concept admirably in a spiral diagram, shown opposite. [109] If we use this idea of a spiral to describe the iterative process, when we come back around to the 'same place', we actually have moved forward, by the distance between loops in the spiral.

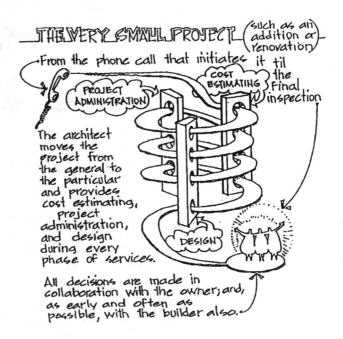

Dr. Juran also uses the spiral as a way of explaining what he calls 'the spiral of progress in quality' [110]. Here is one of his diagrams:

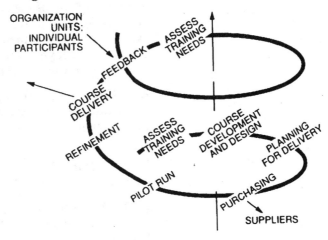

We can think usefully about feedback in this way: What we learn from our experience can be measured by the pitch of the spiral. If it is very tight, we really are only going in circles; if it is open, we have made progress as we went around.

A great leap forward
for Herman

PDCA cycle

A key tool in every system of quality management is the feedback loop; in its simplest form the "PDCA" cycle, introduced in Chapter 4.2.

The PDCA cycle forms the basis for team efforts in problem solving. It represents the four steps necessary in addressing a desired system or process change.

1 **PLAN** - Plan a change aimed at an improvement in the design process. What could be the most important accomplishment of the quality improvement team? What changes in office practice might be desirable? What data can be gathered to study the change? Is new data needed? If yes, plan to record this new data, decide how you will use it, and in what process.

2 **DO** - Carry out the change or the test, preferably on a small scale. Search for data on hand that could answer the questions in Step 1.

3 **CHECK** - Check the results to see what was accomplished or learned. Observe or monitor the effects of the change.

4 **ACT** - Adopt the change, or abandon it if the results are not useful. Try the cycle again, with accumulated knowledge.

Feedback in process flow

If you turn back to the flowchart example on page 155, you will see a number of arrows that 'go back' to some previous step. In a flowchart, these mean that some step hasn't been satisfactorily completed (the test result was 'no'), and the process has to be repeated to get it right.

I made the comment there that 'design may be necessarily iterative, but should not be more iterative than necessary'.

It is obvious when one looks at that flowchart that failing to catch a problem at any one stage will both delay the progress and add unnecessary cost.

The flowchart process is one of the most widely used tools in both TQM and ISO 9000 to improve quality through feedback. This tool can be used to graphically describe any process in any industry, but obviously its use should be restricted to those processes where some real benefit can be gained by creating the flowchart.

How do we know which processes those are? One good way to start is to identify the processes which aren't working as well as you would like them to, or those which annoy you. It is in these situations where you are most likely to learn something new about the processes by flowcharting them: flaws in the way the process is operating, or critical points where you should be testing the process but aren't.

Setting up a flowchart

Here are the steps for setting up this analysis:

1 Identify problem processes.
2 Prioritize and select processes to study.
3 Prepare flowchart of first process.
4 Identify all critical points for success of the process.
5 Describe these points:
   - What is the test of adequacy at that point?
   - Who is responsible for testing adequacy?
   - Does that person know his or her responsibility?
   - Are the tests being carried out?
   - If not, why not?
   - If so, what is happening with the results?
6 Check that the flowchart shows these decision points, and what happens if there is a negative result. If it does not, revise the flowchart.
7 Continue this process until the flowchart is complete and accurately shows what *should* be happening.

At the end of this process the problem will be sharpened and clarified, and the solution may be apparent.

Application of the feedback cycle

The feedback wheel can be used to good effect to study certain relationships. As just one example of that, I did some work for a state governmental client to help them better understand the consequences of varying procurement methods, shown below.

Traditional procurement model

This model presumes a normal 'full services' design contract, with the design professional responsible for contract administration.

Note the importance of post-occupancy evaluation (POE) in this cycle. It is the key activity that bridges the gap between construction and writing the program for the next project.

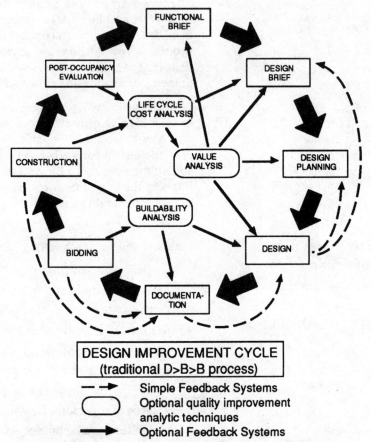

DESIGN IMPROVEMENT CYCLE
(traditional D>B>B process)

- - → 	Simple Feedback Systems
⬭	Optional quality improvement analytic techniques
➡	Optional Feedback Systems

All risk conditions are either internal to this cycle or external to it. Examples of internal risk conditions are inadequate briefing or inappropriate selection of materials. Examples of external risk conditions are inclement weather and political changes.

Normally this process starts at the top, with a statement of a client's needs, and progresses around the cycle. Traditionally the weakest link in this cycle is POE (post-occupancy evaluation). Key reasons for this weakness are a failure by all parties to the process to realise the importance of POE in design improvement, and (consequently) no provision in anyone's brief to provide for collection or analysis of POE data.

Design > document & build model

This model is middle ground between the traditional model and design-build.

In it, the client engages the architect to do the design, then the project is bid, and a team responsible to the contractor does the documentation.

This model is very much the norm in Japan.

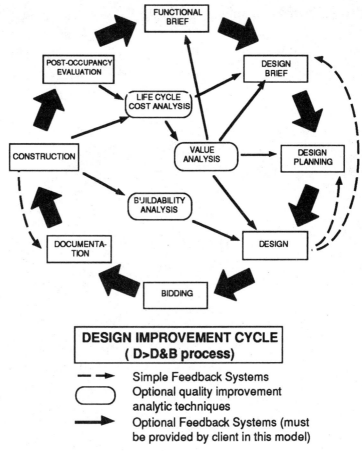

DESIGN IMPROVEMENT CYCLE
(D>D&B process)

- - ▸ Simple Feedback Systems
⬭ Optional quality improvement analytic techniques
━▸ Optional Feedback Systems (must be provided by client in this model)

From a feedback process perspective, the Design > Document & Build model is the weakest of the three common systems. This is because the functional connections do not exist as they do in either the traditional D > B > B system (where feedback loop integrity can be maintained by the design team, through construction inspection) or Design/Build, where feedback loop integrity can be maintained by the builder. As a result, in the D > D&B model, the client has the fundamental responsibility for maintaining the design improvement feedback loop, since the client has structured a system which interrupts the loop.

The only way this feedback loop can be completed is either for the client to faithfully provide the feedback, or to ensure that the design team has access to, and input into, the document/build decision-making process as well as the outcome (results) of that process. This limitation has important consequences in structuring effective long-term risk management programs.

Design/build model

Note how the sequence of activities has changed from the two previous diagrams.

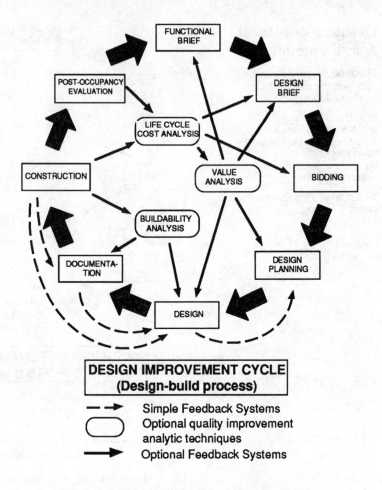

**DESIGN IMPROVEMENT CYCLE
(Design-build process)**

- - →   Simple Feedback Systems
⬭   Optional quality improvement analytic techniques
──→   Optional Feedback Systems

The difference between going in circles and feedback loops is that the latter come back to a new and better starting point, through structured self-education.

The POE connection

The risk management studies above showed how POE was critical to completing the feedback loop, and that in the D>D>B model, this information was generally inaccessible to both the design team and the documentation team, thus creating a problem for all parties in the transfer of education gained through experience.

Fortunately the whole field of POE is beginning to be recognized as an important specialist skill for design professionals.

What we need, however, is a mental shift that drives every designer back to 'the scene of the crime' a year or two after completion to see how the building is aging and whether the inmates are happy. There is a masterful reference available on POE; see *Resources* at the end of Part 5.

Feedback and corporate memory

It is my personal view that the retention of what I call 'corporate memory' is one of the most important aspects of the education-through-feedback process for design professionals. It is the subject of the next chapter.

Chapter 5.1
Summary Checklist

✓ Process feedback, as an action to prevent repetition of past mistakes, is a requirement of both TQM and ISO 9000.

✓ The iterative process is either going in circles or a continuous improvement feedback loop, depending on where you are when you come around again.

✓ Flowcharting a process that could be improved is one of the best ways to discover the sources of the problem and point toward the solution.

✓ POE is necessary to complete the feedback cycle.

5.2   Capturing and Holding Corporate Memory

Specifiers will agree to become 'keepers of the system' and become expert at office information systems. - Mark Kalin [111]

Purpose

To highlight the importance of retaining - and aid the ability to retain and use more effectively - the knowledge that passes through the practice.

Keepers of the system

It's now nine years since I read Mark Kalin's 'prediction No. 6 for 1990' [111], and it rings in my ears as loudly as the day I happened upon it - one of those rare gems that never loses its glint of new light. When he wrote it, Mark was thinking about the future of specifiers, but the real power of his comment lies in the implicit question: WHAT ARE OUR SYSTEMS? He offers a clue: *information*. But what information?

As I've pondered that question over the years, I've come to the conclusion that in most practices, the most valuable information accessible to the practice quietly and surely slips through the fingers of those who guide the firm, and is lost forever. Hence, this chapter on 'corporate memory'. It's all too often more of a 'memory' than 'corporate'.

What is corporate memory and why is it on the loose?

Corporate memory, like personal memory, is what the corporation remembers from its past experiences. How clever the corporation is depends on how much it can remember. Architectural practices, for the most part, remember precious little considering the richness of their past experiences. WHY?

Because, in all but the smallest and most stable practices, most of the firm's prior experiences happened to employees who moved on and took the corporate memory - which was paid for by the firm - with them nearly intact.

Think of that memory as a library of original manuscripts, of which no copies exist.

If the persons leaving took with them a stack of those manuscripts, the directors would get very excited. But that is what usually happens when a person leaves your employ. It's just that the manuscripts were never written down, and you don't see them marching out the door.

But, you say, *"That is the way it has always been; why is it an issue? Besides, the younger architects are really only learning what the senior architects know, and it is part of our professional ethic to educate them."* Quite so, but our profession is evolving at a faster rate than ever before. Today it is more likely that the senior members of the firm do not even understand what the younger members are doing, especially if they work at a keyboard.

Multi-skilling and specialization

Architecture is very rapidly breaking into specialties, whether the generalists like it or not, and to the extent that architects become more multi-skilled; move out into new areas of expertise; the more this specialization will characterize our practices.

It will become increasingly impossible for directors to understand exactly what their best employees are doing, and when employees leave, what they did while with the firm.

New employees, arriving at a firm with an empty corporate memory library, will re-invent their piece of the corporate wheel-rim from their background experience, which at best will mesh with what was done before, and at worst will reverse it (assuming that what came before was good stuff).

The best firms will begin to find efficient ways to capture that corporate memory as it is experienced, sift it, store it, and have it available as an accessible resource, rather like collecting, sorting, processing and warehousing the by-products of manufacturing.

What does corporate memory look like?

How will I know it when I see it? The forms corporate memory can take are as varied as the people who make up the firm. Some examples:

◆ Standard details.

◆ Standard pro formas, such as room data sheets, schedules.

◆ Information about products, especially new products, which isn't in the catalogues.

- ◆ Information on reliability and maintainability of products.

- ◆ Research methods; setting up cost-effective, reliable procedures.

- ◆ Better specification clauses.

- ◆ Design information on specialized building types, such as hospitals or golf courses.

- ◆ Design information on system assemblies, especially high-tech mechanical and electrical systems, and their architectural requirements.

- ◆ Computer routines, especially mini-programs and algorithms which improve standard applications.

- ◆ Knowledge about clients' needs, preferences and attitudes.

- ◆ Access to media contacts.

- ◆ Knowledge of techniques outside 'normal' practice, such as the ability to set up financial pro formas, life-cycle cost studies, cost-benefit analyses, etc.

Benefits

The benefits to capturing more of corporate memory are many, but would include the following:

- ◆ Everybody in the firm will spend less time hunting for extant pieces of corporate memory.

◆ If the process IS efficient, the time savings will outweigh the cost of organizing it.

◆ The firm will be able to respond to new challenges more quickly and be less dependent on the time commitments of its 'experts'.

◆ People will become less indispensable, but at the same time, more highly valued for their contribution.

◆ The departure of a key person is less likely to handicap the firm.

◆ Errors will decrease because of less wheel re-invention. Documentation costs will drop, and contract documents will be more reliable.

◆ Some of the time spent re-inventing new methods of production will be replaced by more time spent on design and original work.

◆ The directors will have a greater understanding of and appreciation for what their employees are up to.

◆ The 'lone wolf' types will find the new environment uncomfortable and will quietly wander off.

More on feedback

In QM-speak, this process is called *feedback*: having a formalized method of learning from everything you do, such that the ways of doing it are continually undergoing evaluation and change to become better. Yes, every firm does that to some degree - usually in a vague, erratic and random way. If you want to have a QM plan that respects either TQM or ISO 9000 philosophy, it will have to be formalized and operate predictably.

Australian feedback system

If you agree with the above logic, what would you do to begin to capture that elusive corporate memory? Here are some ideas:

One highly respected interior design practice in Australia, Geyer Design (Melbourne and Sydney), has used this system for a long time with great success. Members of the firm are expected to show up for meetings wih their corporate memory notebooks, and they do. The firm regards the record of this collected memory as one of its more important assets.

◆ Make corporate memory a priority. Talk about it. Get your staff to talk about it. Focus on the experience your firm has lost in the past, and should have retained.

◆ Make someone responsible for corporate memory (your 'keeper of the system') and ensure that she dedicates some time to it each week. Request that she prepare a summary monthly report.

◆ Get rid of scraps of paper. Buy everybody in the office a cheap, bound notebook, which they are to use as a diary, writing everything in it: phone numbers, details of calls, meetings, anything which falls outside the firm's formalized project reporting procedures. When these notebooks get full, they can be turned into the 'memory minder', where they will form a chronological record of experience of every person in the firm.

The notebooks' creators will want to photocopy parts of them, copy forward some information, etc. That is fine. But the original goes into the firm's corporate memory.

Some people will resist this idea enormously, or will agree to it but never enter anything. Maybe they don't belong in the firm. Maybe they need to understand that one of the reasons they get a paycheck is to create such a record of their work in the firm.

◆ Establish a regular system of filing information at the close of any project, where someone who is NOT part of the project reviews the entire file and sifts out collected data which has a general firm value. If such data is important to the permanent project record, make copies for the file or make references in the permanent project record as to where the removed items can be found.

◆ Institute a REGULAR office procedure of cleaning out the piles on and under desks, returning not only information borrowed from the library, but new information which belongs in the library.

◆ Develop resource profiles on every staff member and circulate them, so that everyone in the firm will know who is specially skilled at what, and can go to them for advice.

♦ Have regular meetings of staff which focus on areas where the firm needs more knowledge to do its job better. Assign investigation and reporting duties to persons who are interested in following up these ideas. Set time limits and parameters.

♦ Reward people who internalize the corporate memory capture process, support it, and creatively support it. In a medium to large firm, this could be dinner for two at a nice restaurant, awarded monthly; or perhaps quarterly in a small firm. Or perhaps a Friday off with pay, or a fine book or set of CD records of the employee's favorite music. Whatever the reward, it should also benefit the employee's spouse/partner.

♦ Believe in it yourself, and set the standard. People will do *amazing* things when someone they respect puts high value on something and creates an atmosphere of acceptant expectation.

This list could go on for many more pages, but you will have the idea. The point is to tailor a program to YOUR firm!

**Chapter 5.2
Summary Checklist**

✓ Think about the value of what is in the heads of your best employees, and what would be the best way to make that knowledge available to other staff.

✓ Act on your answer.

✓ Appoint a keeper of the system.

✓ Check on the results at least quarterly.

5.3 Optimum Documentation: The Fine Line Between Too Much and Not Enough

We produce too many drawings. We can trace the reason for this in the lack of direct relationships and trust between designers, engineers, craftsmen and technicians. - Ray Moxley, Building Management by Professionals

Purpose

To focus on the documentation process and discuss ways to improve it.

Re-thinking the process

In the great majority of architectural practices, no area offers so much opportunity for improvement as that of documentation.

Many practices might doubt this view, but what I have seen in many, many offices convinces me that over-documentation needlessly increases project cost and dissipates the firm's resources, while (often on the same project) under-documentation creates problems during contract administration and may well lead to unnecessary change orders.

The causes of inappropriate documentation

There are a number of reasons why the documentation process, which is the single largest cost to architectural and engineering practice, is a prime candidate for improvement in so many practices:

◆ It is the primary training ground for the inexperienced. Graduates of many design schools are unprepared for the reality of practice, which is that design - while being the most important part of practice - in fact is only a very small part of it.

In most offices, the path to becoming part of the 'design' team goes through the labyrinth of the drafting office, and takes quite a while. From this flow two consequences. One is that the neophyte designer, dreaming of the career he hoped to have, but hasn't yet achieved, puts the mind in neutral while the hands keep busy.

What he does to keep busy is to beautify the drawings: hatch the walls, dot the concrete, draw lovely earth in section, and create perfect lettering.

A collateral problem is that, though wanting to create elegant buildings, the frustrated draftsperson can only create elegant drawings.

◆ A lack of experience, especially with construction technique and the requirements of materials assembly. The conscientious draftsperson draws what he knows best, which is usually the things which least need to be drawn, or draws them in ways they won't (or shouldn't) be built.

◆ The tendency to 'get runs on the board': to show good progress by drawing all the easy things first. More than once I've seen situations where that crucial building section - that would eventually require the scrapping of much other documentation - was kept neatly taped down under other drawings on the senior drafter's desk. There was always an excuse why it wasn't tabled for review.

◆ Specifications on the drawings: There still is a lack of awareness of the line that needs to be drawn between written information on drawings and in the project manual. Not only is the lettering of drawings the stuff of the dark ages - the slowest possible way to convey information - it is also often contradictory to the specification, and can cause problems in interpretation on the job site.

◆ A lack of timely interest by management. *Days* can go by in the drafting department, all the hard questions unanswered, while the practice leaders are busy on site solving the problems that weren't solved in the last project's documentation.

Simple remedies

Fortunately, the solution to better documentation is relatively simple, but requires a clear and definite management commitment. Here are my suggestions:

◆ Talent: Get the right balance of gray hair and learners. The 'chief draftsman' role is one of the most important in practice success, and too often these people are the first to get the ax when the recession hits. Field experience and people skills at the top of the documentation team are crucial to practice risk management.

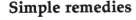

◆ Notes vs. specifications: Have a defined policy, and ensure that all staff understand it and stick to it. The interface between the specification writer and documentation team is very important, especially if the firm outsources specification writing. The specification writer should keep a close watch on the level and content of noting on drawings.

◆ Plan the documentation! It is amazing how often documentation simply 'starts' with no real thought as to total number of sheets, structure of the set, which parts are more important to get done first, etc. This activity requires the full attention of management in the smaller practice, until management has confidence that a realistic plan is in place and working (in this regard, see Chapter 5.5).

◆ Make a clear distinction between the design process, and documentation of the design intent. I know that many architects will argue that design and documentation should be a seamless process; where the design simply continues to undergo further refinement right up to the point of issuing contract documents.

That idea is great, if the designer is driving the process. It doesn't work if the designer is busy on the next design, and the learners are left to 'draw it up'. The latter process invites over-design. There are projects where 100% of the project must be designed, but they are rare. Skill at component assembly is a fundamentally different activity from re-invention of components.

◆ Be 100% clear with your staff as to the level of documentation you want on each project. Do you want elegant drawings, or instructions that are easy to read from dirty, crumpled plans under poor light?

◆ Think about detailing from the corners of the building in, not the flats of the building out, and continuously urge your team to think the same way. It is the corners, especially where three planes meet, that will ultimately shape the details, and cause them to be discarded if the junctions were not carefully considered.

◆ Identify the problem areas - the trickiest parts of the project - and draw them first. If this is not possible, then identify what things must be resolved in order to draw them, and resolve those things first. On major projects, this activity is often worth flowcharting.

Herman's excess documentation

◆ Know what 'industry standard' is for all common details. If industry standard is good enough, don't document it. If you want more than industry standard (and are confident the client wants that too) then document it.

**Chapter 5.3
Summary Checklist**

✓ Over-documentation needlessly increases project cost and dissipates resources; under-documentation creates problems during contract administration and may create change orders.

✓ Get the right balance of gray hair and learners.

✓ Define a policy for dividing drawing notes and specifications.

✓ Plan the documentation!

✓ Distinguish between the design process, and documentation of the design intent.

✓ Define the level of documentation you want on each project.

✓ Detail from the corners of the building in.

✓ Solve the problem areas first.

✓ Don't document where industry standard is good enough.

5.4 Leading Your Team

*First, it is important to recognize that **doing** is not necessarily **managing**.* - David Haviland [112]

Purpose

To review strategies for improving project teamwork.

Team-building

Team-building is not a skill taught in design schools. It is not a skill that the majority of design team leaders are often very good at, despite their long experience in team settings.

Quality management of the consultant team is inferred as being a requirement of ISO 9000, and is implicit in leading TQM theories. Back in Part 4: *TOOLS*, you may have noted that the examples illustrating a number of tools were on the subject of managing other consultants, especially those appointed directly by the client.

Architecture has, for decades, been a diverse business, involving many different disciplines. When all those specialists worked for and were paid by the team leader, control problems existed, but the team leader had a fairly powerful lever to manage with. In recent years, with increasing use of alternative procurement methods, as well as direct appointment of consultant by clients or their project managers, leading the team has gotten more complicated, and the 'lever' of the checkbook is often missing.

Regardless of the legal responsibility structure, the architect typically has express responsibility to coordinate the team. Even where the responsibility is not express, somebody has to do it, and the architect is usually the logical person to take on the role. This role is not always easy. In my work with a variety of practices, the most common complaint I hear has to do with the difficulty of controlling inter-team processes. (By inter-team, I mean the interfaces between project teams in different firms.)

David Haviland has researched and written extensively on intra-team management; [112] his books on process management belong in your library if they aren't in it, so I will not cover the same ground he has already covered so well. (Intra-team means within your own practice team.)

These changes in consultant appointment, procurement, specialization and project complexity have created a situation where an authoritarian approach backed up with checkbook diplomacy is no longer appropriate. The team leader of today needs new skills. How should they be acquired?

Training

Training is a requirement of ISO 9000, and is heavily emphasized by most TQM authorities. In general, the role of training is to prepare the workers and their managers to be able to function in a different cultural environment (that of the TQM organization).

I've specifically not included a chapter on training in this book, in part because it is covered so extensively in other referenced resources, but more particularly because in the design professions, skills training is usually not an issue, is usually appropriately addressed when necessary, and there rarely are any middle managers.

It is in this area of team building skills, however, where (in my view) most practice leaders would benefit from training. It isn't possible in the scope of this book to precisely describe the training needed, nor am I especially qualified to do so. What I can do, from my own experience, is point out the importance of such training, and urge practices to provide it for those whose responsibility it is to take on the team leader's role.

Gaps and overlaps

The inevitable result of the 'gap and overlap' problem is delay, fighting over who 'should have' taken on those responsibilities, and (all too often) work that has to be done over again, almost always without recompense.

One of the most serious problems that emerges in inter-team management comes about when the appointment and briefing process is inadequate; for example when an inexperienced client makes direct appointment of team members, or when a project manager puts excessive emphasis on consultant fees. The results nearly always cause what are called 'gaps and overlaps' in role responsibilities; more often gaps. This means that there are tasks that must be performed, but they are not in any team member's role description. They haven't yet been purchased.

What happens in this situation is that team members assume that 'others' are taking responsibility for some required tasks. By the time it becomes generally known that there are gaps in responsibility, the likelihood that critical design decisions will have been neglected is high.

Task Manager

In response to this problem, in 1985 I developed a system called *Task Manager* for Denton Corker Marshall, one of Australia's leading design practices. This system tracks over 700 consultant tasks, organized into 25 design disciplines, that could reasonably be done by more than one member firm in the design team.

The tasks from one consultant group of this system are shown below. This tool effectively ends the 'gaps and overlaps' problem, and is highly effective for negotiating responsibilities where there is separate appointment of consultants.

Task Manager 02: Structural Engineering

2.01 Prepare time and resources schedule for all structural engineering work.

2.02 Prepare list of all approvals needed for structural work, with probable review time required for each.

2.03 Prepare list of all critical decisions, and the deadlines for making them, to be made by others in order to meet the schedule for the structural design.

2.04 Prepare specification and plan for geotechnical survey.

2.05 Contract for and obtain soil report.

2.06 Review soils report and report to architect/client.

2.07 Obtain information on below-grade walls of adjacent structures.

2.08 Review 2.07 information and report to architect/client.

2.09 Investigate structural requirements of any site structures to remain, report to architect/client.

2.10 Prepare structural parts of demolition specifications.

2.11 Investigate temporary shoring requirements and report to architect/client.

2.12 Prepare temporary shoring specifications.

2.13 Observe and report on demolition operations.

2.14 Observe and report on temporary shoring operations.

2.15 Design/specify hoarding, structures, site hut structures, sign structures.

2.16 Prepare structural reports or investigations required by authorities for approvals.

2.17 File for and obtain all required structural approvals.

2.18 Prepare feasibility analysis of alternative structural systems.

2.19 Prepare wind loadings analysis.

2.20 Prepare spandrel beam deflection analysis.

2.21 Analyze implications of "growth" in precast systems and building compression; advise on joint requirements.

2.22 Perform all structural design with regard to underground tanks, utilities structures, etc.

2.23 Design all structural equipment supports.

2.24 Review curtain wall designs for structural adequacy.

2.25 Prepare guide criteria for locations and maximum sizes of slab and beam penetrations.

2.26 Locate and dimension core, wall and floor penetrations.

2.27 Check all brickwork and blockwork design for structural requirements.

2.28 Design structural connections for curtain wall systems, precast systems, etc.

2.29 Design control and other movement joints needed due to deflections under loading or building sway.

2.30 Review lift and escalator designs for structural requirements.

2.31 Design structural components for building maintenance units.

2.32 Coordinate specifications to architect's standard.

Recently, we have developed this tool as an interactive database running under FileMaker Pro; so that it can be easily customized to a practice, and from there to a project.

Fast-track coordination

In 1982-83 I was involved with a major office building development in Boston where the design team had developed particularly good coordination processes for a project with a complex procurement model.

In this project, which was partially fast-tracked, the structural design and all building services design were performance based, whereas the architectural design was carried out fully (completed while the contractor was doing the pile driving). Also, during this time, the contractor set up a project office for the detailed design of the superstructure and building services.

The services design was developed in conjunction with the architectural team on a floor by floor basis, and signed off by both the design subcontract teams and the design engineers, who had a 'watching brief'. As each floor was signed off, it was released for fabrication and erection.

I'm sure there were a few problems, but from my fairly close involvement as the contract administrator, I wasn't aware of them. It still remains to me a model of a highly successful team coordination approach. The reason it worked, in my view, was the establishing of the project office for coordinating subcontractor design.

Another fast-tracked project that I had the opportunity to experience first-hand proved instructive with respect to what happens when cultural expectations differ. This project, a huge (A $1.0 billion; US $750 million) commercial project in Melbourne, was developed by a major Japanese design/build contractor. The developer set up a project office for all of the design teams, which filled most of a city office building.

There was nothing wrong with the coordination effort, which involved hundreds of design staff in about two dozen disciplines. However, in Japanese custom, everybody was paid directly on a 'cost-plus' basis. That meant that overheads were paid, but that there was no opportunity for profit for the design firms, who had to put many of their best people on the project. It also meant that participating firms had neither incentive nor responsibility for monitoring design costs - it was the client's job.

Where the process broke down was when the 'crunch point' came: the design budget got used up, and the design wasn't complete. Design staff were dismissed in droves, and the work was completed with skeleton crews.

Doubtless those closer to cost control on the project would have their own views on how to prevent this kind of a situation, but it seemed to me that giving some risk, and some profit, to the design firms would have added their experience in controlling design cost to the team, and would have been a good trade-off for the developer.

Document coordination

William Nigro's REDICHECK system, described in Chapter 4.7, focuses on checking the coordination (or lack of it) between the various disciplines, as this area has been found to be a rich mother lode for contractors seeking change orders.

The general guidelines of Chapter 5.3 also apply to the overall team output, but are perhaps harder to coordinate. Using the *Task Manager* is the best way to achieve that coordination, but since you may not have access to Task Manager, you need to carefully *plan* the documentation with your other team members. It is a very good idea to arrive at a mutually agreeable list of objectives and a schedule, and work hard to stick to them. This is an area where *partnering* (see Chapter 4.9) can be tremendously valuable to the design team.

**Chapter 5.4
Summary Checklist**

✓ Provide team-building training to your team leaders.

✓ Focus on eliminating gaps and overlaps in the assignment of tasks to consultant team members.

✓ Give careful thought to potential involvement with complex project procurement models, especially with respect to risk and the value that your unique contribution can add.

5.5 Changing Your Calendar and Other Strategies

The whole focus should be on providing the necessary leadership. To do this managers need to be aware that it is the signals they give which are acted upon, not the words that they use, nor the messages that they write. - Roy Fox

Purpose

To outline a few strategies that may help the reader (you) to create new paradigms in your practice, paradigms which will be appropriate for the times you are in, the markets you face and the future you want.

Chaos theory

Tom Peters, in *Thriving on Chaos*,[113] makes the following extraordinary statement:

"I have studied leadership and strategy implementation for over twenty years, reviewing hundreds of books, thousands of studies, and observing a host of effective and ineffective leaders. Literature on management style is best measured by the ton, as is true for topics such as conflict resolution, consensus-building, 'forging a team at the top,' choosing an optimal structure, and goal-setting techniques. More recently "how to create the 'right' culture" seems almost to have become a boardroom obsession.

"To be sure, many sound ideas have surfaced concerning each of these important topics. Yet I am willing to stick my neck out and state unequivocally that all of them, taken together, pale by comparison to the power of this one: changing your calendar.

"Changing your calendar is not sufficient to bring about desired organizational change. But it is necessary. It is quite simply impossible to conceive of a change in any direction, minor or major, that is not preceded by--and then sustained by--major changes, noticeable to all, in the way you spend your time."

Herman changes his calendar

This idea comes up again and again in literature on quality management, yet nobody that I have read has put it so clearly or (to use his words) so unequivocally.

What happens when you change your calendar? Peters offers compelling evidence that the answer is *'whatever you want'*. We all know that it is not that easy (change never is), but the weight of some of the best thinkers of our time only seems to confirm that Pogo was right; that we are our own worst enemy when it comes to creating changes we want.

In this chapter we are poking around at the outer edges of QM; just inside the fence from a whole range of nearby intellectual pursuits. There is only the space here to open a few gates and point out the first markers; they are yours to follow if you are so inclined. *Resources* at the end of Part 5 lists a number of guidebooks.

Revaluing your talent

The way we price our services traditionally has been based on expenditure of hours rather than expenditure of creative genius. Because of these attitudes, we apportion too little for design and too much for documentation, and then, having created the self-fulfilling prophesy, never have enough for design and permit ourselves to spend more than is necessary for documentation.

Want more info? Our old friend Frank Stasiowski pops his head up once again; he's the expert. See *Resources*.

Owning your niche

The best marketing intelligence we have tells us that unless your practice is one of those firms which really is big enough and resourceful enough to be all things to all clients, the best way to avoid evolutionary extinction is to find and master a niche market. Niche market thinking demands answers to two vital questions:

◆ Is your cave on the path to somewhere?

◆ How crowded is it in there?

Tom Peters has made a lot of money and an international reputation by hyping the idea that the times we are living in are changing so fast that none of the traditional ways of thinking about business evolution will work tomorrow - and he means *tomorrow*, not next year or five years from now.

Is your cave too crowded?

For the very small firm, this means continually researching new opportunities, matching them with your skills, and seizing the ones where the fit is best.

At its simplest, that is niche marketing.

I'm no expert at it, but so far surviving in the game, so I can share the few things I've learned about it:

◆ Caves are like other real estate. The only three things that matter are - yes - position, position and position. The niche market is your cave, your protective hidey-hole until you get booted out by a bigger animal. But where is this cave? Clients may not beat a path to your door; it should be on the path to something they already want, or you'll go hungry.

◆ How crowded is the cave? How many others are you competing with in this niche market? How do their strengths compare with yours? Can you be leader of the pack (hunt at the front)?

◆ Be ready to move. The better the niche, the faster the others will find it and begin to crowd you out.

See *Resources* for suggestions on further reading.

Predestining your future

There is an old saying that when you are up to your neck in alligators, it is hard to remember that the assignment was to drain the swamp.

Albert ponders his future

The future belongs to those who can take a step back and survey it. In football terms, drop back to buy a bit of space and time to see how to advance the ball. While everyone else is butting heads, see what is happening out there.

Most design professionals are too busy to plan ahead, which increases their chances of getting left behind.

Thinkers from widely divergent fields have espoused the idea that a fundamental step in change is to put yourself mentally in the place you want to be. 'Clothes maketh the man'. Put on the armor and those who don't know you will think you are the knight.

There must be a very fine line between stepping over into a better reality that exists, and that you are ready for, and stepping over into a non-reality; a serious delusion. I find this question of self-re-invention to be a most interesting challenge.

Recent books have documented the difference that changing one's image can make - when a movie actor became President, the marketing of the Presidency changed forever.

The question is: Can we peel those spots off the leopard? How can we tell? The answer can only be - yes, but not easily. We have seen from the quality masters that culture change is core to quality improvement, and that personal culture change on the part of management is the only way to effect culture change in the firm.

This journey led Alan Patching (see Part 2: *Resources*, p 83) to conclude that the answer required the study of psychology. What I am certain of, is that this question of personal image re-invention and inner cultural change is inextricably intertwined with successful team management and professional services marketing. *And* quality management.

Improve your negotiating skills

Yup, that's it. Shortest bit of advice in this book. Already well documented by experts; I've nothing to add. See *Resources* for learning recommendations.

Improve your time management skills

I've read a lot of material on time management over the years, and tried some of it. Did the Elizabeth Wood speed-reading course decades ago. Even bought an organizer. Some people are 'clean-desk' people, some are not. I'm not. I know where everything is on my various desks, how far down, in which pile. But I have discovered that at night, the papers play little games, and sneak around and get in other piles.

A time management problem in the making!

Seriously, though, the best and simplest time management system I've ever seen is the one advocated by the hugely successful motivational guru Dr. Stephen R. Covey.[114] I use it. It works. It is a version of the 'classifying quality problems' TQM tool introduced on page 163, so I can recommend this tool as a valid TQM device.

Covey calls this the 'time management matrix'. The way it works is that you draw four boxes, and put all the activities on your list into one of these four boxes:

- Urgent and important
- Not urgent and important
- Urgent and not important
- Not urgent and not important

Some advice on Covey's matrix: Run two diagrams, one weekly and one daily.

Simply put, Covey's methodology says that the Quadrant 2 activities are the important ones, and that if they don't get done in Quadrant 2, they move over to Quadrant 1 and thereby command all your attention. He says that the only way to keep the Q1 list down is to do the Q2 activities before they get to Q1 status, and that the only way to do that is to steal time from Q3 and Q4 activities. Beyond that, I invite you to read the referenced book and/or listen to the cassette tape of the same title.

	URGENT	NOT URGENT
IMPORTANT	Quadrant 1 Activities Crises Pressing problems Deadline-driven projects	Quadrant 2 Activities Prevention Principle-centered activities Relationship building Seeing new opportunities Planning Recreation
NOT IMPORTANT	Quadrant 3 Activities Interruptions, some calls Some mail & reports Some meetings Proximate, pressing matters Popular activities	Quadrant 4 Activities Trivia & busy work Some mail Some telephone calls Time wasters 'Pleasant' activities

**Chapter 5.5
Summary Checklist**

**Added at the insistence of
the illustrator.*

✓ Change your calendar.

✓ Revalue your talent.

✓ Own your niche.

✓ Predestine your future.

✓ Improve your negotiating skills.

✓ Improve your time management skills.

✓ Draw cartoons.*

Herman manages his time

5.6   Great Inventions

Make a better mousetrap and the world will make a beaten path to your door. - a minor paraphrasing of Ralph Waldo Emerson

Purpose

To review some of the systems that other design practices have invented to improve quality of service.

Appropriate technology for your photocopier

The ease with which technology accomplishes some things creates its own quality problems. A prime example is the photocopier. It is very easy to lay large tracings over the platen, print off a number of copies, slap a transmittal on the top, and send them out to all and sundry.

The inevitable result: The transmittal gets thrown away, and those photocopies, sent out to update documents, have no date, no notice of update, no drawing number, no title, no method of identification. The more conscientious firms put a stamp on these copies, but usually there isn't a place on the print to put a stamp, and most people don't bother or forget when they are rushed.

Cameron Chisholm & Nicol, a Canberra practice, has created the perfect answer to this problem, a piece of 'appropriate technology' that costs about 15 cents. Taped to the front of the office copier is an opened manila file folder with a large hole cut in it. On one end is a title block, firm name and address, etc., and a place to put in relevant drawing ID information.

The user simply flips this 'mask' up over the platen and makes the prints. Voilà! Each print has a nice white border, looks like a proper detail, contains all firm ID, and has a clean place on which to identify where it came from. From a QM point of view, nothing could be better. What's more, the practice ensures that its name, address, phone and fax numbers are on *every* document it sends out.

If your copier has front controls that would get in the way, the masks could be hung on a nail behind the machine, and used the same way. Different masks could be created for different projects, to cut time needed to identify each copy.

Ideas from Jones Coulter Young

The Perth-based practice of Jones Coulter Young (JCY), a highly successful regional office of about 35 staff (formerly part of the Australian Philip Cox national group), has developed a number of brilliant, cost-effective strategies for improving quality. We will look at two of them here: storyboards and combining the brief & design drawings.

Storyboards

The idea of storyboards is not new. A great many project team managers use the technique to think through documentation set up, but leave it there. The technique is often used in team-building. If you have a copy of William Peña's *Problem Seeking*[115], on page 57 you will see a picture of 'analysis cards', a form of storyboards.

JCY uses the storyboard technique to program and track progress of documentation. Each drawing sheet is represented by a 6x8 file card, pinned up in the team area, which not only contains the drawing layout and contents, but also start and completion dates and staff assignment. When parts of drawings are completed, those parts of the cards are marked with a hi-lighter.

Advantages of the storyboard technique:

◆ Instant, at-a-glance assessment of progress for the whole project.

◆ The progress of any team member is always on display; a great motivator.

◆ Key drawings, like building sections, can't get 'lost' in the documentation process.

I know that many other practices use versions of the story-board technique. For example, the Boston firm of Childs Bertman Tseckares (CBT) uses a similar system it calls the 'storybook'. CBT uses a double-sided card as shown below:

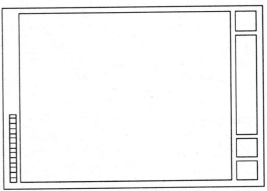

As you can see, the CBT version of this tool adds a cost control feature, by projecting the time needed for each sheet, and recording of actual time.

Combining the brief and the design drawings

In an earlier chapter I noted that a key requirement of ISO 9000 was that the design review had to formally consider whether the client's brief (the program) had been met by the design. The only practical way to achieve this is to have all of the briefing information together in one place; easy to access.

When I first started working with JCY, I found they were using a technique that did just that, and quite elegantly: On certain projects, the right-hand fourth or third of each design drawing was set aside for the development of the brief, such that the full record of meetings with the client, all instructions, relevant code requirements, etc., was all right there. It was updated as needed. This process was continued until sign-off on the design development drawings.

In a real sense, this concept is no more than adding background to the 'revisions' column universally found on designers' drawings everywhere, but the addition is a powerful one, which 'idiot-proofs' respect for the client's brief.

This technique makes design reviews a breeze, and gives the client a great deal of confidence in the process. Great QM!

This concept took me back 30 years or so, to when I worked briefly for the Minneapolis architect Colin Hardenburgh. He had an extraordinary technique of never erasing anything - he kept the doodles and earlier sketches on the finished construction drawings: a 20th century palimpsest where bits were drawn over as the later version.

He acknowledged that it made the drawings harder to build from, but argued that it reminded him of the whole chain of client changes as he went along. I would classify this as a 'lesser' invention, and do not recommend that you adopt it. (It does not conform to ISO 9000.)

Building code analysis

Many design firms set up an outline of the building code requirements for a project at the start of a project. This simple tabulation can have huge dividends, for obvious reasons. It is worth doing on projects of any size. Typically it would include the following information, if applicable to the project:

◆ Applicable code(s)
◆ Use and occupancy
◆ Type of construction (if known)
◆ Allowable areas
◆ Use mix
◆ Fire resistance requirements
◆ Means of egress and requirements
◆ Special requirements if a public assembly building
◆ Protective openings
◆ Required fire ratings of components (floor, roof, ceilings)
◆ Roof covering requirements

This analysis, of course, is part of the 'specified requirements' of an ISO 9000 design review.

Product data sheets

Another true QM tool used by many practices is the product data sheet. Opposite is one example, again from CBT's excellent 'Job Captain Handbook'.

Substitution request form

First suggested to me by architect Charles Chief Boyd of Tulsa, the substitution request form very effectively controls unnecessary requests for substitution, and certainly qualifies as a QM tool. On pp 274-275 is the version I use.

Product Data Sheet

Info. source/ local rep.:

Category:

Collected by:

Date:

Product/process description:

Installation method (See sketches on back):

Costs: Per unit/material:

Total costs
(Note economies available):

Labor/additional materials required:

Sizes available:

Finishes available:

Lead time:

Local examples:

Features:

Problems/ restraints:

General comments:

See sketches on back:

Request for Substitution

This form must be completely filled in with all relevant data by the Subcontractor and submitted to the Architect for consideration before any request to change the drawing or specification requirements will be considered.

Project name: _____   Date of Request: _____

Location: _____   Architect's Job No: _____

Request by (firm): _____

Address: _____

Contact person: _____   Phone: _____   FAX: _____

Subcontract works: _____   Package No: _____

SUBSTITUTION REQUESTED IS FOR: Reason for request: _____

☐ Named product.   _____

☐ Product type, material, finish or formulation.   _____

☐ Fabrication or installation methods.   _____

PRODUCT / MATERIAL / METHOD FOR WHICH SUBSTITUTION IS REQUESTED IS SHOWN ON THE FOLLOWING DOCUMENTS:

Specification: Section No: _____   Page(s): _____   Clause No(s): _____

Drawings: (List No's of all Drawings affected): _____

Describe in detail any alteration to any other part of the Works required by use of the requested substitution:

_____
_____
_____
_____

Total nett cost of any such other required alterations, including overhead and profit: $ _____

Cost of Builder's administration (to be filled in by Builder): $ _____

Cost of Architect's documentation and administration (to be filled in by Architect): $ _____

Total cost of such other alterations (to be filled in by Architect): $ _____

Total cost savings achieved (from page 2, to be filled in by Architect): $ _____

Total cost/benefit to Proprietor (to be filled in by Architect): $ _____

Benefits to Proprietor other than financial: _____

_____
_____

COMPLETE THE REVERSE SIDE AS APPLICABLE.

ATTACH THE FOLLOWING INFORMATION:

1   Manufacturer's technical data sheets on proposed products.
2   Manufacturer's standard form of warranty.
3   Letter on manufacturer's letterhead stating that manufacturer will warrant products as specified, if specification requires specific\ not included in manufacturer's standard form of warranty.
4   Letter(s) from subcontractor(s) responsible for works affected by proposed substitution which state the total cost(s) of all such work, if any alteration of other work is required.

Fill in the following blanks as are applicable to the product, material or method type. As a guide, if the item is mentioned in the Specification as a performance or materials requirement, then information about the proposed substitution is required by the Architect to evaluate the proposed substitution. Requests lacking relevant information will be returned without action.

SPECIFIED PRODUCT, MATERIAL OR METHOD

Description: _____
_____
_____
_____

Product Name: _____

Type: _____

Model No: _____

Fire rating (hours): _____

Thickness: _____

Composition: _____

Availability (time): _____

Country of manufacture: _____

Substrate preparation required: _____
_____
_____
_____

Length of warranty available (years): _____

Sound transfer coefficient (STC): _____

Exposure class: _____

Resistance to chemicals (list): _____
_____
_____

Other specified performance criteria (list): _____
_____
_____
_____

UNIT COST OF PRODUCT / MATERIAL (Must be completed):

$ _____ What _____

Units required: _____ Total value: $ _____

PROPOSED SUBSTITUTION

Description: _____
_____
_____
_____

Product Name: _____

Type: _____

Model No: _____

Fire rating (hours): _____

Thickness: _____

Composition: _____

Availability (time): _____

Country of manufacture: _____

Substrate preparation required: _____
_____
_____
_____

Length of warranty available (years): _____

Sound transfer coefficient (STC): _____

Exposure class: _____

Resistance to chemicals (list): _____
_____
_____

Other specified performance criteria (list): _____
_____
_____
_____

UNIT COST OF PRODUCT / MATERIAL (Must be completed):

$ _____ What _____

Units required: _____ Total value: $ _____

I certify that I have checked the above documentation for the proposed Request for Substitution and warrant it to be substantially complete and accurate:

Signed by: _____

Date: _____

☐ Request approved.

☐ Request denied.

☐ Request approved subject to qualifications per attached documentation.

☐ Refer Variation Order No: _____

Approved by: _____

Date: _____

Comments: _____
_____

More inventions?

You want more inventions?

Herman brings his genie over to Hermione's

I dare say that most design practices around the world have developed one or more great inventions, or a great refinement of someone else's invention. Out of all the possibilities open to us, we would rather re-invent the wheel than do anything else. And not tell anyone else about it.

One of the more astonishing things I have heard in my life was from a Melbourne firm that said it would like to hire me to write its specs, but only if I would agree not to write specs for anyone else. The firm's argument was that it had spent thousands of dollars on their master spec system, and didn't want anybody else to have access to it! I wondered what the firm thought happened to the project manuals it issued for projects.

The reality is that your employees will steal all your best ideas anyway, and sell them to the next employer. Your only chance of survival is to stay one jump ahead of the competition. Hunkering down won't make you a star.

I've come across many inventions along the way; some great, some good, some so-so. For example, I've seen room data sheets used brilliantly. The use of standard detailing - a true QM technique - is so widespread that it doesn't warrant expounding on here.

The point of this little section (in case you haven't guessed it) is to illustrate that our profession has been developing QM solutions for many decades. We've just not labeled them as such. If you took all the best ideas that you sometime used, polished them up and used them consistently, you would likely have a pretty neat TQM system that wasn't far from ISO 9000 compliance. Did you know that?

A key problem is that we use these tools erratically, we do not document their existence, and we have no records of their use. *THAT* is the hard part, which makes what we do *non*-TQM; *non*-ISO 9000.

Chapter 5.6
Summary Checklist

✔ Look in your corporate memory bin, take out and dust off those great tools you already have, and start using them regularly.

Part 5 Resources

References

(109) Franklin, James, from *Getting to Yes Partnering: Project Strategy for the 90's* (work in progress).

(110) Juran, p 162.

(111) Kalin, Mark, *Automation and the Specifier*, The Construction Specifier, January 1986, p 82.

(112) Haviland, David, *Managing Architectural Projects* (4 vols.): *The Process* (1981), *The Effective Project Manager* (1981), *Case Studies* (1981) and *The Project Management Manual* (1984); published by the American Institute of Architects.

(113) Peters, Tom, *Thriving on Chaos*, Pan Books, 1987, p. 412.

(114) Covey, Dr. Stephen, *The 7 Habits of Highly Effective People*, Simon & Schuster, first published 1990.

(115) Peña, William, *Problem Seeking: An Architectural Programming Primer*, 3rd ed., AIA Press, Washington, 1987.

For more help on...

Feedback loops: Cornick, pp 94-98.

Corporate memory: Rose, pp 85-95.

Documentation:

◆ One of the better resources is Keith Styles' *Working Drawings Handbook*, The Architectural Press, London, 1982; and Nichols Publishing Company, New York.

◆ DPIC Companies' *Lessons in Professional Liability* offers excellent advice, especially regarding specifications (Chapter 4).

Leading your team; team-building:

◆ The most comprehensive resource I've found is David Haviland's *Managing Architectural Projects* (see footnote 112).

◆ Peter Senge, *The Fifth Discipline*, Random House, 1990, especially Chapter 9: *Personal Mastery*.

◆ Kaderlan, Chapter 7.

◆ Stasiowski and Burstein, pp 279-282.

◆ Stitt, Fred: *Design Office Management Handbook*, Arts & Architecture Press, 1992, pp 39-41, 48-50 and 277-312.

For more help on...

Leading your team; team-building (cont.):

◆ Quick, Thomas L., *Successful Team Building*, Anacon, American Management Association, 135 West 50th Street, New York 10020, 1992. This is an excellent resource.

◆ For information on Task Manager, contact Building Technology Pty. Ltd., 126 Russell Street, Melbourne 3000 Australia; fax (61-3) 9650-3848.

Changing your calendar and other strategies:

◆ Changing your calendar:

 Δ Peters, *Thriving on Chaos*, pp 412-416.

 Δ Kaderlan, pp 157-163.

◆ Revalue your talent: Frank Stasiowski, *Value Pricing for the Design Firm*, John Wiley & Sons, 1993.

◆ Own your niche:

 Δ Weld Coxe et al. (see footnote 56).

 Δ Stasiowski, *Staying small Successfully*, Chapter 2.

 Δ Peters and Waterman, *In Search of Excellence*, pp 182-186.

◆ Predestine your future: Books in this category seem to multiply like rabbits, of the 'think and grow rich' genre. Select carefully; read with a grain of salt.

◆ Improve your negotiation skills:

 Δ Roger Fisher and William Urey, *Getting to Yes: Negotiating Agreement Without Giving In*, Penguin Books, 1981.

 Δ William Urey, *Getting Past No: Negotiating with Difficult People*, 1991; Penguin Books.

 Δ Paul Steele, John Murphy and Richard Russill, *It's A Deal*, McGraw-Hill (London), 1989.

 Δ Frank Stasiowski, *Negotiating Higher Design Fees*, Whitney Library of Design, 1985.

◆ Improve your time management skills:

 Δ Covey, pp 145-182.

 Δ Stephen R. Covey and A. Roger Merrill, *First Things First*, Simon & Schuster, 1994.

 Δ Kaderlan, Chapter 8.

 Δ Franklin (see page 82), pp 4.11-4.14.

 Δ Patching (see page 83), pp 86-96.

Part 6

THE BOTTOM LINE: Optimizing Your Investment

6.1   The Marketing Edge, Perceived and Real

This lack of interest in perception is understandable. People wanted to get away from the messiness of perception to the solidarity of truth. - Edward de Bono, Water Logic.

Truth is what you perceive it to be - Anon.

Purpose

To consider how the marketplace values the design consultant's ownership of a quality system and to focus on the most important reason for improving practice service delivery: a competitive market edge.

Is QM the latest marketing gimmick?

A decade ago, one often heard the idea that if you wanted to get work, you had to be computerized - that is, you had to have a computer sitting in the corner, whether you could operate it or not, because clients expected the modern practice to have computers. Today, the only computers sitting silently in the corner are the obsolete ones.

Today, something of the same psychology may be working with QM: The client wants you to have it, and hopes you know what to do with it. That scene is rapidly changing, as the clients themselves are digesting the changes that QM brings to their own organizations, and are becoming more sophisticated about their interest in their consultants' and contractor's QM systems (see Chapter 4.4).

In Australia, where implementation of an ISO 9000 QM system is a requirement to get work from most federal and state agencies, and increasingly from the private sector as well, most governmental departments are setting up phasing-in periods, where implementation is permitted to take place over a period of time, some system elements are given priority over others, and systems are not required if fees or project costs are below 'threshold' levels.

Other units of government, for example municipal Councils, are simply requiring an ISO 9000-compliant system, but being fairly lenient about the level of implementation.

QM as an antidote for building failure

There is a widespread belief that improvement in quality procedures will reduce failures in buildings, principally through improved information exchange.

This is well shown by events in the 1980's in the U.K., summarized in the Royal Institute of British Architects' (RIBA) *Quality Management: Guidance for an Office Manual*. In the Foreword, then RIBA President Maxwell Hutchinson notes:

> *"In the early 1980s the government's Building Research Establishment clearly identified that although building assembly is largely concerned with one off projects, building failures are of a repetitive nature. In addressing these findings the RIBA focused its attention on improving construction industry communication and the transfer of knowledge and experience. Firstly the Institute supported the industry-wide adoption of Co-ordinated Project Information; it went on to publish its Guidelines for Sound Practice. The National Quality Campaign focused attention on the International Standard 9001, the model for quality management systems.*
>
> *"In November 1989 the RIBA Council, along with a number of historic measures aimed at quality and competence, unanimously supported the development of a quality management system for architectural practice aimed at providing demonstrable evidence of members' firms' capabilities. The Institute encourages its members to examine their firms' management system and in so doing increase society's confidence in the construction industry's ability to provide building to a cost, within a determined time scale, to measurable and acceptable quality."*

QM as an antidote for marketing failure

The goal here is to improve *'society's confidence in the construction industry's ability'*. Hutchinson goes on to assert the RIBA's belief that:

> *"The demonstrable assessment of quality is a marketing tool for practices of all sizes and all persuasions."*

In the U.S., Stasiowski and Burstein's view, expressed in their book [116] probably typifies current thinking:

"Successful marketing in the 1990s has little to do with fancy brochures, slick graphics, or any of the normal, traditional 'marketing techniques'.

"Instead, it is expeditionary marketing ... taking clients to heights they never before imagined ... giving clients more than they expected, and certainly more than they asked for... and through the most efficient and effective project management systems, focused on quality of delivery, showing them that you are intense and active and focused on their project, and their project alone."

The prevailing wisdom is that marketing success is not likely to come from legal protection of the profession through requirements to use architects or to protect use of the title, however much we prefer such solutions.

Better candidates for success are real cost-cutting through improved service delivery efficiency, reduction of unnecessary work, diversification of services offered, developing expertise in emerging areas of opportunity, and repackaging or re-valuing the way we charge for our expertise.

One clear conclusion is that to the extent the services we offer appear to be undifferentiated from those offered by others, these services will be treated as 'commodities' by purchasers, and selection will be solely on the basis of price.

Since there will always be marginal businesses around, either desperate for work at any price, or willing to 'work for peanuts', to compete on price is a guarantee of professional poverty.

Incentives

One of the interesting developments taking place in Australia with respect to quality system introduction is that some states (Queensland and, probably in the future, Victoria) are taking an incentive rather than a punitive approach to the phase-in period. The idea is that they give a 'handicap' allowance to the firms with approved quality systems, of the order of 5% of fee value. This rewards the firms that have made the investment.

QM as a marketing differentiator

If you accept the above statements, then it follows that QM can be used as a tool to help differentiate the services you offer from those of others.

At first glance, it might seem that when everybody has to have QM to get hired, then it no longer provides any differentiation. In fact, it turns out that the opposite is true.

With over 80 design office QM clients, I've had a very good opportunity to see how they deal with this differentiation issue. What I have observed is that the firms that never bothered to differentiate their services are happy with a 'stock' QM solution; whereas those who care about setting their firms above the common denominator are quite insistent that their QM systems are - and are seen to be - *different* and *better*.

For these practices, being a leader in the implementation of quality management is almost as important as being a leader in design, or so I would judge from the evidence.

Delighting the client

A number of experts insist that to exceed the client's expectations you must understand the client's business better than the client does. This point was reinforced strongly by the Clients' Panel at the AIA's National Summit on Project Delivery in Nashville in September 1995. While this advice may be impossible for most of us with most clients, virtually every practice could do a lot to improve its collection of data about prospective clients and new clients.

Clients' expectations of consultants are rising. This is reflected in the Requests for Proposal (RFPs) one sees. Not so many years ago, clients expected, and got, statements of qualification from firms, and firms were selected largely on qualification.

That situation is mostly history. RFPs are more likely to require proposers to detail how much they know about the client's proposed project, and often limit the quantity of material they will accept which extolls consultants' virtues. Clients are saying, in effect, *"We don't care how smart you are, or how many design awards you have won; we want to know how you are going to deal with this problem."*

Clients are saying they want your practice to be client-centered in its approach. Becoming more client-centered in your marketing is partly a matter of attitude and partly organization. Any good text on professional services marketing will include a chapter or more on this subject (see Resources at the end of Part 6 for suggestions).

Many authorities recommend tools for collecting and organizing information about clients; for example Frank Stasiowski offers a 73-point 'customer profile' pro forma (117).

Is marketing part of QM?

Both TQM and ISO 9000 theory link quality management to marketing; specifically that marketing itself is a quality function in your organization. ISO 9004.2 states that management *"should establish procedures for planning and implementing market activities"*, and identifies the following marketing elements: (118)

◆ Establishing client needs and expectations.

◆ Identifying complementary services.

◆ Identifying competitors' activities.

◆ Reviewing relevant legislation, codes and standards.

◆ Analyzing and reviewing client requirements, service data and contract information.

◆ Confirming commitment and ability to meet quality requirements.

◆ Ongoing research in new technology, changing market needs and impact of competition.

The real marketing edge

If you have developed your quality system with care and implemented it with commitment and diligence, it will provide you with the following benefits:

◆ Better knowledge of your client and his expectations.

◆ Fewer lost documents; less time spent hunting for them.

◆ Less lost drawing time and discarded drawings.

◆ Fewer changes to completed documents.

◆ Less specification of obsolete products.

◆ Reduction in change orders, claims for time extension, and ambit claims.

◆ Less time required to sort out site problems.

◆ Greater harmony in the office.

The degree to which you will reap these benefits is determined by your relative state of disorganization and lack of control before you start. Some or many of the items on this list may already be working very well for you, in which case you already have many of the elements of a good QM system in place (if not so identified).

There will some cost to achieve these benefits, obviously. But if your system is working the way it should be, then these costs will be outweighed by the direct gains in profitability.

You can use that increased profitability either to lower your fees and be more competitive, invest in research and other ways of improving your ability to deliver service, or simply to give yourself a raise in pay.

Chapter 6.1
The BOTTOM LINE

> ✓ Clients have a perception that quality of delivered service will be higher when a practice has an identifiable quality consciousness.
>
> ✓ Depending on the experience and approach of the client, the client may expect to see demonstrable evidence of that consciousness.
>
> ✓ Certification is one, but not the only, kind of such demonstrable evidence. To be effective as a marketing aid, the evidence needs to be what the client expects to see.
>
> ✓ Craft a marketing strategy based on what clients really need, which may not always be what they are asking you to provide.
>
> ✓ A well developed and managed quality system will increase your profitability and lower your risk.

6.2   Quality Costs and Quality Profits

Cost-effective quality management systems mean improved performance, greater client satisfaction, lower PI premiums, and professional peace of mind. - Ron Baden Hellard, former Chairman of the RIBA Management Committee

Purpose

To outline concepts of quality costs and to compare the costs of improving quality of service to the costs of not improving it.

How should we attack the cost question?

There is disagreement at the guru level as to the value or necessity of measuring the cost of quality programs. Most agree that it is important to try to determine value, but the question is: How far should one go? Where is the point of diminishing returns, where more information costs more than it is worth?

It is clear that quality costs something, particularly when implementing a new program. It is easier to measure direct quality costs than indirect costs. As I noted earlier, very few architects track re-drawing costs, or the value of discarded, half-finished contract documents.

It is also not very easy to measure quality profits, in large part because of the 'one-off' nature of design projects.

The cost-benefit analysis itself also comes at a cost, and this cost must be appropriate for the value of the information received from doing it.

Standard models

It is helpful to consider the standard models of quality costs that the manufacturing industry has worked out over many years, because they provide some insight into the issue, and help us to translate these concepts into our own industry. There are two such models, widely used. The first, the Quality Cost Model is shown at the top of the next page.

This model requires a little explanation.

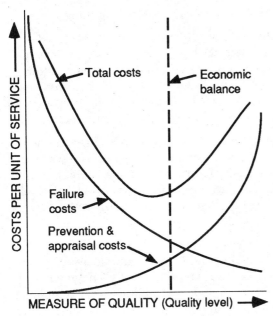

What this diagram shows is that small increases in spending on prevention and appraisal yield huge dividends at first, but as there are fewer and fewer mistakes to find or prevent, the cost of finding and preventing them starts to get higher and higher per unit of work.

The total quality cost is the sum of the failure cost and the prevention and appraisal cost. You can see that the total cost reaches a low point and then starts to climb.

In most cases, there is a point where failure costs equal prevention and appraisal costs, usually at a slightly higher quality level than the low point of total costs.

Authorities suggest the optimum economic balance is somewhere between these two points: increased quality is available at a very low increase in overall quality cost.

The second model, shown below, describes what happens to the various elements of quality costs as the quality system 'matures'. This called the 'Distribution of Quality Costs".

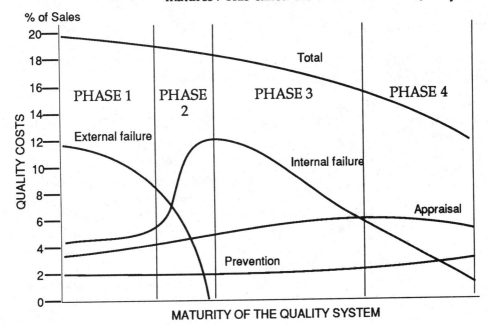

This diagram shows a number of interesting things:

◆ In most industries, total quality costs are about 20% of gross output at the start of a quality program. This cost is made up of about 12% 'external' failure e.g. customer dissatisfaction, returns, defective goods; upwards of 4% 'internal' failure (detected before shipping); upwards of 3% appraisal costs; and about 2% prevention costs.

◆ Phase 1: After introduction of QM: As we saw in the previous graph, very small increases in spending tend to reduce the external failure rate dramatically, but at first there is not that much of an increase in 'internal' rejections. The defective products are discovered in final checking, not on the 'assembly line'.

◆ Phase 2: As the system matures a bit more, the internal processes start taking hold, and manufacturing finished quality starts to improve dramatically - huge gains are made, but there is a high cost, because semi-completed products are still being scrapped or reworked.

◆ Phase 3: As the assembly line processes begin to operate better, mistakes made and discovered have peaked and begin to drop slowly. The combination of prevention and appraisal costs continues to rise slowly. The rate of external failure has virtually gone to zero.

◆ Phase 4: The total cost of quality drops slowly but surely.

Application of these principles to design

Can we meaningfully translate these ideas into our own industry? Let's consider them in turn.

External failure

In the building design industry, external failure includes:

◆ Interpretative design failure: misinterpreting the client's needs and requirements.

◆ Endangering the public, through bad structural design or selection of materials that could cause injury, such as using smooth tiles in sloped exterior walks.

◆ Mistakes in contract documents: dimensions that don't add up, calling up a product as one thing one place, something else in another.

◆ Discrepancies and ambiguities between the drawings and the specification that could cause confusion and result in claims for extras.

◆ Failure to coordinate the work of different design disciplines, causing any of the above.

It is important here to understand the difference between external failure and the *cost* of external failure. In our industry, the cost of external failure includes:

◆ Cost of professional liability insurance.

◆ Cost of deductibles paid when there is a claim.

◆ Loss of senior professional time spent defending the firm when there is a claim.

◆ Loss of senior professional time spent resolving problems to prevent claims from being made.

◆ Cost of re-drawing to instruct contractor to correct error.

◆ Loss of income through client's refusal to pay.

◆ Loss of future profits if a repeat client goes away.

We can see quickly that the first item would not change much if external failures decreased substantially, and the second and third items would be reduced but not eliminated (because of 'shotgun' claims), but the remaining items are closely linked to the level of external failure.

Internal failure

In design, internal failure almost always consists of re-drawing time when an error or coordination failure is discovered, but depending on when the problem is discovered, can also include things like reprinting and re-sending of documents.

The costs of internal failure, then, include:

◆ Re-design and/or re-documentation.

◆ Re-checking (appraisal) of the revised work.

◆ Communicating of revisions to others in team, and possibly to client and/or contractor, including printing, binding, shipping.

There often are flow-on effects caused by internal failure, such as when the necessary revisions imperil the schedules for other work, or the client or contractor claims delay costs due to time slippage of the delivery of the documents.

Appraisal costs

Appraisal costs include labor to perform:

◆ Design reviews.

◆ Internal checking (of your own work).

◆ External checking (coordination with work of others).

Prevention costs

Prevention costs include:

◆ Personal time of management required to instill a greater quality consciousness and build motivation.

◆ Time required to establish and maintain the quality system.

◆ Training.

◆ Employing more experienced people.

◆ Project quality audits.

◆ Team reviews at project completion.

◆ Post-occupancy evaluations.

It is interesting that quality management authorities peg the costs of prevention at a constant 2% of turnover, as shown on the 'Maturity' diagram above. So far, there is not sufficient evidence to know if that figure would be appropriate for the design industry. I have heard reports of firms spending up to 5% of gross on prevention, but I suspect that would include the start-up, one-time costs of initially developing and implementing the quality system.

One of the things that typically happens when a firm puts a QM system in place is that a number of other functions get updated, and these costs are seen as being caused by introduction of the quality system. An example is that piles of obsolete forms get thrown out and replaced, which should have happened anyway.

Can we get a handle on these costs?

Herman gets a handle on quality costs

If your practice is typical, you could implement a quality system and never know whether it was costing or saving you money. Why? Because, if you are like the vast majority of design professionals, you have *no idea* what you presently spend on quality.

Do you track the cost of re-drawing? Of course, all re-drawing is not 'doing things wrong', or even avoidable. But much of it is.

If we never begin to measure how much re-drawing we do, we will never get to the question of how much of it is avoidable, or how to avoid it.

Do you track the amount of time you spend resolving discrepancies during construction? Not likely!

Quality cost systems for designers

A quality cost system won't prevent mistakes, but it will help you understand where the problems are, and where you need to focus your attention in order to prevent them.

If we don't start analyzing the coordination errors found before and after issuing documents for construction, we will never find out which ones could have been prevented. Here are my recommendations for finding out what your quality costs are now:

- *Everybody* fills in a time sheet. No exceptions.
- Add two new categories to your time sheets:
    Δ Re-work due to internal error.
    Δ Re-work due to consultant coordination.
- Explain the importance of tracking re-work to your staff; monitor the change and spot-check results.
- Estimate, as well as you can, the past average annual cost of preventing and defending claims.
- Profile your quality costs *now*, before you implement a quality system, so you will be able to evaluate the benefits later.

Chapter 6.2
The BOTTOM LINE

✓ Quality system improvement costs money, but if managed properly, can save more money than it costs, through efficiencies and elimination of rework.

✓ Implementation costs must be planned and budgeted, just as the acquisition of any other new resource.

✓ The direct incremental benefits to the practice will vary according to level of system confusion in the firm before implementing better systems.

✓ Intangible benefits, such as better marketing opportunities and reduced practice risk, inevitably cancel out any direct net cost to the practice.

6.3   Risk Management

Design professionals and owners could benefit from taking a more 'global' view of risk than they sometimes do at present. Enhanced and broadened cognizance of a wide range of risks in the design and construction process would presumably manifest itself in better informed and more prudent designs, improved specifications, improved project relationships and communications, and enhanced construction contract administration practices. It is axiomatic that all of these, of course, should contribute to fewer misunderstandings and unfulfilled expectations, less acrimony, and therefore reduced exposure to claims - bona fide and otherwise - against the A/E. - Roger J. Smith Esq. [119]

Purpose

To come to a preliminary conclusion on the question of whether implementation of a quality management system could increase practice risk, to outline the relationship of quality management to risk management, and to consider options to reduce risk related to quality.

Is quality management a two-edged sword?

The question has been asked: If I adopt a quality program, which implies or states explicitly that our practice will have a higher level of quality control than others, or than we previously had, will this increase our exposure to claims? In other words, is this a 'quality cost'?

Fair question. While there is no real evidence to date, expert thinking is that the possibility exists, especially in regard to the already present problem of certification.

There has been a growing tendency for clients to require that design professionals warrant the efficacy of their designs and documents and/or to require that they certify that the built result complies with the design. There are many versions of these warranties and certifications, and they are all a danger for the unwary, to a greater or lesser degree.

The following quotation from *Guidelines for Improving Practice* [120] illustrates the point:

"The great weight of judicial opinion holds that, in the absence of express language, one who provides professional services does not guarantee or warrant a particular result. It is, therefore, incumbent upon you to avoid contractual language which is, or amounts to, a guarantee or warranty. Language expressing or implying a guarantee or warranty may well be hidden and overlooked by the unsuspecting. Note that such clauses may not contain either of the terms, nevertheless they have the same effect. For example:

"'The design professional agrees and represents that his design, plans, specifications, and all drawings prepared and services rendered shall be free from defects and faults.'

"Clearly, this clause is equivalent to and has the same effect as if it began with: 'The design professional agrees and warrants that his plans, ... ' By executing such an agreement, the design professional places himself in an entirely indefensible position without regard to the cause or circumstances giving rise to any defect or fault.'"

Solicitors for clients have been crafting these deep pits covered with leafy branches along the architect's path for years.

What is new now? What is new is that for the first time, the profession is asked - and often required - to 'develop, implement and maintain' a quality assurance system which theoretically should ensure that defects in the architect's design and documentation process will largely be prevented, and any which somehow sneak through the QM prevention net will be caught in the final checking.

No case has been reported yet which takes advantage of this situation, but it is entirely reasonable to imagine a negligence suit where the client points to the architect's QM Manual and says it was the reason for giving the job to the firm; that the client relied on the special level of quality performance extolled in the Manual, and that such representation in fact amounts to a performance 'free from defects and faults' (to use the above expression).

This line of thinking suggests it may be prudent to include some qualifications in one's quality manual, especially those parts of it that are public.

In any case, the demand for the architect to take some responsibility for the quality of the finished result is not likely to go away, and architects need to be particularly careful about accepting any such obligations - *especially* when they are coupled with a partial services fee agreement. It is foolhardy in the extreme to certify something you did not observe continuously and carefully.

This does not mean that architects should avoid taking responsibility. Rather it means that demands for performance must be evaluated carefully for their risk factors.

The *Guidelines* monograph cited above notes:

> "We must start with the premise that there exists a level of competency within the design professions which renders them uniquely qualified to offer these expanded services on a professional basis. By implication and experience we all know that each individual does not necessarily, or by some magic stroke of his professionalism, automatically become qualified to perform all of the services being suggested.

> "It is, therefore, incumbent upon you to evaluate what demands are being made, in what manner they are to be performed, and whether or not you and your staff alone, or together with available outside consultants, have the necessary expertise to render the services in a professional manner."

If the answer is *no*, then DON'T DO IT! If the answer is *yes*, then ensure you will be appropriately reimbursed for the responsibility you accept and appropriately protected so that the responsibility you accept is not subject to expansion.

Trying to do the impossible

Sometimes agreements require the unqualified certification by the architect that certain results have been achieved, or will be achieved, that the architect certifies that the structure has been built in 'strict accordance' with the plans and specifications. There is no way possible for you to issue such a certificate. Be careful of clauses requiring certification in terms of *strict compliance, in every respect*, or similar language.

Sometimes certifications are a necessity, and such certifications must be worded in such a way as to be precise about what you are certifying; and suitably qualified so that they cannot be interpreted to mean *more* than you are certifying.

For example, you might reasonably certify that *'during the course of occasional site inspections, no construction was observed which was in violation of building code requirements; provided however that such certification is not made with regard to construction which was covered or otherwise not apparent at the time of such occasional site inspection'.*

The following steps may be of help in resolving certification requirements:

◆ Discuss any such requirements with your solicitor before accepting the commission. Resolve the wording of the agreement in a way acceptable to your lawyer and the client before signing.

◆ Have the form of the certification drafted by your lawyer and have it approved by the client early in the project.

◆ Avoid any letters or other communication which would have the effect of increasing the scope of the agreed level of certification.

Refer also to *Resources* at the end of Part 6 (pp 313-314).

Quality management and professional liability insurance

In Chapter 4.4, I discuss a new approach to structuring QM, calling it 'the swell that signals a sea-change'. Another breakthrough in QM thinking has just come to my attention; this time from the professional liability insurer DPIC Companies of Monterey, California.

DPIC is working on a stunning new program called QMS (for Quality Management System), that combines superb merging of ISO 9000 and TQM concepts with generous reductions in the cost of PI insurance for those who undertake the program.

This program, due for release in the spring of 1996, has two 'modules', completion of each of which will earn their insureds a 10% premium reduction.

The first module is a self-administered assessment form which asks a series of questions across 32 topic areas organized into six broad areas of practice. To each question, users rate themselves both as to where they are now, and where they want to be, their 'preferred future'.

The difference between these is the 'gap' or distance the firm must go in practice improvement to have the future it wants to have.

The second module is called 'Practice Improvement Projects'. In this model, users select four areas where they want to focus improvement, and undertake a structured process to implement the change. On completion, to DPIC's approval, insureds receive a 10% premium reduction.

DPIC has made a bold and carefully considered commitment to quality improvement in architecture. I'm sure that they will be closely monitoring the claims history of firms that undertake this program, compared to those who do not. This information could provide one of the clearest arguments yet for the value of structured quality system improvement for design professionals.

Chapter 6.3
The BOTTOM LINE

✓ Certifying that over which you have (or should have) control is accountable architecture.

✓ Certifying that over which you do not have control is asking for trouble.

✓ With authority over processes comes responsibility for them.

✓ The bag of money, and an equal bag of risk, goes to the party who takes responsibility.

6.4 Accountability

In the final analysis, each firm's principals must decide what course they will chart for the future. Will their firm become more and more defensive, afraid to take risks for fear of legal repercussions? Or, will it strike out boldly, with an objective of becoming the best it possibly can be? - Stasiowski and Burstein.

Purpose

To re-examine the accepted premise that the architect/engineer should take care to avoid any responsibility for the methods and means of building.

Retreat from accountability

Fear of blame, claims and pains has caused design professionals to retreat from the management of the construction process that they routinely exercised from a century ago until as far back as we have any records of their work.

A century ago, Louis H. Sullivan wrote in his *Kindergarten Chats:*

"It is really startling to reflect that every building one sees implies a definite personal responsibility and accountability on the part of someone not seen, probably the architect..." (122)

Perhaps 'full rout' would be more apt than 'retreat'. As a result, the influence of the profession is substantially weakened. One writer who has tackled this subject is British architect Ray Moxley, the designer of Chelsea Harbour and the International Exhibition Centre at Rainham, U.K. In his 1993 book *Building Management by Professionals* (121) he notes:

"Many British architects and engineers are good at producing design, production drawings and details... But their role has been diminished to the extent that they are, for all practical purposes, excluded from the direction of the work on site. This 'Ivory Tower' position is slowly emasculating their practical knowledge of construction, and in the long term may reduce their role even further."

I believe that the issue of accountability is one of the most pivotal in all of architecture. Professional design societies around the globe have struggled with this in the face of two movements which have been difficult to respond to:

◆ Consumer protection legislation, especially when coupled with excessive punitive damages.

◆ The treatment of design services as a commodity, to be purchased at the lowest possible dollar.

THE BUCK STOPS HERE

'Passing the buck' is the metaphor for avoiding responsibility. Harry Truman will be remembered for many things, but high on the list will be that notice, which he kept on his desk. It signaled to America, and to the world, that he accepted responsibility.

Responsibility for what? In 1945, the year Truman was suddenly thrust into the Presidency by Roosevelt's death, the country was asking some very fundamental questions as to what responsibility it had toward the rest of the world. His Truman Doctrine and the Marshall Plan rebuilt a shattered Europe. Harry Truman's simple motto meant something powerful.

Does this memory have any meaning for the practice of architecture half a century later?

Do your clients believe you when you tell them that you can get their project built on time, on budget?

Do you know how to achieve that, or do you see it as someone else's responsibility?

The design-build trend

World-wide, there is a rise in clients' preference for design-build, as a way of controlling cost and time growth due to (or thought to be due to) the separation of responsibility of the designer from the building process. To its credit, the AIA has tackled that issue directly, and has taken the lead in getting its members' heads out of the sand, and giving them some tools for the new order.

However, the Institute's preparation of standard agreements for design-build procurement is tacit acknowledgment that this sea-change is probably permanent.

What is the designer's role in the design-build model? There are some success stories where the collaboration is genuine and the results are excellent. There are plenty of other instances where the designer is not much more than a trained poodle, turning out 'free' designs for the contractor's marketing scheme.

Alternative solutions

There have been a number of experiments toward resolution of the problem of design accountability, and my guess is that the experiments will go on for some time to come. As noted in Chapter 5.1, some governmental units in Australia are using the design > document/build model that is common in Japan.

There are two problems with this model, one made obvious by the feedback cycle shown on page 245: this model interrupts the transfer of construction knowledge back to the design function, confirming Ray Moxley's prediction.

The other problem is that the designer's knowledge of how the design is interpreted in documentation is limited or non-existent. Chuck Thomsen's 'bridging' model solves this problem brilliantly (see below), but it might take a while for clients to see the value in paying the designer to be guardian of the design intent. Some - maybe most - never will.

The novation model

Another model, experimented with on many projects in Australia in the late 80's and early 90's, is 'novation'. In novation, the client hires a design team, which takes the design through the preliminary design phase, and sometimes through partial documentation for some elements such as the structure. Then the project is bid competitively, and the winning bidder takes the design team on board, pays them thereafter as in design-build, and delivers the project on a lump-sum basis.

The main problem with novation is that the design team is in an inherent conflict of interest from the point of novation onwards, regardless of the fine language of the agreement. The team is paid by the contractor, and may have no alternative but to compromise the design to stay within the contractor's price (into which it had no input).

The bridging model

The bridging concept is the brain-child of Chuck Thomsen, president of Houston-based 3D International, and George Heery, formerly head of Atlanta-based Heery International, who now heads up three other design, development and consulting companies.

Bridging is similar to the novation model, except that the original design team stays on, in the employ of the client, to ensure that the design is executed faithfully.

The project is bid at the end of the design phase, and the builder takes over the responsibility for documentation, employing its own design completion and documentation team.

The stunning elegance of the bridging model is that it preserves the accountability of the design team, it avoids any conflict of interest, it preserves the vital feedback connection, and it still has all the cost/time-control benefits of the design > document/build model. What a winner!

The future

Herman at the gate, and ready

I said above that I thought that experiments with better procurement methods would continue for some time to come. But will the design professions *lead* the charge, or tag along behind it? The answer to that question *will* define the ultimate viability of our time-honored design professions.

The answer to this question of accountability - literally, being willing to 'stand up and be counted'; to step forward into we know not what - will be the decisive factor.

Chapter 6.4
The BOTTOM LINE

✓ A perception of accountability is crucial to exceeding clients' expectations. How is that perception created? How is it maintained?

✓ Clients want someone to take responsibility. If the architect doesn't take responsibility, the client will hire someone who will, and the architect will end up working for her.

6.5   Can You Hear Your Clients?

It is crucial ... for you to manage the client's expectations so they are consistent with yours, and with your ability to perform. That involves three steps. The first is consciously creating an accurate image in the client's mind of what your practice is and what it can do. The second is understanding the client's expectations. The final step is negotiating any differences to reach a mutually acceptable agreement. - Norman Kaderlan

Purpose

To make a final re-focus on the importance of improving communication with your clients.

By way of summary

The sum of my research indicates that, for our industry, no single element of quality improvement is so important or so much needed as improving communication at all levels of the organization: with your staff, other consultants, and your clients.

In Chapter 1.6, we sampled some of the thoughts of other writers on this subject. In Chapter 3.6, we considered briefly the subject of internal communications. In Chapter 5.4 we looked at a few ways to improve coordination of the project team. This chapter discusses three key steps for successful management of interactions with the client.

No delusions, no illusions

Design professionals have a particular problem with respect to client values. It is brought on in part by the educational process, which powerfully reinforces the importance of *design*. We get out of school knowing how to 'design', but not how to do much else. We want to 'get some clients', so we can design something for them.

Every graduate, having put in the minimum time required to become registered, has a basic decision to make: To either continue to gain more education by working for others, or to gain more education at the expense of his clients. The more impatient take the latter course, but they immediately run into the classic problem that all young practices face: their clients want to see *experience*. (The clients aren't dumb.)

How do you get that experience, that first chance to prove that you really *can* design that child-care center, school extension, what have you? The obvious thing to do is 'puff up' whatever experience you have, as much as you can, to give your prospective client confidence enough to give you your chance.

BAD START! Let's consider Kaderlan's first point from the quotation above:

Create an accurate image in the client's mind of what your practice is and what it can do.

If you do not do this - if you stretch the reality - you will confirm, or raise, the client's expectations to a level that you will be struggling to meet every step of the way. You will have fashioned your own noose.

What is the answer, then, to 'breaking into' a new line of service? To answer, I'll tell you about a project I heard of recently, from a person who was on the selection committee to design a new child-care center. The committee had decided to put only firms with demonstrated experience in similar projects on the short-list. Its advertisement for a registration of interest drew over 60 applications, including over a dozen with suitable experience.

The committee put five of the most promising contenders on a short-list, and then decided to add a sixth, a firm which had the most interesting proposal out of this huge group. This firm said that they had no prior experience in child-care centers, and for that reason they would give it their best effort.

The committee members were so impressed with the proposal, including the firm's candor and honesty, that they decided to interview the firm, but agreed they wouldn't offer them the job. Result: the firm was just as impressive in the interview, and it won over the committee, and won the job.

By the way, confirming your ability to meet the client's requirements is a mandatory requirement under ISO 9000.

Where is the client coming from?

Now we will turn to Kaderlan's second point, highlighted below. In Chapter 6.1 I noted that clients' expectations are rising, and that clients expect their consultants to have a *client-centered* approach.

Understand the client's expectations.

What is a client-centered approach? It means, simply, that you have to think about the project from the client's point of view, rather than from yours. Some of our more illustrious architects of the past have been openly contemptuous of the clients' ideas; the architect 'knew best' and that was that. Those days are history, and just as well.

In my early days I worked for a while for a Minneapolis architect who went through 'phases', as do some painters. When I was there, he was in his 'copper period', and every project I worked on for about two years had a copper roof whether the client wanted it or not. This may be 'managing the client's expectations' (they would finally give in), but it was a pretty heavy-handed way to do it.

The only way to understand the client's expectations is to ask a lot of questions. And more questions. And listen carefully to the answers. [123]

How can you tell if the client understands you? Several authorities, including Kaderlan, recommend asking the clients to tell back to you, in their own words, what they understood from your explanation. Listen carefully to that telling: if it is different from *what you meant*, then you're still not communicating adequately.

Sometimes you will have to be creative in finding ways to communicate adequately with your client. I am reminded of one Boston client who simply could not visualize anything - floor plans, sketches, perspectives just didn't do it. The project was a large, new kitchen. In the end, we mocked up the whole kitchen, full size, in cardboard, in her garage. She walked in, and her face lit up. Suddenly, she understood the whole design - and approved it.

Reaching closure

Too many design professionals are uncomfortable with any differences between their clients and themselves, so they try to ignore these differences in the hope that they will go away. Some make the really stupid assumption that when the clients see the design, they will immediately understand the importance of good design, and forget all objections.

What is more likely to happen is that on seeing the design, the client will be calling his lawyer.

In selling, the process of resolving all impediments to the sale is calling 'reaching closure', and it is a specialty in the marketing game. Essentially, reaching closure is pure negotiation. As I noted on page 266, you should improve your negotiation skills. If this advice is not pertinent, then you are a rare designer indeed.

We have come to the the third of Kaderlan's points:

Negotiate any differences to reach a mutually acceptable agreement.

Here I would like to emphasize the word *mutually*. If the best that you can negotiate is not really acceptable to you, then think very hard about whether you really need that project. You are capable of true negotiation only when you have the ability, both financial and mental, to walk away from the deal.

There are only so many hours in the day, and in your professional life. You owe it to yourself to use them the best way you can, and - except in the rarest of circumstances - you should *not* use them up on projects that will be a burden to you.

**Chapter 6.5
The BOTTOM LINE**

- ✓ Offer your clients uniquely designed services that fit what those clients need. You are much more likely to get fees appropriate to the cost of providing the service than if you are perceived to be offering 'commodity' design services.

- ✓ Create an accurate image in the client's mind of what your practice is and what it can do.

- ✓ Understand the client's expectations.

- ✓ Negotiate any differences to reach a mutually acceptable agreement.

6.6   Change and Flowing with the Times

It is clear that among the challenges which design firm management must tackle, the one that will involve more changes in the next few years will be the management of change itself. - Weld Coxe

Purpose

To consider some issues for an attitude toward change in the way we practice, which will ensure our survival in the rapidly evolving market for our services.

Are you ready for change?

Either the best thinkers of our era are wrong, or we are in the midst of dramatic evolutionary change; change which will irrevocably alter the way we have to see our immediate and long-range future, if we are to have a viable role in that future. Below is a quick look at the thinking of two prophets of change, plus a few thoughts about directions we are heading (or being pulled) toward.

Water logic

Partway through researching this chapter, I discovered Edward de Bono's little book *Water Logic*, which seems to be its own complete metaphor for what this chapter needs to accomplish. de Bono begins his investigation with a study of perceptions, which are key to understanding the relationship between quality management and marketing (see Chapters 6.1 and 6.5).

de Bono's work is a model for planning, specifically for understanding and organizing one's inner perceptions, into what he calls 'flowscapes'. de Bono contrasts 'water logic' with 'rock logic', which he says is the model that most of us learned early, and live by. de Bono says *"Traditionally we have tried to get away from perception to deal with the 'truth' of reality. It is time we looked directly at perception."* (124)

de Bono defines rock logic as being based on 'is' and identity, whereas water logic is based on 'to' and 'what does this flow to?' Thus, water logic is related to 'eastern' approaches to life; rock logic is embodied in 'western' thinking. What does de Bono's new logic do for us?

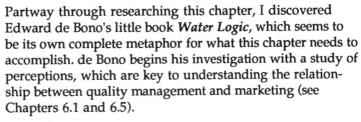

I think it is very useful to set aside a certain amount of quality time to challenge one's mind, to expand one's thinking.

de Bono is one writer (among many) who will challenge your thinking. It is only through this conscious testing of your thinking habits and assumptions that you will be able to recognize the quiet sea-changes that shape our destinies, before they become obvious to everybody else.

If you are a small practitioner, working in a niche market, you need to be working at the crest of the wave, not in the trough. And it will take more than good design skills.

Peters, thriving on advice about chaos

Then we have Tom Peters' authoritative rampage through corporate thinking for the future, *Thriving on Chaos*. What are we to make of his 560 pages of advice for 'a world turned upside down'? Does Peters have a real crystal ball, or is he just good at selling books? All I can say is that if you take him even half seriously, his points demand a lot of thinking about the future.

The future role of QM in design practice

There is very little doubt that some form of quality management system will be a requirement for practice, globally. My own experience and research indicate that ISO 9000 thinking and TQM thinking will move toward each other, in all likelihood to be generally seen as aspects of a single concept. That, indeed, is the premise of this book.

In this model, the need for quality system certification is likely to be less important than is perceived today, and professional societies will likely establish their own certification bodies, which will set standards for quality performance much as they now set standards for ethics.

The PQP - a management tool for both clients and designers

If for any reason you skipped it, go back and read Chapter 4.4.

Typically, where government agencies have begun to require that consultants have QM systems, these agencies develop detailed requirements for project quality plans which often go well beyond the requirements of ISO 9000.

What is happening is that clients are using the designer's PQP as a tool to control the design process, with the goal of reducing the risk of cost and time growth attributable to design. You might not like that concept much, but it certainly is the situation in Australia and the U.K. If you accept that the client has a legitimate interest in tighter cost and time growth, then this trend is quite logical.

In effect, ISO 9000 gives the client the basis for demanding a higher level of performance from its consultants. This may be one reason why governments in some countries have been so quick to adopt ISO 9000.

Revolutionary increases in productivity

As the world stumbles erratically but surely toward a global economy, the overwhelming pressure for western nations to remain competitive has forced dramatic increases in both productivity and quality of output. The U.S. has risen to that challenge in manufacturing, but at no small cost to both those who lost out and those who stayed in the race.

While CAD has changed many design practices, it really only is a new tool that simplifies many routine operations. The design industries have not seen anything like the changes that have characterized manufacturing. We are still doing things more or less the way our ancient forefathers did them. I don't yet have a clear idea of what these changes will be, but I am 100% positive they are coming.

Smart Asian nations are welcoming western designers, but only to learn what they can from them. When that learning reaches a certain maturity, they won't need the example any more. I'll let you work out the rest of the thought.

Continued evolution in design and building procurement

In Chapter 6.4, I discussed some recent trends in design and building procurement; in Chapter 5.1, some of the problems associated with some of these models. This evolution is guaranteed to continue, because clients want more certainty of time, cost, and value. Partnering will feature in this evolution. Be ready for it.

Chapter 6.6
The BOTTOM LINE

✓ Continually look for new and more efficient ways to meet clients' needs. Re-examine every step of the process.

✓ Learn all you can about new trends in practice. Take that learning to the next step.

6.7   Next Steps

Do it over again. - Philip Crosby's Step Fourteen

You and I, and Herman and Hermione, are completing this iteration of the journey, this quest to see how the principles of TQM and/or ISO 9000 can help us to practice better. Let's look in on our two friends, and see how they are doing.

Their research

Besides their journey through this book, H & H have done a bit of research. Herman, always keen on the TQM idea, borrowed Deming's *Out of the Crisis* and Juran's *Juran on Quality by Design* from the library, but found he couldn't get through either of them, so he's 'gone off' TQM a bit. Hermione, who has contacts in London that may lead to some consulting in Europe, is more interested in ISO 9000. She bought a copy of ISO 9001, read it twice, and is thinking about what the rules would mean to her practice.

Their conclusions

Both H & H felt they needed to reduce the TQM and ISO 9000 concepts to their very cores. After a long discussion they decided that, while TQM relies heavily on *measuring*, ISO 9000 relies heavily on *recording*.

They also concluded that these are, in fact, only two sides of the same coin: recording what is measured in TQM is implicit, otherwise the measuring would have no purpose, and that the recording emphasis in ISO 9000 depends on having something to measure, so that there is something worth recording.

Their commitment

H & H have decided that they *will* go forward, and develop and implement a quality system in their practices. They have also decided that they will work together on this project, to develop a system they both can use.

They will devote every other Saturday to this effort for as long as it takes to get their systems working well. They've tentatively agreed to allow 12 months for this.

Their tools

H & H have allocated a budget for some resources, which they will share on a 1/3 each basis with Henry, a landscape architect in Hermione's building. (Henry may join the Saturday QM planning sessions.) Their list of books to buy:

- ✓ Franklin, James: *Current Practices in Small Firm Management.*
- ✓ Kaderlan, Norman: *Designing Your Practice.*
- ✓ Mears, Peter: *Quality Improvement Tools & Techniques.*
- ✓ Nelson, Charles: *Risk Management for Design Professionals.*
- ✓ Rose, Stuart: *Achieving Excellence in Your Design Practice.*
- ✓ Stasiowski, Frank: *Staying small Successfully.*
- ✓ Stasiowski and Burstein: *Total Quality Project Management for the Design Team.*
- ✓ Thomsen, Chuck: *Managing Brainpower.*

Their QM structure

This was not so easy; H & H spent the whole of the first Saturday discussing this. Despite his finding the TQM texts too daunting, Herman was holding out for TQM. Hermione, mindful of the prospective project in Europe, wanted to be sure that her system could be certified under ISO 9000 later if need be. In the end, they agreed that the *Ten Keys to Quality* gives them both what they need, and they have adopted that structure.

In their second Saturday working session, they hammered out the details of that structure; which can be seen at the end of this chapter.

Key quality activities

H & H found that they shared some needs and not others. Here is their focus for the next six months:

- ◆ **Audits:** Although neither H nor H has any present thought to seek certification, they believe that the audit concept will benefit them greatly, and force them to more consistently implement their system. They will do audits for each other.

This makes Herman nervous, because he knows he is not very organized, but he thinks he will benefit from Hermione's more meticulous approach.

◆ **Document and data control; quality records:** Hermione has a tidy mind and a tidy office; Herman has neither. Top priority for Herman (see his schedule below); but background for Hermione.

◆ **Marketing:** Herman is quite happy with his client and project mix; marketing doesn't concern him. It does concern Hermione, who wants to completely review her approach to marketing and get bigger and better projects, as well as crack the off-shore market. While Herman gets his mess sorted out, Hermione is going to work out a new marketing strategy.

◆ **Measuring performance:** H & H are unsure how far to take ideas about trying to measure productivity and quality of output, but they have agreed that they will add *'re-drawing due to internal error'* and *'re-drawing due to client change'* to their time sheets, and track these items on a monthly basis. (Herman has agreed to start filling in his time sheets.) They have also decided they would keep track of the number of errors found in pre-bid checking to try to gauge improvement in the processes. They will review these decisions after 12 months.

◆ **Partnering:** Both want to know more about it, and will speak to their local chapters of the AIA and ACEC to suggest they jointly sponsor a partnering workshop, and to contact James Franklin FAIA (formerly the AIA's Resident Fellow) about running it.

◆ **Peer reviews:** Both want to take part in the peer review process, especially with regard to their QM implementation, and will arrange it through the ACEC.

◆ **Risk management:** Herman has already taken the DPIC risk management workshop, and Hermione has signed up for the next Schinnerer workshop. They will compare notes and exchange course materials.

Their schedules

Their systems might be the same, but their implementation schedules reflect their different interests and needs. Here is Hermione's:

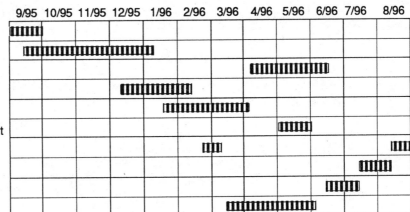

	9/95	10/95	11/95	12/95	1/96	2/96	3/96	4/96	5/96	6/96	7/96	8/96
1: Mgt. commitment	▓▓											
2: Service to clients		▓▓▓▓										
3: Purchasing								▓▓▓				
4: Process				▓▓								
5: Quality control					▓▓▓							
6: Service improvement									▓			
7: Cont. improvement						▓						▓
8: Training											▓	
9: Work environment										▓		
10: Document control								▓▓▓				

And here is Herman's. They are working on their goals and objectives, after which they will start on their procedures.

	9/95	10/95	11/95	12/95	1/96	2/96	3/96	4/96	5/96	6/96	7/96	8/96
1: Mgt. commitment	▓▓											
2: Service to clients				▓▓								
3: Purchasing								▓▓▓				
4: Process			▓▓									
5: Quality control					▓▓▓							
6: Service improvement									▓			
7: Cont. improvement						▓						▓
8: Training											▓	
9: Work environment										▓		
10: Document control		▓▓▓▓										

On the next page is H & H's QM system structure. If you compare this structure to the table on pages 40-41, you will see that their overall structure has a TQM orientation, but that the substructure satisfies the requirements of ISO 9000. Some ISO 9000 system elements are not listed; they are satisfied by others e.g. 4.8: *Identification and traceability* is covered by 10A: *Document and data control*.

Note that H & H have chosen to break up ISO 9000 element 4.4: *Design control* into subelements, which are located in Keys 4 and 5. This illustrates the flexibility available to design practices in structuring quality systems.

Herman & Hermione's Ten Keys to Quality

1 Management commitment:

Management must establish, inspire and lead quality system implementation.

1A   Quality policy
1B   Quality system structure

2 Service to clients:

Drive planning and delivery of services from a thorough understanding of client needs and expectations.

2A   Marketing
2B   Contract review
2C   Client contact
2D   Partnering

3 Purchasing:

Base purchasing (inward services) on value rather than cost.

3A   Subconsultant coordination
3B   Coordination of client's consultants

4 Process:

Develop process controls which ensure that quality requirements can be met.

4A   Project quality plans
4B   Design planning
4C   Design process
4D   Documentation
4E   Contract administration

5 Quality control:

Monitor processes to ensure that quality requirements are being met.

5A   Design review
5B   Quality checking
5C   Design change

6 Service improvement:

Provide processes which improve the service as it is being produced (in-process improvement).

6A   Corrective action
6B   Risk management

7 Continuous improvement:

Evaluate the effectiveness of process controls and operate a positive feedback process to ensure increased capability of quality delivery.

7A   Management review
7B   Preventative action
7C   Quality audits
7D   Post-occupancy evaluation

8 Training:

Institute a program of continuous training, to adequately respond to changing markets.

8A   Office manual
8B   Training

9 Work environment:

Provide a work environment which motivates staff to do their best.

9A   Leadership
9B   Premises and equipment

10 Document control:

Keep good records to demonstrate quality capability and performance.

10A Document and data control
10B Quality records
10C Technical library
10D Master specification

Chapter 6.7
The BOTTOM LINE

✓ ISO 9000 focuses on recording while TQM focuses on measuring.

✓ There is almost unlimited flexibility in how you can design and implement a QM system.

✓ Start by identifying your needs and meeting them.

Part 6 Resources

References

(116) Stasiowski and Burstein, p 13.

(117) Stasiowski, pp 112-116.

(118) ISO 9004.2:1991: *Quality management and quality system elements*; Part 2: *Guidelines for services*, pp 12-13.

(119) Smith, Robert J. Esq., *Allocating Construction Risks: What, Why, How & Who?* Vol. XVII, No. 5, *Guidelines for Improving Practice*, published by Schinnerer Management Services.

(120) *Guidelines for Improving Practice*, Vol. III, No. 4.

(121) Moxley, Ray: *Building Management by Professionals*, Butterworth Architecture, London, 1993, pp 1-3.

(122) Sullivan, Louis H., *Kindergarten Chats*, Dover Publications, 1979 reprint, p 25.

(123) Norman Kaderlan has an excellent section on verbal and non-verbal communication in his book - read it. Chapter 6.

(124) de Bono, Edward, *Water Logic,* Penguin Books, 1994, p xii.

For more help on...

The marketing edge:

- Stasiowski, *Staying small Successfully*, Chapter 3.
- Weld Coxe, *Marketing Architectural and Engineering Services* (Van Nostrand Reinhold, 1983), 2nd ed., pp 45-159.
- Gerre Jones, *How to Market Professional Design Services* (McGraw-Hill, 1983), 2nd ed.

Quality costs:

- Stebbing, Chapters 2 and 3.
- Crosby, pp 101-107.
- Stasiowski and Burstein, pp 265-271.

For more help on...

Risk management:

◆ Charles Nelson, *Risk Management for Design Professionals*, RAIA National Education Division, 1991; available from Architext, 41 Exhibition Street, Melbourne Australia 3000; fax (61-3) 9650-3587.

◆ *Lessons in Professional Liability*, DPIC Companies (see page 234, footnote 103 for address).

◆ *Guidelines for Improving Practice*, Schinnerer Management Services, Two Wisconsin Circle, Chevy Chase MD 20815-7003 USA. Vol. XXIII, Number 1 of this series, *Certifications and the Response of Design Professionals: The Dangers of Unqualified Certifications* is the best source in print for advice on the issue of certification of the completed project.

Accountability:

◆ Ray Moxley's 'Advanced Methods of Management' system is designed to increase the design professional's control over quality of built work (see footnote 121).

Hearing your clients:

◆ Kaderlan, pp 94-107.

◆ William B. Martin, *Quality Customer Service*, 3rd ed., Crisp Publications, Inc. (Menlo Park). An inexpensive, superb general workbook on improving service quality.

◆ Rose, pp 48-69.

◆ Stasiowski and Burstein, pp 235-263.

◆ Stasiowski, pp 103-134.

◆ Stitt, *Design Office Management Handbook*, pp 154-165, 199-203.

Change:

◆ de Bono, Edward, *Water Logic*.

◆ Kaderlan, pp 151-164.

◆ Weld Coxe, in *Design Office Management Handbook*, (Stitt, ed.) pp 30-32.

◆ Peter M. Senge, *The Fifth Discipline*, Random House (Sydney), 1992.

◆ Tom Peters, *Thriving on Chaos*.

Index

About the author...

Charles Nelson is an American architect with an international perspective. Married to an Australian teacher of English as a Second Language, he has lived for much of the last decade in Melbourne. The proprietor of a 'very small multi-national practice', he has offices in Melbourne and Goffstown, New Hampshire. His niche market is provision of management consulting services to other design professionals.

Nelson is a member of the American Institute of Architects, a Fellow of the Royal Australian Institute of Architects, and a member of the Construction Specifications Institute, the American Society for Testing Materials, the Design & Construction Quality Institute, and Standards Australia.

He is also the author of *Risk Management for Design Professionals* (published by the Royal Australian Institute of Architects), and numerous articles on the practice of architecture.

...and the illustrator

Michael Lindell is a Fellow of the Royal Australian Institute of Architects. For 51 years he has had difficulty in communicating with words and thus relies on his 'pictograms'. He is based in Melbourne with Woods Bagot, and has the privilege of working throughout the magic place that is 'the Pacific'.